# Making Ryan's Daughter

*Paul Benedict Rowan* was born in Dublin in 1963. His first book, The Team That Jack Built, *was published in 1994 to considerable critical acclaim. Paul has worked for a number of newspapers in Ireland, as well as the BBC World Service, where he was a producer, reporter and presenter for eight years. He has worked for* The Sunday Times *since 2000, for the sport, news and travel sections. He has been travelling to Kerry since before he can remember.*

# Making Ryan's Daughter

## The Myths, Madness and Mastery

Paul Benedict Rowan

NEW ISLAND

MAKING RYAN'S DAUGHTER
First published in 2020 by
New Island Books
16 Priory Hall Office Park
Stillorgan
County Dublin
Republic of Ireland

www.newisland.ie

Print ISBN: 978-1-84840-765-7
eBook ISBN: 978-1-84840-766-4

British Library Cataloguing in Publication Data. A CIP catalogue record for this book is available from the British Library.

Typeset by JVR Creative India
Cover design by Old Mill Cottage Design
Index by Fergus Mulligan Communications, www.publishing.ie
Printed by PUP Introkar, Poland, www.introkar.com

New Island Books is a member of Publishing Ireland.

*To Marla,*
*Will you marry me, again?*

# Author's Note

This book is based on recorded interviews with more than sixty people closely involved with the making of David Lean's 1970 film, *Ryan's Daughter*. I conducted most of the interviews during a four-year period between 1999 and 2003 in Spain (where some of the crew were living), Los Angeles, south-east England and Kerry. Kevin Brownlow, David Lean's official biographer, kindly gave me access to a wealth of unpublished material including letters and interviews. I also leaned on contemporary reports and observations from local and visiting writers who visited Dingle during that period, along with a few of my own impressions from growing up in Ireland and regular visits to Kerry. A complete list of interviewees and sources are included towards the end of the book. I've done my best to write this story in such a way that will give you, the reader, a feel for the cloistered conditions which the filmmakers experienced on the Dingle peninsula during the 18-month shoot and the hostile world which they returned to afterwards. My narrator is a curious conservative with catholic tastes. I hope you enjoy the story he tells.

# Contents

# Introduction

Sir John Mills won an Oscar for his role in *Ryan's Daughter* and said he could have written a book about what happened during the filming of the movie on the wild west coast of Ireland from 1968 to 1970, but he probably would have told only half the story. Were he of the mind, he could have shared the whole, extraordinary lot, for he could hardly have been better placed. He played the part of the fool or village idiot, Michael, who, watching mute from the sidelines, sees everything and is first to sniff out the infidelity that forms the basis for the David Lean film. In fact, the film had been called 'Michael's Day', before the title was changed to focus on the role played by Sarah Miles, whose husband Robert Bolt wrote the screenplay and was determined to make her an international star.

It's also true that in real life Mills was at the centre of everything. He was offered his part in Rome, where Lean and Bolt wrote the film over a ten-month period, and during the filming of *Ryan's Daughter* was given honorary membership of the director's tight inner circle, known as the Dedicated Maniacs, a club normally restricted to senior crew members. When the 'David Lean Project', as it was also called at one point, moved to Ireland for filming, Mills was invited into Lean's caravan regularly to discuss the day's shooting and listen to recordings of the scene in question made for the director by Bolt. Lean even had an affectionate nickname for Mills: Nob. And Mills took Lean's side in the director's lengthy and damaging stand-off with Robert Mitchum, which lasted for virtually the entire eleven months that the iconoclastic American actor was trapped in Dingle.

Careful with his money, even when he was on a day off, Mills would drive to the set in his Mercedes with his wife, Mary Hayley Bell, to avail of the excellent lunch that chef Roger Jones and an army of caterers were cooking up and to catch up on all the latest news. Behind the cheery, chipper exterior, Mills missed nothing, and he had a good memory, but in a way he was too close to what was going on. His instincts would have been to gloss over the scandalous goings-on, which shocked and titillated even the Hollywood set that had decamped to Kerry for that crazy eighteen-month period. The actor had, after all, made light of his own near-demise when he had been concussed and almost drowned when swept out of the currach he was rowing in treacherous seas at Coumeenoole Cove, in Dunquin, at the start of filming. 'Sue the bastards,' the Irish actor Niall Tóibín thought. 'Sorry for messing up the shot,' were Mills's instincts.

However, they clearly worked, as Mills had a survival mechanism that ensured he remembered only the good times, so that anything enjoyable or amusing remained crystal clear in his mind, whereas the unhappy events quickly became clouded. David Lean was the same. And there is no getting away from it, *Ryan's Daughter* was an unhappy film.

In fact, one could quite easily ask: who was most hurt by the making of *Ryan's Daughter*? David Lean went into the project as the most marketable film director in the world and emerged from it dismissed as yesterday's man. A successful and innovative British director since the 1940s, in the ten years before the Irish venture Lean had been embraced by Hollywood and enjoyed a phenomenal run of international success, from *The Bridge on the River Kwai* (1957) to *Lawrence of Arabia* (1962) and on to *Doctor Zhivago* (1965). The ailing giant that was Metro-Goldwyn-Mayer Studios (MGM) had been rescued by the revenue from *Doctor Zhivago*, which had made Lean a personal fortune and a star in his own right. Then *Ryan's Daughter* was critically mauled and ridiculed, leaving him badly wounded, as everyone had assumed he was cranking out another sure-fire winner.

Lean's right-hand man and creative partner, Robert Bolt, was an intellectual who also had the Midas touch. Bolt had written *Lawrence* (along with Michael Wilson, it later emerged) and, away from Lean, had also won the Best Screenplay Oscar for *A Man For All Seasons* (1966), which was directed by Fred Zinnemann (another loser, as it happens, from the *Ryan's Daughter* project). No wonder the contract that Lean and Bolt signed with MGM to make *Ryan's Daughter* was the most expensive in movie history. However, Bolt's career too was about to plateau on the mountains of Co. Kerry, before going into decline. His marriage to the leading lady also collapsed after he was cuckolded by a writer from *Time* magazine, David Whiting, who was masquerading as a white knight come to rescue the couple from the critical opprobrium that *Ryan's Daughter* received. Sarah Miles even claimed that Bolt's attempts to revive his career contributed to the stroke that so debilitated this kindly man in the last years of his life.

And where do you begin with Sarah? Carefully, for a start, for she is still very much alive and in rude health, a walking advertisement, it could be said, for the benefits of drinking one's own urine, of which she is a practitioner and advocate. Sarah claimed that she never really wanted to be a star, and her behaviour suggested as much. This highly talented young actress had a reputation for being difficult that caught up and consumed her as the flames licked around *Ryan's Daughter*. Talk about life imitating art. Bolt, a schoolteacher before he became a writer, had created a storyline where Mitchum's character, the schoolteacher Charles Shaughnessy, dolefully accepts that his wife Rosy, Miles's character, is having an affair with a British army officer. Six months into shooting, with the film in the doldrums because of bad weather, the irony was not lost on the restless crew when word spread that Mitchum and Miles were intimate. Sarah found it hard to resist Mitchum's 'bearlike proximity' and 'animal magnetism' and would admit years later that she did have an affair with him, but only after *Ryan's Daughter*, when she was divorced from Bolt.

The other losers? Those Irish actors who spent more than a year in Dingle earning money the likes of which they hadn't seen before, and who drank themselves to death, literally, within a few years. At the other end of the spectrum were the money men and distributors at MGM who were relying on *Ryan's Daughter* to help stave off impending bankruptcy, and whose top brass were stonewalled by Lean every time they came over to Ireland from their New York office trying to hurry him along.

*Ryan's Daughter*, which was supposed to be an intimate love story, ended up being given the epic treatment even though the storyline was slight. Cheaper, edgy productions such as *Medium Cool* (1969) and *Easy Rider* (1969), the latter of which cost $360,000 to make, provided storylines modern audiences could relate to, and were far more successful. Lean was weighed down by his decision to shoot in 70mm rather than 35mm, which required a much larger technical support crew. A huge travelling circus clogged up the roads in Kerry for more than a year, sometimes even running into itself as locations were changed at the last minute and trucks and caravans U-turned on bogs and beaches.

Some fared better from *Ryan's Daughter*. Lean's right-hand man, Eddie Fowlie, found himself a young Irish wife whom he whisked away from Dingle to a life with the jet set. The producer, Anthony Havelock-Allan, fell out badly with Mitchum, but could live with that as the cheques finally started dropping through the letterbox. He did well out of it even though he was a producer in name only, there as a friend of Lean rather than the martinet needed to crack the whip and drive the production through as Lean dallied endlessly.

Disciplined, happy and healthy, Mills had a ball in Dingle with his beloved family around him, scarcely believing his luck as shooting extended months beyond his contract, and lucrative overage payments kicked in. The Oscar statuette he won for *Ryan's Daughter* sat proudly on the baby grand piano in his living room when I met Sir John in 2002 at his home in Denham, West London. At that stage it was clear that he wasn't going to be writing any book. Even talking for any great length of time had become a struggle.

The filming of *Ryan's Daughter* was finished off in apartheid South Africa as Lean couldn't get enough sun in Ireland. 'What was South Africa like?' I asked Mills.

'Lovely. I seemed to have liked everything, didn't I?'

'Ye were an eccentric bunch, weren't ye?'

'Yes, there was a lot of drama offstage. David didn't get on well with Mitchum. He could be a bit of an old aunty and Mitchum went out to shock him. And then Sarah cared for him, though perhaps I shouldn't say that. So it was quite a hothouse of emotion.'

Our conversation was entering its twentieth minute and Mills, who was 94, was getting tired. The time had come to wind things up.

'I'm rather boring for you because I like everything,' Mills said, by way of a closing statement. 'That is my trouble.'

No trouble at all, Sir John. No trouble at all. Let me be your fool.

# 1. Roughneck in a Rolls

Eddie Fowlie loved breaking rules, so what better time to make a move than during siesta? He had already emptied much of the contents of his caravan into his large automobile, noisily at times. Otherwise, Carboneras was silent in the early-afternoon sun, save for the lapping of the Mediterranean Sea against the shore. Fowlie ignited the straight-six engine of his Rolls-Royce Silver Cloud 1. He steered it through the whitewashed village and headed out on the road at the beginning of a journey that would take him from the southeastern tip of Spain to the most western point of Ireland and another sleepy place: the town of Dingle.

Fowlie had worked out that the journey would amount to nearly a week of hard driving over some two thousand miles, but he was relishing the prospect. Carboneras and the caravan were all very well, but he yearned for the excitement, the adventure, the challenge that came with making big motion pictures, and especially big motion pictures with David Lean.

Fowlie was Lean's dogsbody or right-hand man, depending on who you spoke to, and was the most dedicated of the director's Maniacs. Lean didn't have many friends and Fowlie was probably the closest one. He was also considered to be Lean's alter ego, with a degree of influence over the director that some others in Lean's tight circle resented. Lean first met Fowlie in Ceylon (now Sri Lanka), on the set of *The Bridge on the River Kwai*. Lean was swimming in the river under the bridge when Fowlie dived in, re-emerged and exclaimed, 'Bloody millionaire stuff', an outlook that hugely impressed Lean at a time when most of the crew and actors were complaining about the hazards of working in Ceylon's steaming jungle. Fowlie was Lean's property master, special effects man and location finder, and those were just his formal roles. He was known to knock down telegraph poles when they were in the camera's line of sight by driving into them with his Land Rover. He would locate and strangle cockerels when their crowing was disrupting filming. He was regarded as animalistic yet had an artistic side that belied his brutish manner. He was Lean's go-to man and problem-solver, albeit one who could create new ones just as quickly.

He sometimes wondered whether he had been spoiled by David, and certainly he copied him. He shot stills using a Leica, the make of camera favoured by his employer. Fowlie had estranged himself from his children of former relationships, like David, and joined the Lean tribe that went from film to film.

As he steered the Silver Cloud past the whitewashed cottages and then entered the desert landscape of Almería, his mind drifted to what had brought him to this place – *Lawrence of Arabia*, curiously enough, and in particular the staging of the sacking of the city of Aqaba by Arab forces led by Lawrence. Lean's crew had built a magnificent replica of Aqaba just outside Carboneras and afterwards Lean, his assistant John Box and Eddie himself had bought land in the area, or practically been given it by a local businessman. Box and Eddie were two of Lean's most Dedicated Maniacs, like family even. Here, they were all going to settle in the sun, away from Britain, away from the bloody trade unions and the taxman, who the socialists at Number 10 had unleashed to bleed dry those prepared to make themselves a few quid. In the Spain ruled by General Francisco Franco, they got to keep what was rightfully theirs. They liked Spain, and all it stood for, so much so that Lean came back to film *Doctor Zhivago* near Madrid, even though it was the story of a Russian poet who never left his own country.

As the road to the town of Venta del Pobre straightened out, Fowlie checked his speed dial. A steady 80mph. It was good to get the Rolls on a long journey at last. He had been poking about in it since David had given it to him after *Zhivago*. A rare smile spread across Eddie's face. David had been in a particularly expansive mood back then. One or two vital members of the crew had received cheques of $50,000 as a personal thank you from the director. Lean had also treated himself to a Rolls-Royce upgrade, from the Silver Cloud to a burgundy-coloured convertible Silver Shadow. *Doctor Zhivago* was making even more money than *Lawrence*, and there was no Sam Spiegel about to divert the proceeds either. Eddie wanted Lean's Silver Cloud and had written him a cheque, which David had returned with a message scrawled across it: *I always thought you'd look good in a Rolls-Royce*. And Eddie did look good. Bloody good. He felt good, too. England, where he had to stop over on his way to Ireland, was an attractive prospect when you only had to spend a few days there. Things had been getting a bit too hot and heavy back at base. He'd been putting away too much booze of late and the rows with his young wife Conchita were getting worse.

Eddie thought also of Barbara Cole, the continuity girl David had met in the Jordanian desert on *Lawrence* and invited to share his mobile home. Barbara had put body and soul into building a magnificent house on Lean's land in Carboneras and was awaiting Lean's arrival, when he had scooted off with another woman. She was tough, Barbara, but Eddie couldn't help thinking of Miss Havisham every time he looked up at the house. He had mentioned David's name once to her in the street and she had started weeping. Yes, he could do without Carboneras for a while. It being a David Lean film, he knew it would be a long while.

Eddie's first inkling that something was moving came when a cable arrived from Rome and was delivered to the caravan. He knew David was there and he had opened the telegram the way he had ripped open his Christmas presents as a young boy. 'Don't take a job,' Lean had written. 'Robert and I are writing a little gem. Phone.' From the telephone box in Carboneras he had done so immediately and been summoned to Rome. There, he found David and the Robert in question, Robert Bolt, in the largest suite of the Parco dei Principi Grand Hotel behind a fog of cigarette smoke, poring over papers, with empty coffee cups and overflowing ashtrays surrounding them.

David had emerged to take him and Robert to dinner, and over Parma ham and Lobster Thermidor Lean put a proposition to him. While Robert – a Red – bolted down his food and gave out about what the Yanks were doing in Vietnam, Lean told Eddie that he wanted him not just to be property master but to find locations for his next movie. This would be a love story set in Ireland. 'Michael's Day' was the working title. The following day Lean briefed him further back at the hotel and he was introduced to the producer, an old friend of David's called Anthony Havelock-Allan, an aristocratic type of whom Eddie was immediately suspicious. Havelock-Allan handed Eddie an envelope full of Italian lire, telling him to pick up his next payment in London.

Fowlie had been told that filming would take place in Ireland, but past experience told him that Lean movies had a habit of spilling out into other countries, and Spain itself, with its variety of landscapes and abundance of technical talent and cheap labour, was one of Lean's favourite locations. It would be just like David for the whole bloody thing to end up back here. After two days driving west through Andalucía and then north along the border with Portugal, Fowlie scouted north-western Spain, thundering along the Bay of Biscay from San Sebastián to Gijón. From what he had read of the script and from what Lean had told him, he knew that the film had a dark, moody side, and what he saw was too green and too blue. He drove on, through France, and took the ferry to Dover.

Exactly a week after he had pulled out of Carboneras, he settled into the Royal Garden Hotel in Kensington. All the while he enjoyed the stares he was getting, particularly when he had reason to speak to someone. He knew he looked and sounded like a rough-neck in a Rolls; the huge build, the large sensuous mouth, the shock of white hair. Eddie was back where it had all started, but he remained nostalgia-free. He wasn't keen on returning to his home town of Teddington, nearby on the banks of the Thames; his priorities lay elsewhere.

Fowlie visited Bartholomew's map shop in Charing Cross. There he bought ordnance survey maps of Ireland and took them back to the hotel, where he spread them out on his king-size bed. He had been all over the world making movies but, like so many Brits, he had never hopped across the Irish Sea to Ireland before. His brief was not so much Ireland but more the West of Ireland, facing out to the Atlantic Ocean. As he studied the maps, his eye was quickly drawn to the Dingle Peninsula. For a start, it reached far out into the Atlantic. Then there were the three little islands further offshore; the Blaskets, they were called. Just the sort of background David wanted when he was shooting. The map's contours told him there were mountains in the area, not very big ones, but of promising shapes and sizes. The Dingle Peninsula, he decided, would be his first port of call.

On the way out of London, he collected spending money from MGM Studios at Borehamwood. Though he was itching to get to Ireland, on the way to the car ferry he scouted the coast of Wales as another alternative location. Fowlie then got the ferry to Dublin and headed west straight away. He and the Rolls crawled through village after village after town – motorways hadn't arrived in Ireland – and the countryside in-between all looked too green and too pretty. By the time he reached the Dingle Peninsula, 200 miles on, night had fallen and he was feeling tired, but his spirits curiously began to rise as he looked about him. Driving along in the Silver Cloud, he could see the dark shapes of mountains to the right and a great flat expanse of what must be the ocean to the left, with a few lights twinkling in the distance. In the blackness he couldn't see the water, but when he wound down his window he could smell the sea breeze and taste the salt on his tongue.

He was on the very edge of Europe, the most western point. If he'd been able to keep on driving, his next stop would have been New York. As it was, he reached Dingle close to midnight. It was late summer, but Dingle was deserted and damp, with just the odd parked car out on the street. What type of people lived here? He went into a pub called Ashe's and ordered a whisky. The owner, Tom Ashe, had time to fill him in on some local history as the place was quiet. This was a small market town and a fishing port, but the harbour had become badly silted up so big boats now stayed away. From Dingle's most thriving period in the sixteenth century, when it had been an important trading post, the town had gone into steady decline and had a dwindling population that relied to a large degree on handouts from the state and those who had emigrated to the United States but hadn't forgotten their loved ones back home. Touching.

Fowlie retired to his hotel on the outskirts of the town. The Skellig Hotel was still not fully completed but had opened, was of a reasonable standard, a good size and would provide an adequate place to stay. He took that as a good omen. Although David had spent nearly a year living in a caravan in the desert in Jordan for *Lawrence*, Fowlie knew that the director valued his creature comforts more as an older man. That night Eddie Fowlie became one of the Skellig's first guests. The girl behind the counter was charming and helpful, with the most delightful lilting accent. He could have stayed there all night listening to her, but instead delayed just long enough to get a name and location for the local estate agent, who could act as his guide. She recommended the local stout and after a couple of delicious, creamy pints in the hotel bar, he retired for the night.

Fowlie slept with the curtains open and daylight revealed a place sent from the heavens. The morning was bright and sunny and from the hotel window he could see what he could only guess at the night before: the dramatic, dark mountains that ran down to a vast expanse of ocean. In the blue sky hung great towering fortresses of white, fluffy clouds. Walking out of the hotel, it also dawned on him that the landscape was more brown than green, or purple where the heather covered the mountains. His senses tingled. As he continued to gaze, he noticed that the combination of water, mountains, clouds and sun was generating the most wonderful quality of light. This place was full of drama, full of atmosphere. David would love that.

At John Moore's estate agents, he found Joe Mahoney happy to shut up shop and swap the comfort of the office for the front passenger seat of the Rolls. What Eddie saw on their journey increased his excitement. Ten miles out the road to the west he came to the wonderfully rugged Slea Head and clapped eyes on the first of the Blasket Islands, a mile or so out to sea. He was excited, not only by the sight of them but by the realisation that he had been right in his assumptions when he'd looked at the map back in London. The islands would offer depth of field and a stunning background when David needed one. Eddie could already picture David filming the blurred images of the islands held in puddles on the road. At Coumeenoole Cove there was another boon, a narrow road steeply descending to a small beach carved out of the black cliffs and battered by great Atlantic rollers. The film called for an arms landing by Irish rebels. This would be perfect, he thought. And, as a clutch of other beach scenes were called for, Mahoney directed him to Inch Strand, about thirty miles back along the peninsula, a vast promenade of golden sand and dunes stretching for miles out into Dingle Bay. At another, Banna Strand, Fowlie was in typically irascible form, ignoring 'Private Property' signs and Mahoney's protestations as he found something else called for in the script that only God could create: a cliff overlooking the beach. Mahoney directed him to a plinth nearby dedicated to one Roger Casement. Turns out it was the same beach where Irish rebels had attempted to stage a landing of German arms in 1916 and in doing so had delivered Casement into the arms of the British army and the hangman.

This area had everything, he concluded, and all locations were within an hour's drive of each other. Anything not provided by God, Fowlie knew he and his team could build. Still, he had the rest of Ireland's west coast to scout in case there was something even better. It had been a fruitful couple of days. The one drawback was the unpredictability of the weather and the large amount of cow dung getting thrown up into the undercarriage of the Rolls. His car was plated underneath, but still. Fowlie hired a Mercedes and found a hayshed in which to stash the Rolls. Then he travelled up and down the length of Ireland's west coast, from Cork to Donegal, not once but two or three times, almost running the rented Merc into the ground before dropping it back at Sean Moran's garage in Dingle.

# 2. Passage to India

All this time, Lean had been working away on the script with Robert Bolt at the Parco Dei Principe in Rome. Also at his side was 21-year-old Sandy Hotz, who was providing not only moral support but also the creative spark for what would become *Ryan's Daughter*. Lean, at the age of 60, was three times older than Sandy, and his crew were understandably curious about how the liaison had come about. Was it her looks, for she was certainly striking? Jocelyn Rickards, the costume designer on *Ryan's Daughter*, who visited Lean at his hotel, spotted a pair of low-heeled black patent-leather shoes in the suite, which she reckoned must belong to his new girlfriend, and was rather struck by the young woman herself when she came into view: 'Tall and supple, Sandy was a little like a pre-Renaissance Madonna, with pale honey-coloured hair, a high forehead and long, delicately rounded limbs. She seemed half-girl, half-woman, was utterly in love with David and fresh from her convent education, waiting for everything that he could teach her about life, filmmaking, growing up, living and loving.'

Rickards had heard all about Lean's reputation when it came to women. When Lean met Sandy, not only was he still married to an Indian woman, Leila Matkar, but his steady lover Barbara Cole was already earmarked as the fifth Mrs David Lean. It was a Gordian knot that would take some time to cut.

Lean had met Leila on a voyage of discovery to India and then married her in Paris in July 1960. He was at the sharp end of a few difficult relationships back in London at the time, and he liked the eastern way in which Leila sat at his feet and lit his cigarettes. Leila became his fourth wife but was made what Lean called a 'celluloid widow' by *Lawrence of Arabia* and *Doctor Zhivago*, only appearing in her husband's company intermittently. Living out in the middle of the desert in Jordan in a caravan, with the rest of the crew under canvas, David had embarked on an affair with Cole, who had succumbed to his ardour even though she realised that if it cooled, she could lose her job as continuity girl on the film. For Lean, it was pretty much all business. When taking on a new movie project, he found himself energised by starting a new romance. He was of the opinion that finding the right new woman could make the movie better by at least 50 per cent, though it is not quite clear how he arrived at that figure.

Lean was a handsome and virile man. Apart from directing one of the most ambitious and difficult movies in the history of the industry, he would spend his nights making love passionately to Barbara in his caravan out in the desert when his wife was elsewhere, which was most of the time. Leila suffered bouts of depression, which were a hindrance to David when he had a movie to make, as she would be slumped in a chair on her rare visits to the set while he bustled around the place. Barbara, who was in her early forties, was a highly practical New Zealander and knew her role, on and off the set, accepting that filmmaking would always be the love of Lean's life, and that she could assist him not only in a job she loved but also filling in the gaps around it. The passion was still there when *Lawrence* passed and *Doctor Zhivago* came along. Leila was still around too, but Barbara was patient.

After making *Zhivago*, Lean went back to India to be with Leila, but her depression had worsened and David couldn't bear to be near ill people, his wife included. Instead, he threw himself into researching a project he had nurtured for more than ten years: the filming of the life of Mahatma Gandhi. He planned to make this with Bolt, seeing it as the natural progression of their work after *Lawrence* and *Zhivago*. Then a letter arrived from Bolt in August 1966 that took Lean by surprise.

His brilliant cohort was having his own domestic difficulties. It was more than a year since they had last met, and in that time Bolt's marriage had collapsed, partly, the writer would claim, because Lean had placed so many demands on his time and company on location. His wife, Jo, had found another role for a carpenter, Gordon Riddett, who had come to their house in west London to install a modern kitchen unit while her husband moved up in the world.

Bolt was devastated by his wife's adultery and concerned about their three young children, but he found love again at a dinner party in London when he met a young actress seventeen years his junior called Sarah Miles. They quickly moved in together and then briefly visited Lean in India, where Bolt was researching the Gandhi project. However, Bolt started going in a different direction, partly as a result of the critical mauling that *Doctor Zhivago* had received, and also because of the fresh and exciting twist in his love life.

In letters to David at that time, Bolt argued that their next collaboration should be on a smaller scale than *Lawrence* or *Doctor Zhivago*, which was based on the Boris Pasternak novel, and which Bolt said was like 'straightening cobwebs' when it came to adapting it for a screenplay. Bolt now made it plain that he was tired of ruthlessly condensing great literary works into two- or three-hour movies, as he had also done with *Lawrence* – 'cable-ese', as he called it. It was time to get away from the epics, Bolt argued, and do something more along the lines of the love story that had established Lean's name, *Brief Encounter* (1945).

'I'd like our next to be . . . what? I don't know,' Bolt had written in January 1966. 'But something simpler in its mechanics, with more emphasis on atmosphere (like *Brief Encounter* if you like), less sheer strained ingenuity of story-telling. A simple but grand theme that could be told at lesser length.' A month later he introduced a caveat: 'I forget exactly what I said in my last, but I don't mean *Brief Encounter* in the sense of anything as small as that; it ought to be a simple story with an important or exciting theme. Simple so as to give us room, important or exciting so as to give us impulse and energy.'

*Brief Encounter* – a story of suppressed love between two people who are married, though not to each other – touched a nerve in David. In recent years he had affected to despise 'those beastly little British films', complaining that the 'wretched' *Brief Encounter*, an intimate, restrained film that marked his breakthrough as a director, kept being revived and spoken about by critics who disliked much about his more recent films, which were strictly in epic mode. David saw an ideal opportunity to show those critics who said he couldn't do anything on a more human scale that he still had the talent that had once produced *Brief Encounter*.

Norman Savage, who had edited *Zhivago* with Lean and would go on to do the same job on *Ryan's Daughter*, was dining in Madrid with a friend, Peter Miller, who had worked on *Bridge on the River Kwai* as an assistant director. David was on a short visit to the city and happened to be dining in the same restaurant, so he joined them at the coffee and brandy stage and they talked into the early hours. 'We discussed amongst other things a movie which he intended to shoot in ten weeks,' said Miller. 'Seeing the total disbelief in our eyes he told us very firmly that he'd done it in the past and was going to show everyone that he could do it again.'

Still, it was a struggle. As part of this change in direction, Bolt wanted to put *Gandhi* on the backburner and instead write a part that would catapult the 24-year-old Miss Miles to international stardom. Back in England, Bolt made an attempt at a screenplay of Jane Austen's novel *Emma*, which he tore up. He then turned to *Madame Bovary*, by the nineteenth-century French novelist Gustave Flaubert, an account of a provincial girl who dreams of romance while trapped in marriage to a mediocre, middle-aged man.

The tone of the Bolt letter that reached Lean in India was rather breathless: 'I'm going to do a script of *Madame Bovary*,' Bolt wrote to Lean on 31 August 1966. 'Do you know it? Besides being a "classic", it's an immensely disturbing account of frustrated passion and romantic longing. Very intimate, dramatic to the verge of melodrama, and yet implacably realistic. Sarah for Madame Bovary of course. It would have to be shot in France. Does it interest you? You're the perfect director for it. If not, can you suggest who would be second best?'

Lean found it impossible to share his thoughts properly with Leila, but he was dismissive of both Bolt's project and Miles when he wrote to Barbara, who was supervising the building of the house in Carboneras, in southern Spain, where they planned to live together. 'Isn't it a bugger darling?' Lean asked in his letter of 15 September 1966.

> I don't know the book, but I bet it's good. Dear old Robert must be in a temporary madness. Aren't we all, from time to time? I can't believe that Miss M has the weight for such a character and unless he gets somebody like me, I don't think a distributor would back her little-known name in such a huge title role ... I'm afraid he must write the part for her and *her* character. I can also imagine what rehearsals would be like with Miss M knowing more about Robert's intentions than anyone else, including me.

Lean didn't share that withering assessment with Bolt, and nine months later, when Bolt's finished script arrived in his mailbox, he was far more favourably disposed towards the idea, as his love life had taken a twist of its own. Unable to cope with Leila's worsening depression, which now confined her to a room in an Old Delhi hotel with the curtains drawn all day, Lean had visited the Taj Mahal at Agra, which also featured in his movie-making plans. With him was the art director Alexander Trouner. Their rented car had broken down just outside Agra, and he and his friend had an extended stay there at a colonial-style hotel called Laurie's.

While at the hotel Lean had become intimate with the tall, white girl who brought him, and subsequently his afternoon tea, to his room. This was Sandy Hotz, the 20-year-old daughter of the hotel's proprietor.

Sandy had just seen *Lawrence of Arabia* and had immersed herself in Western art and fashion through reading magazines and books. She was bright, cheerful and vivacious, the perfect antidote to Leila, in Lean's view. What had been planned as an overnight stopover for Lean turned into a five-month stay.

He wrote again to Barbara on 18 November 1966, this time in full confessional mode, as though struck by temporary madness himself. 'I have fallen in love with a young girl. In my bloody arrogance, I used to say I could never understand such a thing, that I was immune, above the common crowd. I feel almost as if I don't understand anything any more. It's a sort of final fall from my too arrogant pride.'

A married man thirty-seven years their daughter's senior wasn't what the Hotzes had in mind for Sandy, no matter how many millions of dollars Lean had, but they were powerless to stop David and Sandy from eloping to Europe just after her twenty-first birthday, in February 1967. The couple flew to Zurich, where David had business with his bank, and then on to Spain, where David picked up his new Rolls-Royce. Sandy made herself scarce while David met Barbara in Madrid, where they said their goodbyes and his now former continuity girl tried not to cry.

David was back to having just two women in his life. The lovers meandered through France and northern Italy before arriving in Naples in July 1967, from where David planned to show Sandy the island of Capri. David didn't have a residence or even a house. In one way the Rolls-Royce was his home, with a boot containing a few shirts, a few pairs of trousers and – as Alec Guinness once noted – his Oscars.

It had been that way now for more than a decade for this air-conditioned gypsy. When he wasn't working or travelling he took a hotel suite, usually in either Venice or Rome. David had been living the life of an international itinerant since the messy break-up of his marriage to his third wife, Ann Todd, fourteen years previously. The divorce settlement had resulted in punitive tax demands from the Inland Revenue and the loss of his splendid mansion in Kensington, West London. After being so ghastly to Barbara, he wasn't going to kick her out of their new house in southern Spain, so he continued the life of flitting from one five-star hotel to the next in cities across the world.

He and Sandy were ensconced at the Excelsior in Naples when Bolt's completed screenplay of *Madame Bovary* was delivered to their suite: 'Even if you don't want to do it,' Bolt had written in an accompanying note, 'please write and tell me what you think.' Bolt had become an admirer of Lean's intellect, even if others weren't, including David himself. Lean's insecurities stretched back to the sibling rivalry of his childhood. His younger brother, Edward, had overtaken him and gone to Cambridge University, whereas David plodded through school, regarded himself as a bit of a dud when it came to learning and always had a suspicion about 'intellectuals'.

David's talent emerged in an unconventional way. He had come up through the technical side of the industry, ever since, really, an uncle had presented him with a Brownie box camera as a present for his eleventh birthday. When he found himself able not only to take good pictures but to develop them in his home-made dark room, his self-confidence grew. The hobby became his all-consuming passion and reflected the two sides of his family background: art and technology. His father came from a line of academics and painters; his mother was descended from Cornish engineers. Both were Quakers, who encouraged David's photography but banned him from the cinema, which was considered immoral. A cinema-going nanny had corrupted him with her hilarious Charlie Chaplin impressions at the kitchen table. When David finally reached the age of consent, he found the movies were a glorious escape from his drab surroundings growing up in the South London suburb of Croydon, where there was much domestic unhappiness after his parents divorced. His father, an accountant in a London firm, had got him a job in the City when he left school, but eventually admitted defeat and used his contacts to get his teenage son a job as a tea-maker in a West London film studio. Lean enjoyed escaping from the constraints of his Quaker upbringing, but always remained with his shirt buttoned up to the neck.

A love of nature and the outdoors, imbued from an early age from reading, was another blessed release for David, and he always thought of himself as a bit of a boy scout. However, his talents stretched further than that, into the intellectual sphere, even if he didn't recognise it himself. Bolt said of Lean that, 'Little by little he read. Here was an amazing thing: You would give him something like *Madame Bovary* to read and he would deliver so fine and far-reaching a critique of it and he didn't think anything of his ability to do that.'

Lean's latest adventure to the island of Capri with Sandy was put on hold once Bolt's script arrived in Naples. What followed for his young girlfriend was a stark lesson in where she stood in the David Lean pecking order. She had watched while Lean sat down and read Bolt's script with an intense concentration. When he had finished – Lean was a slow reader – he prepared a ten-page letter explaining to Bolt why he wouldn't make the film. Still, his mind was in overdrive and he was clearly preoccupied. He then tore up the letter and started on a much longer one to Bolt. The whole process took weeks, with David only rising from his typewriter to take dinner with Sandy in the hotel dining-room – often silently – or to go to bed. Sandy hated the suite they were staying in. It had high ceilings and chandeliers but was still gloomy and reminded her of a mausoleum. While other women might have stamped their feet or packed their suitcases, she quietly accommodated her man. Sandy managed to find a bookshop in Naples that had a handful of novels in English and read François Rabelais's *Gargantua and Pantagruel* over a weekend. David finally emerged after nearly a month of drafting radical changes to Bolt's script.

Sandy was young, but she was well-educated, perceptive and a fast learner. David had told her about Robert's relationship with Sarah Miles, and she quickly realised that David too was being drawn to Flaubert's novel because he found much in it that mirrored his relationship with her. Rather than dismiss the Bolt project completely, Lean wanted to devise what would be presented as an entirely original story, using *Madame Bovary* as the source.

He had been speaking to Bolt on the telephone and then announced to Sandy that they were going to Rome to meet the writer, forthwith. Once there, Lean laid his hat at the Hotel Parco dei Principi, overlooking Rome's botanic gardens. 'I never did get to Capri,' sighed Sandy, 'but that was the start of *Ryan's Daughter.*'

Bolt mourned *Madame Bovary* but was prepared to live with *Ryan's Daughter*, particularly as Lean had accepted that Sarah would play the title role. Miles was there to stay; the couple had married months earlier and she had just given birth to their son, Tom, in October 1967. All the while Bolt beavered away, not just on *Madame Bovary* but on *Gandhi* as well, a film that Fred Zinnemann was also interested in directing, but when Bolt wrote to his other great collaborator on 29 December 1967, it was clear that all roads led to Rome and David Lean. 'In about a fortnight's time I expect to be working with David again on an "original". It will be loosely based on the Bovary idea, but very loosely, bearing about the same relationship to Flaubert as *Stagecoach* did to Maupassant.'

MGM weren't quite so sceptical. On the basis of an outline of the plot, Lean and Bolt secured what was potentially the most lucrative deal ever for film-makers. Under the terms of the contract signed on 23 January 1968, Lean would receive $1 million, paid into his Zurich bank account immediately, plus a massive 35 per cent of net profits and a living allowance of $1,000 a week. Bolt would get $400,000, plus 10 per cent of net profits and a similar living allowance. He had just become the highest-paid scriptwriter in the world, outstripping the likes of William Goldman and Tennessee Williams, who was paid $200,000 for *Boom!* (1968). MGM had just purchased the hottest creative team in Hollywood and would expect plenty of bang for their buck.

Bolt and Sarah took an apartment in Rome, just to keep their distance, but Miles then injured her leg and couldn't use the stairs, so they moved into the same hotel as Lean and Sandy, the Parco dei Principi. The director took over much of the top floor, which overlooked the zoo in Rome's Botanic Gardens. Lean was visited in his top-floor suite by fellow director, Richard Lester. 'You'd wake up in the night and hear these bloodcurdling sounds,' Lester told Lean's biographer, Kevin Brownlow, about when his sleep was disturbed by roaring lions. 'I thought to myself, "Is this his life? A couple of green-and-white-tiled rooms on the top floor of the hotel, after all he's achieved?"'

Adventurer he may have been, but Lean lived the life of an inflexible Englishman abroad. Visitors to his suite noticed his Zenith Intercontinental radio tuned to the BBC External Services. The hotel prepared Lean's travelling pack of Wall's pork sausages for breakfast every morning and he had English marmalade on his toast. He spoke scarcely a word of Italian, nor any other foreign language for that matter. For the first time since he had left England, he indulged his passion for gardening on the balcony of the hotel. Most evenings, he and Sandy would drive just under a mile to dine at the same five-star restaurant, Cesarina, a choice made not just because it had fine cuisine and an accomplished pianist but also because he knew the way there at the wheel of his soft-topped Rolls-Royce. More than anything, he worked tirelessly on the script with Bolt, who had taken rooms on the floor below with Sarah and their baby son, Tom.

While Sarah and Sandy went shopping, or swam in the hotel pool with Tom, Lean and Bolt got down to work.

Bolt would arrive into Lean's suite every morning with his pipe and a triple pack of Benson & Hedges and swig down the first of many espressos. They were considered the most potent filmmaking partnership in Hollywood. Lean had made Columbia studios a fortune with *Bridge on the River Kwai*, but when he teamed up with Bolt for *Lawrence of Arabia* and *Doctor Zhivago*, the financial harvest had been even more bountiful. *Zhivago*, in particular, which had cost $11 million to make, had already grossed more than $150 million dollars, out of which Lean had amassed a personal fortune, which was remarkable, given that the movie had been panned by the critics.

This success didn't come out of nowhere; Lean was a painstaking taskmaster who immersed himself in every stage of the filmmaking process. On *Lawrence*, he had originally worked on the script with Michael Wilson, the screenwriter blacklisted under the communist purge of Senator McCarthy and working incognito. The pair had collaborated successfully on *Kwai*, even if Wilson was uncredited, but they had a major falling out on *Lawrence*, and Bolt was then drafted in by the producer, Sam Spiegel. After some teething problems the pairing flourished. Lean laboured over the script almost as intensely as Bolt, whom he regarded as a dialogue expert. Lean did the visualisation and edited the film in his mind as the script took shape.

Bolt was fresh from his own triumph with *A Man For All Seasons*, which was based on the successful stage play he had written, and both he and Lean decided that their latest collaboration would be presented as an original screenplay. Their first job, therefore, was to get the story out of France and away from Flaubert. They considered the Shetland

Islands, but then ruled out Britain as they were both anxious to stay away from the taxman. India was also given brief consideration, as Lean thought it would be fun to do a version in which the glamorous hero was a young maharajah. However, he soon talked himself out of that idea when he realised that, big country though it was, it would inevitably lead to closer contact with his wife, who was still stricken with severe depression in Delhi, not to mention Sandy's parents.

It was Bolt who suggested Ireland. He had visited several times, and as a former history teacher he had a good knowledge of the country. Its troubled past suited the story well, because they needed an outsider to come over the hill and affect the characters. They would set the story in the year 1916, when the Easter Rising against British occupation had just taken place and the First World War was raging.

Neither was keen on filming back in Britain. Good socialist though he was, if Bolt stayed in the UK, taxation levels meant that for every additional £100,000 a year of income, he would receive around £15,000 into the hand. Stay out of the country for a year and he would get to keep the lot. Bolt had similar considerations when it came to a black Lamborghini sports car Lean had presented to himself and Sarah as a wedding present, after his new wife had put her eye on it in a Rome showroom. Bring it back to England and he would have to pay 40 per cent tax on it. Ship it to Ireland instead and he could avoid that. 'Bolt is money mad! Money mad!' his agent Peggy Ramsey used to exclaim.

Bolt didn't mention it to Lean, but he knew Sarah would like Ireland as well, for the simple reason that she would be able to bring over her four precious dogs with her on the boat, without having to quarantine them.

Despite his extensive travels, Lean had never been to Ireland before, except when he had a stopover at Shannon Airport on his way to the United States. Nor did he have any great inclination to visit the country, but he was convinced when Bolt pointed out that an Irish location would play well in the United States, and would give them the chance to cast American actors in some of the big roles. The location also meant that there would be an abundance of good British technical talent at hand, while at the same time the film industry trade unions, which David despised, could be kept at arm's length.

It was at this point that Eddie Fowlie was despatched to Ireland, while Robert and David continued to work away. With them periodically was the producer Anthony Havelock-Allan, who was in Rome working on *Romeo and Juliet* with Franco Zeffirelli. They held daily conferences together over the script, with Lean agonising over every comma and full stop. Bolt grew exasperated, sometimes having to rewrite scenes five or six times. Month after month dragged on. Lean tested his writer, just as he did his costume designers and actors, to what he thought was his breaking point.

Another man Lean wanted to get on board was his peerless cameraman, Freddie Young, who had brilliantly realised Lean's vision on *Lawrence* and *Zhivago*. Lean paid him the compliment of writing to him at some length – a twenty-two-page letter despatched on 16 July 1968 – setting out in the process the plot they had arrived at:

A girl marries a teacher who, because he has taught her about great men and their music and their romantic imaginings, she believes he has similar heroic greatness. He has none at all: he is just a simple, good man and no match for her youthful imaginings. Their bed does not set off a Brock's Benefit [fireworks display] in the way she supposed it would.

Into this situation comes a real-life hero from the Western Front; a shell-shocked VC [Victoria Cross], a strange, withdrawn man who thinks that life is over. Explosion of Brock's Benefit. Running parallel is an IRA sub-plot of gun-running of German arms. Gun-running partly thwarted by a storm and totally arrested. But what no one knows is that in the aftermath of the storm floats a box of dynamite at the feet of the cuckold husband who knows about his wife's infidelity ... the VC is blown up and there is a happy ending which should be really touching.

While Bolt was getting restless, Lean was happy to work away in Rome. However, Fowlie had been on to him. He now had hundreds of photographs he wanted to show to Lean, and a swathe of beautiful locations, though he had failed to find one central element: the village. Lean had told him this needed to be a run-down, grey place to reflect the mundanity of peasant life that Rosy seeks to remove herself from.

'David, I've got a lot to offer you, except for the village,' Fowlie recalls telling Lean over the phone from Ireland. 'They're all too bright and colourful or there's a petrol station or supermarket in the way or something. We're going to have to build a village.'

'Eddie, you find a place to build it.'

Into Fowlie's mind's eye came an instant vision of Lean accusing him of choosing the wrong place.

'No, David, I need you to come over and pick the site. If you don't come, we can't start next spring as you planned because it will take a long time to build the village. I want you and an art director who's going to build the thing. I've reserved a nice suite of rooms for you in the best hotel in Kerry.'

'But Bob and I haven't finished the script,' Lean replied.

Fowlie then played his trump card. He knew that Lean loved open fires.

'In the private sitting room there's a nice big turf fire.'

There was a brief pause.

'I'll come.'

# 3. A bit of a fillum

The first that local people got to know about the village being built on the small mountain outside Dingle was when a bright-orange helicopter landed in the area in October 1968. An alien spacecraft could hardly have caused a greater stir. The helicopter settled on a dry patch on a boggy, windswept mountain, populated previously only by sheep and those who occasionally went to check on them. Now a group of men spilled out of the helicopter and roamed around the immediate vicinity. At the centre of them was a tall fellow wearing a cream-coloured mackintosh. As he moved, the group followed him and there was much pointing going on, most of it by him.

A couple of locals took it upon themselves to find out what was happening, and on closer inspection the picture became a little clearer. One of the men was recognised as Eddie Fowlie, the crazy Englishman with the unkempt white hair who had already turned heads dashing around the place in his top-of-the-range automobile. For a while the man in the mackintosh moved away from the group and stood motionless, hands on hips, staring out onto the ocean below, in the direction of the Blasket Islands. He was a handsome man, with a luxuriant sweep of greying hair lashed back by the wind. Completing the profile was a powerful nose, square chin and ears large enough for a baby elephant. A couple of locals who had gathered knew the group was part of a film crew, and the man looked like he might be a dashing actor, but one sage pointed out that he was David Lean, the famous film director. Lean and the group charged around for a further half an hour, looking at maps and continuing to point all the while, and then returned to the helicopter and were gone.

In their place came a flood of rumours that a movie was about to be shot in the area, and two weeks later this was confirmed when a group of local stakeholders gathered in the Ó Sé household in the hamlet of Dunquin, at the foot of the mountain, for a meeting with the film's Irish fixer, Bill O'Kelly, or Lieutenant Colonel William O'Kelly, as he liked to call himself. O'Kelly was a former Irish army officer, with a keen interest in amateur drama, who had used his impressive array of contacts to smooth the passage for several other foreign films made in Ireland pre-Lean, such as *The Blue Max* (1966) and *The Italian Job* (1969), the prison scene of which was filmed in Kilmainham Jail. To the locals who had grazing rights for their sheep on the mountain, O'Kelly offered £15 each for six months' rental. They were, he told them, 'going to make a bit of a fillum' and needed to construct a village set on the land they were renting. He also held out the prospect of plenty of work for the local men in building the village set. O'Kelly's offer was quickly accepted. It was the start of boom times in Dingle.

By October 1968 there were two Rolls-Royces driving around the town. One was Fowlie's, the other Lean's. One pulled up outside Fitzgerald's Hardware Store on Main

Street in Dingle, with a Land Rover alongside, and ordered a truckload of 4x4 stakes. Tom Fitzgerald was on his uppers and didn't have them in stock, but he nodded and then put in an order to a hardware store in Cork for the supplies, which would be delivered the next day. Fitzgerald was dealing with the film's construction manager, Peter 'The Duke' Dukelow, a gruff East Londoner and another of Lean's Dedicated Maniacs. Dukelow, who had served in the British army, was responsible for the realisation of two of Lean's big building projects, the bridge in *Kwai* and the city of Aqaba in *Lawrence of Arabia*. Dukelow had mixed feelings about the elevated siting of the village, which Bolt was calling Kirrary. Here was what was meant to be a fishing village, situated halfway up a small mountain. Dukelow had loads of Irish relatives and knew that an Irishman wouldn't walk his dog up that mountain on a winter's day, never mind build a village there. When he voiced his concerns to Lean, he was told that such an anomaly could be banished by sleight of the director's hand.

Lean liked that the site could be easily sealed off and was as safe from prying eyes as any built in a studio. They could work unhindered in a controlled environment while still achieving a look that was perfectly authentic. Lean had particularly bad memories of filming *Summertime* (1955) on location in Italy in the mid-1950s – his first movie filmed outside Britain – when Venetian traders had banged dustbin lids together to disrupt filming, as they sought more compensation for loss of business. Had they filmed *Ryan's Daughter* in Dingle itself, the only interference from the locals would have been the sound of cash registers ringing and shopkeepers yelping as they did cartwheels to the bank. However, Lean and MGM were happy to undertake a big set-piece construction project that would demonstrate the breadth and daring of the director's filmmaking skills and ambition.

Dukelow, aware that any structures built along the lines of the back lot at MGM Studios would be blown off the mountaintop within hours of being constructed, decided that the houses would have to be made of real stone and slate. Particular care and attention would be given to the construction of Shaughnessy's schoolhouse at the bottom of the mountain, which would feature prominently. That meant several months of hard work, which was why they needed to start now, even though winter was approaching, so that the village would be ready for shooting the film on the site by the following spring.

First, Dukelow and his crew built the road snaking up the side of the mountain to the site. Then, on 1 November 1968, the first load of timber went up the mountain, and that night a storm knocked down several telegraph poles, making locals more adamant than ever that it was an act of insanity for a village to be built there. However, if David Lean wanted to throw his money away, who were they to argue with him?

Finding the necessary labour wasn't a problem, given the huge money the company was offering and, like Jesus's apostles, the local fishermen, who could turn their hand to anything, tied up their boats and followed Dukelow, to complement the tradesmen and labourers who suddenly came flooding into the area. A construction crew of 200 men was quickly assembled. Most of the workforce was drawn from the local area, where peasant life was a grind.

The prospect of carving out a better life elsewhere meant that emigration was rife and the population was declining. Many of those who stayed relied on handouts, from relatives living in the United States or from the state in the form of unemployment benefit, which amounted to £4 9s 0d a week. For some, working on *Ryan's Daughter* saw their money increase tenfold or more, to £40 or £50 a week.

A union representative from the Irish Transport and General Workers Union (ITGWU) in Dublin came on site and tried to get the local workers to join up. A strike notice even went up at the foot of the mountain. 'What could a union do for us?' one local labourer, Tommy Mitchell, asked. 'We're getting four times our normal wages and all they would do is take a couple of quid off us a month.' Fowlie was delighted to see that the 'Strike on here' sign, which had been posted on a telegraph pole, was quickly removed and the union guy sent on his way. Fowlie gleefully recalled: 'This big fella said, "Since these fillum people came, the sun's been shining on us. You get yourselves back to Dublin or you'll be hanging from a tree".'

Dukelow had enormous drive and treated his workers with respect – and they repaid him by working through the most horrendous conditions. There was no such thing as rain time. In the worst of the weather they donned capes like Batman's and got on with it.

Dukelow, an enormous man with a big red birthmark on his left cheek, had two major failings – he was virtually illiterate, which meant he couldn't read the drawings, and he was prone to disappear on drinking binges. By Dukelow's side was the young art director Roy Walker. Working off the brilliant sketches (storyboards, as they are known in the business) by the production designer, Stephen Grimes, Walker would draw up the plans and then go through them with Dukelow. Walker wasn't long out of art school in London, but for *Doctor Zhivago* he had looked after the construction of the Moscow street that had been brilliantly mocked up north of Madrid, which, at half-a-mile long, was one of the biggest sets ever built. The one-street village of Kirrary on the patch of sheep-grazing land at the back of Dingle was on nothing like that scale, but it presented a different set of problems.

'We fought battles all the time with the wind and rain,' says Walker, who had learned the hard way that erecting mere façades, like on a normal film set, wasn't possible on this barren mountainside.

> The walls were built of stone to stand up to the winds, which were coming all the way from New York. There was a gap in-between two of the buildings. I saw guys with stones which weigh almost a hundredweight and they would be blown off their feet with the power of the wind as they walked through the gap. The hut we built for administration purposes, drawings and the like. We built it with steel on the top of it and concreted it into the ground to stop it blowing away.

A place of refuge, when the wind was howling and the rain was blown in off the ocean like horizontal stair-rods, was the British army barracks being built as a set a short way down the mountain. It consisted of a series of semicircular, corrugated-iron Nissen huts. One of the huts was turned into the catering area, where the officer class of the construction army could enjoy eggs and bacon while the rain lashed against the windows. When things got really bad, or as an occasional treat, they retreated to the only bar in Dunquin, Kruger Kavanagh's, where pigs' trotters, smoked by the locals as they drank their pints and puffed on their Player's, were the speciality of the house. The building crew worked a six-day week, Monday to Saturday, 8.00 a.m. to 4.30 p.m., or when darkness fell. David came up every now and then to check on progress and chivvy everybody along before disappearing down the mountain and back to Dingle.

The fruit of their labours was Kirrary. While it stood, it was the westernmost village in Ireland, and therefore in Europe, depending on how you looked at the map, and that is overstating its uniqueness only slightly. Fifty-five permanent structures, some of them equipped with toilets, offices, kitchens, the lot. A pub that served beer. A large community that worked there daily for nearly a year. If it wasn't a village, it was as near as dammit.

Down in Dingle, the transformation wasn't as jaw-dropping, but it was spectacular nonetheless. The population of the town was 1,400 and dwindling, but now suddenly the pavements hardly seemed wide enough. Every vacant office space was taken by the production company, which, since most of the commercial properties were pokey, spread out across the town. The headquarters for Faraway Productions (the Lean company set up to make the film) was at No. 2 The Holyground. Next door, No. 1 The Holyground was Tom Long's pub, which would have its own stories to tell in due course. No. 2 was a substantial two-storey property with a big backyard, but nowhere near spacious enough to cater for all the different departments that came with such a big film. The associate producer, Roy Stevens, took up a lot of space with a big desk he had installed beside David Lean's office and took to chomping on cigars, *à la* Sam Spiegel. The art department, headed up by Stephen Grimes, was also housed there, but others had to spread their wings.

The special effects team took over the railway station of a disused train line that once ran from Dingle into the county's administrative centre, Tralee, a moutainous route a little more than forty miles that had taken nearly two hours to navigate back when it was in operation, which hadn't been for some considerable time. Eddie Fowlie's props office was on Main Street, a few doors down from Ashe's pub. Across the road, an editing suite was installed in an upstairs office, where the editor Norman Savage and his assistant Tony Lawson were to mark up and store the film. Around the corner was the publicity office headed up by a 28-year-old New Yorker called Bayley Silleck. The overflow from the Skellig Hotel stayed in Benners Hotel on Main Street or, if you were further down the food chain, in the scattering of bed and breakfasts around the small town. Space was at a premium as another fleet of adventurers was in town, trying to recover gold from the sunken wreck of the *Santa Maria de la Rosa* in the Blasket Sound. They all mingled in the pubs and with the cast and crew not slow about getting to the bar and getting the drinks in, any ice was quickly broken.

While Lean was adjusting to life in this cold and remote part of north-western Europe, Robert Bolt had returned from Rome to his Surrey mansion, the Mill House. He had left the Lamborghini in storage in the French port of Le Havre and made arrangements to be reunited with it in Ireland in a few weeks' time. Now was time for some recuperation after the exhausting months in Rome working with David on the script, though first he had one small job to do. George C. Scott had turned down the part of the teacher Shaughnessy, much to the disappointment of Lean, who shared the Hollywood establishment view that another actor under consideration, Robert Mitchum, was too much of a 'freewheeler'. Mitchum was Bolt's choice – 'if he's half what Roy Stevens says he is to work with, he'd be easy to have about the place, whereas Scott is, so they say, a bit neurotic and given to sudden violent tempers' – Bolt wrote to Lean on 22 October 1968. So it was time to go with Bolt's choice. And rather than Lean or Havelock-Allan, it was Bolt who put a transatlantic call through to the home in Bel Air, California, of Robert and Dorothy Mitchum.

Mitchum had already read the script, and he liked it. He found it a lyric, literate piece of work that, as he put it himself, gave 'room for dwelling'. He knew that with three genuine heavyweights of the movie industry collaborating – Lean, Bolt and Freddie Young – the chances of something worthwhile emerging at the end of it were extremely good. However, Lean's films demanded an enormous commitment of time and energy from those who got involved, and Mitchum wasn't prepared to make the effort. After seventy movies and feeling old and worn out though still only in his early fifties, he was considering retirement rather than putting himself at the mercies of the world's most painstaking film director. The first time Bolt called, Mitchum was out of the house and Dorothy answered. She told Bolt her husband would ring him back. 'You told him wrong,' Mitchum retorted when he returned home.

Nevertheless, when Bolt called again, Mitchum took the call. It was an important conversation in more ways than one. Not only did Bolt charm Mitchum into accepting the role, but in doing so he made promises that Mitchum would throw back in their faces as the movie progressed. What was said, according to the *Los Angeles Times* reporter Harry Lee Bowers, who interviewed Mitchum as he prepared to head for Dingle by downing cocktails in a Beverly Hills hotel, went as follows:

Bowers: What's the Lean film about?
Mitchum: (Taking a sip of his double Ramos Fizz) It's an entertainment. I don't know what it is about.
Bowers: What part do you play?
Mitchum: A husband. A yoke carrier. If it had been made long ago – who was the actor who played the perfect husband, the one who was always married to Joan Fontaine? – well that's who'd have played it.
Bowers: The Lean picture. Why are you doing it? You didn't want to work and you don't need the money. I read you're worth $5 million.
Mitchum: I read the script and I said that character works every day. So I say, 'No Way. I haven't been out of work in two years. I want no part of it.' The phone rings. It's Bolt. So before he can say anything I start saying, 'Anytime, OK, fine, I'll do it.' [Here Mitchum puts on an effete English accent] 'Hello,' Bolt says. 'Is it the extended tenure of the project? We've found through working out the schedule the

spots where you can be off for 10 days.' 'Spots,' I answered. 'No it's not that. I had just planned to commit suicide. No further questions, alright?'

[Again in an effete English accent] 'If you'd first do us a favour,' Bolt says, 'and do the picture, we'll take on the expenses of the burial.' So I told him I'd do the film if he was that serious about wanting me.

Bowers: How about the story? What's the character?

Mitchum: (Eyes widening, eyeballs rolling, chest expanding like a rooster) I just told you! A husband who shows up whenever the call sheet calls him. I won't tell the story unless we're naked in bed. (He orders another double Ramos Fizz.)

Bowers: How long will you be shooting?

Mitchum: How long did it take to shoot *Doctor Zhivago*? I'm playing a little Jewish lady. In the time of The Troubles. A husband! I'm going out of my \*\*\*. This is no way to be a movie actor. I think it will be my swan song physically. (To his press agent) 'They permit walking in Ireland, don't they?'

When Mitchum reached London in early February 1969, and was recuperating from the flight in his suite at the Dorchester Hotel, he was still spinning out the Bolt suicide yarn, this time for *The Observer* newspaper while dressed in white kimono pyjamas, dark glasses, black socks and a smoking cigar. A waiter wheeled into the suite an enormous trolley of drinks.

'Lot of people coming for drinks, sir?' the waiter asked
'Just me.'

The freewheeling was just starting.

Mitchum had picked up a new Porsche 911 direct from the sports car manufacturer's plant in Stuttgart, and after his sojourn in the Dorchester he drove to Ireland and joined Lean and other members of the crew and cast as they assembled at the Great Southern Hotel in Killarney, fifty miles from Dingle, on 18 February 1969. It was at the elegant Great Southern that Lean was enjoying his creature comforts, before taking the plunge into Dingle and the movie he was about to make. Also arriving, in his Volkswagen camper van, was the actor Leo McKern, who had excelled in Bolt's *A Man for All Seasons*, playing the part of Thomas Cromwell, and was now cast as the publican, Tom Ryan. He was clearly expecting a long haul, as he had also arranged for his thirty-foot pleasure yacht *Nutkin* to be sailed over from Southampton.

Bolt and Miles had also driven over with their son, Tom, and four dogs, Addo, Gladys, Arthur and Betty. In the lobby of the hotel, Mitchum met Sarah Miles for the first time and presented her with a rose. He asked her why she hadn't showed in Kenya for a previous film, *Mister Moses* (1968), in which they were supposed to star together. Sarah explained that she wouldn't leave her dogs in England. Mitchum's mood changed somewhat. 'Women and their fucking hounds,' he exclaimed, before strolling off.

Mitchum had briefly met Lean the year before in Rome, where the actor was shooting the war film *Anzio* (1968) and they renewed acquaintances at a get-to-know-you dinner that night in the hotel. Normally, dinner with Lean was like the captain's table, with the director at the top of it and his crew filling subordinate roles. Gentlemen wore jackets, at least until such time as David said they needn't. This time, Lean had asked his associate producer and confirmed

44

Dedicated Maniac, Roy Stevens, to host it. Stevens knew Mitchum, having worked with him in Australia on *The Sundowners* (1960).

Stevens got the impression that David didn't host the dinner because he was wary of Mitchum's insouciance. David didn't sit next to Mitchum, or opposite; instead he sat a bit further down, beside his girlfriend, Sandy. 'David hardly said a word,' said Stevens. 'And that went down very badly with Bob, so he started messing about and talking about his Quarter Horses and this, that and the other. David didn't know what he was talking about and you could see that he was getting very annoyed.' Lean's trusted second assistant director, Michael Stevenson, had also been invited to dinner because he knew Mitchum, and was left disappointed that the two men he admired so much hadn't clicked: 'Robert couldn't wait to get in the bar with the boys and David wanted to be alone with Sandy.'

Tensions at the top table hadn't seeped down to the production office on the Holyground, where the mood the following morning was expectant, almost giddy. Sarah swept in with her unleashed dogs, one of whom urinated on the electric heater. Through all the bustle, what hung in the air along with the mist, damp and smell of dog piss was the sweet scent of Oscars. David Lean's previous three films, *Bridge on the River Kwai*, *Lawrence of Arabia* and *Doctor Zhivago*, had won a total of nineteen Academy Awards. No wonder actors and technicians scrambled to run away with the Lean circus. Ernie Day, a director of photography, was happy to be demoted to camera operator just to be on the film. Peter O'Toole had fallen out with Lean since starring as Lawrence, but that didn't stop him sniffing around, trying to get the role of the village idiot Michael, which had Oscar written all over it. And the costume designer, Jocelyn Rickards, for all her bohemian mannerisms, craved industry recognition as much as anybody.

Phyllis Dalton, the designer who had won an Oscar for *Doctor Zhivago*, was unavailable for *Ryan's Daughter*, and Rickards had stepped in. Rickards had just finished a gruelling film in Co. Galway called *Alfred the Great* (1969), and had started work on another in London with Peter Sellers when the call came from Lean. It was an opportunity that might never come around again, and she had dropped everything and high-tailed it back to Ireland.

*Alfred* had been full of flea-ridden extras who didn't wear underpants, Rickards remembered, and David Lean's film promised plenty more (although Rickards's dealings with Lean would in time prove to be more unpleasant). Their initial meetings in London had gone well. Rickards had explained what she thought people of peasant stock from the early twentieth century would be wearing, and Lean had been enthusiastic. For the part of Rosy Ryan, Rickards then drew every combination of skirt and blouse, period dress, wedding dress, shoes, underclothes and fabric. Rickards and her assistant had taken the costume drawings to Lean for a meeting at the Ritz Hotel on Piccadilly and he had loved them all, or so he had said. Rickards had wanted Lean to attend a fitting for Sarah in London, but the director was too busy, and so all of the different options for the clothes had to be finished and sent to Ireland without Lean having seen them. This was a recipe for trouble, which arrived before Sarah had put on a stitch.

Rickards didn't exactly fit the profile of one of David's Dedicated Maniacs. For a start, she wasn't ex-British army.

She was also a little too flamboyant for David's tastes, drinking fizz in the production office, her long scarf flowing behind her as she made her way about, champagne flute and cigarette-holder in one hand. It was a minor detail, but Lean paid attention to minor details.

First into the office at the Holyground that morning, for his fitting in front of Lean, was Trevor Howard, playing the part of Fr Collins, the priest who tries to keep young Rosy and the rest of his flock on the straight and narrow. The priest's outfit had already caused some grief. Lean had offered the part to his long-time cohort, Alec Guinness, a practising Catholic, who had objected to the historical inaccuracy of the character wearing a soutane, the full-length flowing robe that was banned by the British authorities in Ireland at the period in history in which the film was set. Guinness was also disdainful about one unrealistic scene in the script, in which the priest goes out in a tiny boat in a wild sea. David must have thought, to hell with smart Alec, because he cast Trevor Howard instead.

While he had issues with the part and the length of time he would have to stay in Dingle, Trevor had no qualms about the outfit, and after being fitted out by Rickards and her assistants, he presented himself in front of David looking like the Bishop of Cork. His collar was gleaming white and the soutane was the perfect length, flowing down to his immaculately polished black brogues. David, however, wasn't about to bend down on one knee and kiss the holy ring. He took a pensive look at the attire, a look that said, 'we have some work to do on this'. The priest was a simple man living in a poor rural community without any domestic help and not above doing menial work to make ends meet. Let's put some dirt in that soutane, David said, and cut the sleeves, roughly, halfway up the arm. Give him a pair of fingerless gloves with holes in them. David turned to his long-time make-up man, Charlie Parker. 'Charlie, this man cuts his own hair, so cut his hair in a terrible way. He drinks a lot, so let's put some red veins around his nose and a cushion around his stomach.' David was so concentrated on the work that he couldn't see Howard's face, but Trevor was getting increasingly agitated as he was pulled hither and thither and dragged around the place. Finally, Lean looked up. 'That's it, thank you very much, Trev,' and Howard stomped off in a mood.

On the way out, Howard bumped into Mitchum. There was none of the same bonhomie when Howard had been reunited with his old drinking buddy a few nights previously in Ashe's pub and had cuffed him playfully around the ears. Now, Howard stormed past in his stained rags.

'So that's how you're going to play it, Jewish, huh?' Mitchum remarked after him.

Lean was only getting started, and Mitchum was next. The American actor had already attended a fitting session at Berman's costume house in the West End of London a couple of weeks previously, arriving for his fitting straight from an eleven-hour flight from Los Angeles. As befitting one of Hollywood's biggest stars, most of the staff at Berman's were hanging out the windows, waiting to catch a glimpse of him as he pulled up outside the Soho office in his limousine. By the time Rickards got to the fitting room, she had already been told that Mitchum was wearing a black hat, dark glasses, black trousers, a black polo-necked pullover, black socks, black shoes, a black raincoat and a long thick gold chain. Every inch the Bishop of Cork, in fact. Rickards introduced herself, and with her assistant, Ruth Myers, started the fittings for the part of the schoolteacher character played by Mitchum: suits, shirts, collars, nightshirts, an unlined grey alpaca jacket for when Mitchum was in the classroom, a raincoat and a tweed jacket. As Rickards worked, Mitchum picked her brains about the crew, the actors and the location, with which he was about to become acquainted. Rickards noted that, throughout the London session, Mitchum had his back to the mirror and was turned towards her. Rickards asked him if he wanted to have a look in the mirror. 'I figure you know what you're doing, no sense in my interfering; everything's comfortable,' Mitchum told her.

Being one of Hollywood's famous tough guys, much of Mitchum's don't-give-a-shit persona had been shaped around hard-boiled stories about the costumes he had worn in his career as an 'actress', which he frequently stated as his occupation in case anybody thought he was taking himself too seriously. On his first screen appearance decades before on the *Hopalong Cassidy* series, he had been given the hat of an actor, Charlie Murphy, who had died that day when his skull was crushed by a horse-drawn wagon in an on-set accident. The wardrobe man had scraped the gore off the rim before handing it to Mitchum, or so the actor liked to tell everybody. When he went on to establish himself as a star of noir cinema, his output was prodigious, and he spoke of making forty films 'in the same raincoat'. He had a freakish wasp-like physique, huge chest and thin waist. Get the fitting wrong, he frequently warned, and he would look like a 'Bulgarian wrestler'.

Mitchum felt Rickards would avoid such a mistake, but satisfying Lean at the second fitting in Dingle was another matter. On his way to becoming the most marketable director in cinema, Lean had started in film as a tea boy at Cineguild in London and worked in virtually every area of production, including a spell in the costume department. His attention to detail was already the stuff of legend. David had relied on a costume change for one of the big dramatic moments in *Lawrence*, when the character switches from Western to Arab attire. On *Doctor Zhivago* he had insisted on an outrageous pink outfit for Geraldine Chaplin at a Moscow train station, even though it was wholly impractical for a long-distance journey, but it made her teeth look white rather than yellow and created a bit of a 1960s fashion sensation.

There was no way he was going to give a costume designer *carte blanche*, and he was prepared to fine-tune endlessly. Mitchum was now finding this out, as he had to mismatch and put on different collars and suits. The producer Anthony Havelock-Allan watched on with an inkling of dread. 'David took it very seriously and Mitchum didn't. He said: "What is this? I've never done a dress parade in my life before. Give me the clothes and I will put them on. I'm not a tailor's dummy."' Lean insisted Mitchum look at himself in the mirror and give his opinion. Mitchum thought the bowler hat he was wearing gave him an Oriental look. 'I look like Charlie Chan,' he replied, referring to the bulky Chinese television detective. David was not amused. 'What *is* he saying?'

Havelock-Allan had wanted Gregory Peck for the part, and Peck was desperate for it, as his grandmother came from Dingle, along with scores of cousins. These early signs made Havelock-Allan yearn for Peck. 'Mitchum has a cynical disregard for films,' he remarked. 'It's a job, that's all. For David, it's an art.'

Havelock-Allan had other worries. He could see the 'little gem' of a film Lean had promised turning into a monster before his very eyes. In the normal director-producer relationship – such as the one Lean enjoyed with Sam Spiegel – this was something he could have put a stop to, but his was really a titular position, and Lean was effectively producer as well. The ten- to twelve-week shoot Lean had talked about had already been pushed out to five months, as MGM wanted Lean to think big, and the director wasn't inclined to disappoint his paymasters in New York. In his epic 'make it marvellous Freddie' letter to Young of 16 July 1968, David had told his director of photography that he wanted him to use his great technical skill so that some of *Ryan's Daughter* 'should have the voluptuous quality of an erotic thought', but then there was also the wider panorama to consider: 'Most of the beach stuff should look extremely beautiful in contrast to the almost sordid village and its mostly second-rate inhabitants. Small rooms and claustrophobia set against great stretches of wild coastline which, on the screen, could perhaps have the grandeur of Wadi Rum,' which brought us back to one of the dramatic desert landscapes in *Lawrence of Arabia*. Bolt was concerned about the direction Lean was taking, and so was Havelock-Allan.

'David thought it was going to be a little film, like *Brief Encounter*. What he hadn't realised was that by that time he had got into the mode of being a big picture maker. He was in epic mode,' Havelock-Allan said. 'That is why it took so long.'

Unlike Lean, most members of the cast and crew had a home to go to and loved ones waiting. Completely immersed in the filmmaking process and expecting others to be the same, David was happy to stretch it out. The first tell-tale sign was Lean's pre-production decision to revert to shooting using 70mm rather than 35mm film. Widescreen 70mm had been used in *Lawrence*, but they had then shot *Doctor Zhivago* in 35mm, and done so with relatively swift despatch. The negative had then been enlarged at MGM's world-leading laboratory in Culver City, Los Angeles County. Lean wasn't completely happy with it, though Freddie couldn't tell the difference, and the two statuettes sitting in the display cabinet of his home in West London suggested he had a point.

'What was wrong with *Zhivago*?' he asked Lean.

'Nothing,' replied David, 'but I want to use 70mm.'

'Okay,' Freddie replied.

For Young, 70mm created problems he could do without. For a start, it was far more expensive, and Young was a good company man, having worked for MGM for decades. Shooting in 70mm meant that everything had to be much bigger and heavier – not just the camera itself, but all the paraphernalia around it: the crane, the track, the tripods and (particularly) the lights. Young got on to Lee Electrics in London, telling the owner, John Lee, to prepare a crew and inventory for every possible contingency. If Lean was insisting on perfection, Young wasn't going to be the one caught out cutting corners. As 70mm required far more lighting than 35mm, Young ordered twelve Brute lamps, each weighing three hundredweight. 'Make that a baker's dozen,' he said. The stands for the lamps were another three hundredweight. The Brutes needed a huge amount of electricity, and hundreds of feet of heavy copper cabling running to big generators also constituted tons more weight. For every Brute, an electrician was needed, and so it was quite a convoy – thirteen vehicles in all, most of them Land Rovers – that set off from Lee Electrics in West London in February 1969 to hook up with Young in Dingle.

There was snow on the ground, so caution was the watchword. However, the electricians were to be christened the clowns of the Lean circus, and it wasn't difficult to see why. At the head of the convoy was the chief electrician or gaffer, Bernie Prentice, driving his yellow soft-top Jaguar E-Type, the only vehicle not towing a trailer. A ferry strike had forced them to come on a circuitous route from West London to Larne in Scotland to Belfast, then across the border and on down to Kerry. A few miles from Dingle, Prentice sped ahead in his E-Type to get a cup of tea and a sandwich laid on for the boys. When he got to No. 2 The Holyground, the first thing the people in the production office said to him was, 'What's the damage to the generator that overturned?'

'What overturned gennie?' an indignant Prentice replied.

Turns out that once Prentice had left the convoy and sped ahead, the drivers behind him had started a race to Dingle. One of the sparks, Denis Brennan, tried to take a bend in the Land Rover just outside Dingle at about 40mph, and didn't make it. 'We hadn't even started the job,' Prentice noted ruefully. 'That's why I had kept in front of them all the way, because I knew what they were like.' One electrician, who could turn his hand to anything, Bertie Hughes, was immediately taken off normal duties and told he would be a full-time mechanic, his first job being to fix the broken generator before word filtered back to head office in West London.

Prentice located a warehouse, just beside Ashe's pub. Soon the crew had retired to Ashe's for the evening. One drink followed another. Prentice's assistant, Bob Bremner, then heard a commotion upstairs. Granny Ashe had been smoking in bed and a small fire had started. The fire was extinguished, the mattress went out the window and the lady was brought downstairs to have a drink. The local fire brigade, made up of volunteers, duly arrived and, with everything having returned to normal, they decided to quench their thirst instead. 'Two o'clock in the morning, we're all pissed. One of the farmers said he was off and he took the fire engine home for safe-keeping,' said Bremner.

Gaffer Prentice sensed there were more incidents just around the corner. Lean had picked a remote spot on a bog road for the first day's filming, the scene in which a local policeman is shot by rebel gun-runners after he realises that they are not the tinkers they are claiming to be. Access to the spot from the road was poor, and on the recce the night before the Land Rover had got stuck in mud. Prentice warned Freddie Young that if they were going to shoot there, they would have to do so without lights, as the Land Rovers carrying the generators wouldn't get through the mud.

Lean didn't want to hear excuses: 'This is where I'm shooting and we start at nine o'clock in the morning'. Construction manager Peter Dukelow intervened, assuring Prentice that everything would be okay. Dukelow had thirty-tonne dump trucks backing up the lane late into the night, dropping their loads of gravel from the local quarry, with Caterpillar tractors spreading it out. All the way, for several hundred yards, so that they could get a generator some of the way down and cables the rest.

And so it was that shooting began – officially, at least – first thing Monday morning, 24 February 1969, a crisp winter's day.

# 4. Not waving, drowning

Waiting back at either No. 2 The Holyground or the Skellig Hotel, poised for 'Acc-shun', was Trevor Howard. When it didn't arrive, there were serious issues. It wasn't Mitchum who was the problem early on, it was more so Howard, who appeared to be doing his best to have himself removed from the movie. If Mitchum was drinking heavily, his alcohol intake was matched at least by Howard, who, unlike his American friend, quickly became a very messy and public drunk. Furthermore, he was nursing a grudge against Lean. Howard hadn't worked with Lean since *The Passionate Friends*, which was released in 1949, and he was annoyed with the director for overlooking him for parts in other movies since, particularly *Kwai*.

While he accepted the role in *Ryan's Daughter*, Howard wasn't particularly enamoured with the Fr Collins part either, complaining, after reading the script, that the priest was always trying to catch up on the action. At the back of the set one morning he made his feelings known to Lean, telling him, 'You know I am only doing this because of you'. Lean suggested they go for a walk, away from the others, during which he explained what Bolt and himself had been aiming at with Fr Collins: an unbending disciplinarian but a wise and benevolent man whose flock was lucky to have him.

The priest's virtues amplify Rosy's dilemma, as she turns her back on what he has taught her and nurtures her forbidden desires, in the process betraying not only her husband but her way of life.

Convincing Howard of the value of the role wasn't even half the battle, however. Howard's actress wife, Helen Cherry, had theatre commitments in London, meaning the actor was on his own, which was a recipe for alcoholic mayhem. In the cloistered environment of Dingle, that was always going to be problematic, particularly since Howard, Lean and as many film people as could fit had moved from the Great Southern to the fifty-room Skellig Hotel in Dingle as work got underway in earnest. Howard's unhappiness deepened, as he was on call every day, and required for make up at 6 a.m., but remained stuck at the hotel until he was stood down in the evening without getting his face in front of the camera.

Josie McAvin, the art director from Dublin who had taken a job as a set dresser to work with Lean, spotted the warning signs before most.

Trevor was dressed every single morning in his priest robes and he wasn't used for six weeks. So he'd get drunk as a coot. Instead of letting him loose saying, 'we don't want you for the day', the production department would be afraid to say to David, 'why don't you let him away?' just in case David changed his mind and Trevor was needed. When we would get back to the hotel at night, Trevor would be there roaring, and he really did roar like a lion. As you can imagine, this upset David Lean.

Finally, there was some shooting on the beach, but that ended up going disastrously wrong. Lean and Fowlie had picked out Coumeenoole Cove, on the westernmost tip of the peninsula, a remote, wild spot. The small beach of golden sand was surrounded by rocks on one side and black cliffs on the other but was accessible by a slipway that led down from the main road. It was one of the spectacular locations that would look wonderful on celluloid but was also a dangerous place to work. Not only was the Atlantic Ocean beating in on it, but the stretch of water known as the Blasket Sound had dangerous currents and eddies. Enchanted by its ruggedness, Lean wanted to shoot much of the action on this beach, including the storm scene, even though he had been warned about its hazards by the art director, Roy Walker, who had almost lost his family there on Christmas Eve 1968, during preparations for the beginning of shooting.

Lean had asked Walker to stay on in Ireland over the festive season and get some photographs when the seas were rough. Walker had driven to Coumeenoole in the Land Rover with his wife Sue, son Laurence and their pet Yorkshire terrier. Walker told his family to stay back while he climbed some rocks closer to the sea to take a few photographs.

I was taking a shot and I suddenly felt wet. I was up to my knees in water and it was rapidly getting deeper as a huge wave had come in. My wife and son were gone. I could see the bundle of red which was Laurence's anorak in the surf. My wife managed to grab him and then the little Yorkie. We were all covered in sand and seaweed. Then there were these weird locals who lived on the hill above the beach.

They hadn't moved, they didn't come and help us or anything.

Walker and family beat a retreat back to their hotel, soaking and covered in sand and bits of seaweed.

'The girl at the reception desk said, "Ah Mr Walker, how is it then? You look a bit wet.'

'We nearly got drowned. At Coumeenoole.'

'"It's a dangerous place, to be sure," she said.'

David came back after Christmas and asked to see Walker's photographs.

'When I told him the story he said, "I don't believe you". I said, "David, it's a death trap." I went back and I sat on the slipway and watched. There was a sand bar way out and it would build up. And every twenty minutes this huge wave would come and you could set your watch by it.'

David decided to erect a Jacob's ladder from the top of the cliffs down to the beach, which was like a lift shaft built with scaffolding, in this case for getting personnel and supplies onto and off the beach, in a hurry if necessary. It could also serve as a platform for filming the storm, in which actors and extras were due to retrieve an arms shipment from the boiling seas. The actor Leo McKern, who played the role of Tom Ryan and had a big part to play in the storm scene, was another who looked on aghast at what Lean was doing. McKern, a keen and competent swimmer and sailor, had already got to know how treacherous the sea around Dingle could be, but he quickly realised that the people who were going to put him and others out in a storm hadn't done their own homework.

McKern had assumed that with so much expertise about, Lean would have worked out how to shoot the storm. He was alarmed by what he saw at Coumeenoole as they busied themselves with the construction of the Jacob's ladder and drilled eye bolts into the rocks to strap down cameras. In the pubs and on the quayside he had been talking to the local fishermen, and his worst suspicions were confirmed when he saw the marks left by a high tide and the shape of the shoreline. 'It became pretty clear that it would be very interesting indeed to witness shooting at this particular place in a full gale as actors, camera, lights and crew would be working under twenty-foot waves,' McKern noted. 'Nobody seemed to have realised that in a gale force 8 or storm 10, the seascape would be changed beyond recognition, even at low tide.'

Lean persevered with the preparations.

'Four days later there was a huge storm and nothing was left of the Jacob's ladder except twisted metal,' said Walker. 'So I said to him, "Forget it. You'll kill people".'

The storm had also wrecked some currachs that had been left on the beach in preparation for shooting, and all for nought, as the unit hadn't captured any footage due to concerns about safety that were quickly borne out. The storm would have to be shot elsewhere. Still, Lean loved the location, and wanted to use the beach on calmer days. An early scene where the priest and the fool Michael sweep up to the beach in a currach and then haul it ashore, where they meet Rosy, was one such straightforward scene – on paper – that he had in mind.

On 11 March, Howard was finally called from the hotel to the beach, and the wind was picking up when he got in the boat with Mills. All he had to do was sit there and let Mills, who was a competent and powerful oarsman from previous adventure roles, do the work. On the first take, Mills pulled on the oars, caught an incoming wave, headed towards the camera and disembarked. No sooner had he done so than a wave broke behind them and turned the boat sideways, filling it with water and slamming it broadside into the beach. Howard and Mills were sent sprawling into the shallows, but both were willing to continue. Setting up the shot was a lengthy process, and an hour later, as Lean tried a second take, the wind grew even stronger. The actors couldn't hear the crew's instructions, even though megaphones were used. The flag was raised for Mills to start rowing to the shore and the lightweight craft rose up on the crest of a wave and surfed beautifully towards the Panavision camera. Then, as if from nowhere, a twenty-foot wall of water struck the boat on the port side, lifted it up like a toy and flipped it upside down. Howard was thrown through the air and hit the sandy bottom, but came quickly to the surface. Mills was less fortunate. The starboard gun-whale of the currach came crashing down on his head and left shoulder, knocking him unconscious and trapping him under the overturned boat.

Frogmen – actually two assistant directors in wet suits trailing safety lines – rushed into the water and dragged the two actors ashore. Mills was out cold, and his limp figure was placed on a stretcher. He then regained consciousness and refused to go in the stand-by ambulance, preferring to be driven home. He also refused to be seen by the unit doctor, local man Donal Savage, who was fond of a drop and somewhat shaky of hand. Instead, Dr George Lyons had to leave his post some forty miles away at Tralee General Hospital and drive over the Conor Pass to Dingle to treat Mills. Howard was shaken and just needed a drink, observing that in the old days they used to do this sort of thing in studio tanks with special effects men whipping up the waves. Howard then made an extraordinary claim: 'David Lean wasn't concerned about our "death" at all, because we had only just started on the film and we could have used two other people later. What he was concerned about was people coming to save our lives who ran across the sand, making footmarks, which would have wasted time for people to have to put right.'

It was true that footprints in the sand caused all sorts of problems, but the rest of it was a slight exaggeration. Two weeks later Howard was in the wars again, this time very much as the villain of the piece. Any residue of sympathy from his boating accident had quickly rubbed off, as he was again roaring like one of those lions from the zoo in Rome as he waited on call and sank innumerable pints of stout. Niall Tóibín, the Irish actor who played the part of The Political (O'Keefe) involved in the gun-running, was also in the throes of alcoholism, but even he was taken aback by Howard's behaviour, which he witnessed as a fellow guest in the Skellig.

Trevor had been there for a couple of months drinking his head off and he'd been called only once and didn't get his face in front of the camera. David Lean had gone to bed early because we were shooting the following morning and Trevor came up the stairs pissed out of his fucking mind. I was in one of the bedrooms down the corridor. Trevor took off his shoe and started belting Lean's door with it. 'Come out, Lean, you fucking cunt. Come out, you fucking bollocks.' And he's fucking and blinding. And Lean says, 'Go away, Trevor. Sober up. Stop acting like a child.' They were being very nice, humouring him. What Howard was doing was trying to get fired before they shot on him.

And he almost succeeded, in the most comical of circumstances. After a Saturday night party, a group had reconvened in a Dingle pub on the Sunday morning, the second assistant director Michael Stevenson among them.

There was a goose on the bar, in a bag, eggs. All the locals. Charlie [Parker, the make-up man], Bob [Mitchum], Trevor, myself. These young guys, they were like gypsies, came in on horses, bareback. It was like a western the way they tied them up and came into the bar. Bob invited them for a drink. A half an hour went by. Bob was making remarks about Charlie and the goose. Out of the corner of my eye I saw Trevor.

'Chinamen, you are all Chinamen. All sweet-smelling Chinamen.'

'Yeah, Treas [Mitchum's nickname for Howard], sure we are,' said Mitchum.

We carried on drinking. Suddenly Howard leapt on one of the horses and took off.

Mitch said: 'We better get him off that horse. He ain't a good rider you know.'

Howard had spent much of his time on a horse in his previous film, *The Charge of the Light Brigade*, but Mitchum knew what he was talking about. Stevenson watched while the gypsies jumped up on their remaining horses to chase Trevor.

The more it was chased, the faster it went. Trevor was hanging on for dear life, roaring like a lion. We're all in different vehicles, Bob and myself and Charlie, going after Trevor. As he was going past the houses people were waving and he was roaring, 'Get me off this horse'. All the Irish people were saying, 'Oh look, there's Mr Howard from the fillum. There he is. There's Bob Mitchum.' In the end the horse realised he had a fool on his back and he just tossed him into a field. The next day we saw Trevor with his legs up in the air in the hospital in Tralee. There was Father Collins, in the bed.

Howard had broken his shoulder and cracked a couple of ribs.

'Whatever you do, don't make him laugh,' said Mitchum, who arrived at his bedside.

Somebody else said: 'Whatever you do, don't give him a drink.'

Sarah Miles said Howard fell off a donkey rather than a horse, and others said that Howard had been trying to show off his riding skills to some local girls, but everybody was agreed on one thing: that Howard was in danger of getting chucked off the film, as Lean had clearly been pushed too far. 'Trevor wasn't supposed to be on the horse, that's what caused a lot of problems with the insurance claim. He was drunk in charge of a horse,' said the art director, Roy Walker.

At one point, Trevor's sacking looked like a foregone conclusion, with names of replacements being bandied about, Lee J. Cobb being one of them.

'Well David, if you get Lee J. Cobb, is he going to play it Jewish?' Mitchum asked. 'If he does, maybe I should keep my shades on.'

Richard Boone's name came up, too. A fabulous actor, but a massive drinker.

'They think they have a problem with me; wait till they get an eye full of Richard,' Howard remarked.

Sarah Miles, who had warmed to Howard's eccentric ways and was a huge admirer of his acting ability, spoke to her husband, who also had the actor's back. Bolt went to see Lean and convinced him that none of them would be as good as Howard, who for good measure managed to get himself out of hospital and back on call.

Still, something had to change. The solution involved evicting Howard from the hotel, so that he was out of Lean's eyeline and earshot, except when he was required in front of the camera. The change was handled in such a way that Howard didn't lose face. Not only was Howard moved elsewhere – to a private rented house in the town – but the production company took the opportunity to have a general clear-out. The company had the run of the Skellig for the winter, but there were existing summer bookings that had to be fulfilled, and it was only Lean and about a dozen others who were able to stay.

David and Sandy took up a lot of space, for the company had got its people in to knock out a couple of internal walls and put three rooms together to create the hotel's only suite and make things more comfortable for them. The harsh and noisy strip lighting in the bathroom was removed and replaced by softer-pink glowing lamps that presented David in a more flattering light. This was hardly a challenge for the film's construction manager, Peter Dukelow, who after all had been responsible for overseeing the construction of that bridge over the river in Ceylon, which involved chopping down trees in the surrounding jungle and having them hauled to the construction site by Indian elephants.

Dukelow and the *Ryan's Daughter* construction crew had enough to be getting on with building their village on the mountaintop, and now there were other irksome 'and while you're at it' jobs once houses were found for the actors and crew within a twenty-five-mile radius of the town. It was then that David Lean's settlement of the Dingle Peninsula began in earnest.

The Dingle folk mostly had outhouses where they performed their daily ablutions, but this wasn't thought good enough for the visitors, who knew they were in for a long haul the way everything was shaping up. The crew got a set per diem rate when it came to accommodation, so instead of paying for hotel rates, most opted to rent instead. Roy Walker took a small house in Dingle, and one of the bedrooms was converted into a bathroom. He became known locally as 'the bloke with the bathroom'.

Jocelyn Rickards and others had similar renovations carried out – repainting, heat installation, new windows fitted, you name it. The work was undertaken either by crew from the film or local builders employed at the expense of the production company. In at least a dozen cases – probably more like two or three dozen – local families moved out of their homes and in with relatives or otherwise went mobile to avail of the unexpected financial windfall coming their way.

Leo McKern was delighted to be able to rent a newly completed bungalow from a local couple, Tommy and Ursula Sheehy. As Leo told it, the couple were building their new home bit by bit, but a six-month rental paid in advance by the film company on his behalf provided them with the necessary cash to complete it in one spell. The McKerns – Leo, Jane and their two young daughters – were the first occupiers of the Sheehy home. The Sheehys themselves took up residence in a caravan in the garden with their children. For the McKerns, the process of settling in was eased when their two young girls were quickly accepted into local schools. Lessons in this Gaeltacht area were taught *as Gaeilge*, but everyone coped, and the young blow-ins quickly picked up the Irish language.

Mitchum had an equally holistic arrangement, albeit on an entirely different scale. His personal assistant, Reva Frederick, had briefly come over from Los Angeles and picked out a small hotel across town called Milltown House, which Mitchum ended up renting out in its entirety from another family of Sheehys. Milltown House was more like a guesthouse, perched on the edge of Dingle Bay and accessible from the town across a narrow causeway. It would achieve almost instant notoriety, becoming known as the 'Dingle Brothel', much to the horror of landlady Margaret Sheehy, but it was so much more than that. It was more like a drop-in centre for locals who Mitchum had befriended, and an oasis for crew, actors and stand-ins. Living with him was his 'man' when he filmed in Europe, an ex-British guardsman called Harold Sanderson, whose loosely defined role encompassed doorman, stand-in, drinks mixer, fixer and bodyguard. Mitchum regarded the hotel with a typically bemused air. 'It had nine rooms numbered one to 10 – I never could figure that out.

Upstairs, at one end of the hall, the sign said "Bath" and "T-I-L-E-T" at the other. It was $450 a month. Furnished it with a bunch of directors' chairs.'

Mitchum had visitors, many of them over from England, where he had worked and played on numerous occasions, and he would inform folks on the set that 'number 7 is hot tonight' based on who was occupying that particular room at the time. He had other stories with which to amuse the crew. The telephone at the front desk of Milltown House remained in operation during Mitchum's stay, and while he waited for Lean to call him to the set, he would end up talking to people on the telephone from places like Liverpool and Leeds.

Could they have their usual room, please? The family was coming.

Mitchum would respond: 'You can have room 9.'

'We were in number 6 last time.'

'Number 6 is occupied.'

'What's happened to Mrs Sheehy?'

'Oh, she's moved on. It's run by a rich American now and he's turned it into a nudist colony.'

If the Skellig Hotel was the official residence of *Ryan's Daughter*, then Milltown House was its disreputable, outrageous cousin – during Mitchum's time – where all and sundry were drawn. Oiling the wheels of discourse were cases of whisky, brandy and other spirits delivered to the house by the drinks giant Seagram's, who had a stake in MGM at the time.

Mitchum put the socialising down to research, as he had come over a month before he was needed for his first scene to settle himself in and work on his Irish accent.

He did this by inviting locals around for drinks. Amongst his guests would be a senior member of the local Gardaí, the parish priest or the doctor. They would come in for a tipple and be there for four or five hours. The conversation would occasionally stray into politics or the wars in Biafra or Vietnam (Mitchum wasn't long from a celebrity tour of duty in South East Asia), not to mention the growing tensions north of the Irish border, which the actor was following closely. Mitchum studied his history and liked it to be known that he wasn't just a he-man; he was a highly literate he-man. While he was supposed to listen, he also ended up doing a lot of the talking, so his Irish guests had to adjust their ear to his hipster, jazzman talk.

Mitchum told them about his time working on the aircraft production line at Lockheed during the Second World War, when he became fast friends with a red-headed Irishman, Jim Dougherty, who used to share the lunch box prepared for him by his teenage wife, Norma Jean Baker, later to become Marilyn Monroe. Then there were his numerous run-ins with the law – 'sassing the cops' – which resulted in him doing time on a chain gang in Georgia after being busted for vagrancy during the Great Depression, when he rode freight trains around the US for years. Grass grew wild on the side of the line, and he later picked up another jail sentence for 'conspiracy to possess' marijuana, a famous Hollywood scandal that had forged his reputation.

Half the time his guests didn't know whether the stories he told them were true or not, but they checked out, even if he liked to give them a twist. His guests were surprised by how well read he was, and how he could quote at length from poems by Keats and Shelley.

When Mitchum and his wife Dorothy had the flu, he called the unit doctor and renowned storyteller, Donal Savage. The doctor arrived with a female companion and had a drink. After a couple of hours swapping yarns, Doctor Savage said: 'You never did meet my wife, did you?'

'He then introduced Bob and me to his wife,' says assistant director Michael Stevenson, who was also there that night. 'Then he left without even offering any medicine. Bob says, "How about that shit? He drinks my Scotch. You never did meet my wife, did you?"'

Some of his guests left so shit-faced that Mitchum would watch to see whether they could make it over the narrow bridge across the Milltown River, which led from beside his hotel back into Dingle, without crashing their bicycle or car into the wall.

His living room was quickly stacked with magazines, books and records. On call once filming started, Mitchum settled down to read Christy Brown's *My Left Foot*, after being introduced to the writer by a mutual friend, a solicitor named Joe Grace, who brought them all off on a pub crawl of Dingle. Crippled by cerebral palsy, Brown trusted Mitchum to wheel him around, as the actor had friends in wheelchairs who had returned badly injured from the fighting in Korea and Vietnam. Mitchum would later start an impromptu Christy Brown admiration society with the broadcaster David Frost.

'In the heat we went out and had a few jars,' he told Frost, putting on an Irish accent before getting serious.

I have some friends who are paraplegics and have no use with their legs. And one of them is a big cat, 245 pounds, and I have to wheel him around in a wheelchair. And he is very delicate around the lower back, around the coccyx, because if he snaps again, then he's really had it.

At the same time, you can't be too delicate in a wheelchair because it is like balancing, like a furniture mover. Christy found out that I was at least acquainted with movement, with handling people in wheelchairs, so he felt confident. And we were both drunk, let's face it, with all these Irishmen going from pub to pub.

Joe says [puts on heavy Irish accent], 'Yer man Christy, he's written a book.' So I thought, what sort of book? Cat sitting there stoned, all twisted up. And I thought something by a child in crayon, as dim as I am. And it dawned on me that he was a very inquisitive and assimilative man.

When not filming during the day, which was most of the time, Mitchum developed a routine where he would go shopping around the town, which was a short walk from his lair. He would hop delicately from one store to the next with a wicker basket tucked under his arm, exchanging pleasantries with the shopkeepers and others, mostly getting goods on credit, and his wife Dorothy would then come around to pay the bills the next time she was in town. In the evening, Mitchum would sometimes go for a drink at one of the estimated fifty pubs in the town. It was then that he had a couple of run-ins with the locals, one of which curbed his socialising.

A set of neighbours across the road from Milltown House were two bachelor farmers, the brothers Timmy and Stephen Kelliher. Like many of the local people, Stevie had a sideline or two, in his case at the wheel of a hackney cab, and he had found work on *Ryan's Daughter* as the driver for Peter Dukelow. It was a job Stevie excelled in, as he knew every pub and its owner within a fifty-mile radius, and Dukelow was a thirsty employer who appreciated that his driver could find him a drink at any hour of the night or day. Stevie was on call all hours, but the rewards were phenomenal – £28 a week plus all the drink that Dukelow would buy him, and when it came to payment, there was no such thing as 'I'll see you tomorrow, Stevie'.

The Duke told Stevie that he would be needed for the best part of a year, and the two Kelliher brothers had agreed that Timmy would take over most if not all of the farm work. Stevie was an amateur actor himself, and loved the whole buzz surrounding the fillum. Brother Timmy had no time for it. Traffic had doubled, a nuisance when Timmy was bringing the cows in for their daily milking. They had fifteen cows up the way, in the field past the graveyard, and the journey of about 200 yards along the road took about ten minutes. Not long for a driver to wait. No matter who you were.

Timmy hated drivers who came too close to the cows. He didn't much like cops either. And at first glance he took the guy who sped around the corner in a big Mercedes, causing a few of the cows to bolt, for a cop. Until the man wound down the window and opened his mouth.

'Could you take those steers to one side? I need to get by,' the man said in a broad American accent.

Timmy also had a bit of a downer on Yanks. This man wasn't being rude, but the accent grated. He ignored the request and concentrated on settling his cows.

'I'm running late.'

'I've as much cause to the road as you,' Timmy replied.

The man in the Mercedes tried a different approach. 'I'm living up there in Milltown House. I'm Robert Mitchum.'

'You could be Robert Emmet for all I care.'

Mitchum immediately understood the reference to the renowned eighteenth-century Irish rebel, laughed, and a few seconds later he had edged past and was on his way.

Timmy later set off on his other daily walk, to his local. He was aware that some of the fillum people had taken it over, but just like on the road earlier that day, he wasn't one to allow himself to be pushed to one side. When he entered Thomas Ashe's, all eyes were on him, and Mitchum pointed him out playfully. Drinks were bought.

'What did you say to the big man today?' asked the publican Kate Ashe.

Timmy Kelliher wasn't looking for a story to tell his grandkids, because he wasn't going to have any. Someone who *was* looking for local kudos turned up when Sarah Miles and Robert Bolt threw a party at their place on Holy Saturday, 5 April 1969, going into Easter Sunday. The couple weren't staying far from Dingle, except there was a large mountain in-between, negotiable only over a tricky stretch of road called the Conor Pass. The idea was that Bolt was at hand when Lean needed him but still had the solitude to work on other projects. Fermoyle House became Mr and Mrs Bolt's place of residence. It was a large nineteenth-century grey stone mansion set in a sizeable garden with stunning views of the Atlantic Ocean, the perfect house to open the doors and throw a big party, or so the glamorous couple thought.

The actors and crew were all invited, and word of the party spread on the bush telegraph. The Bolts, accustomed to more refined mores as they socialised around London, were unaware that gate-crashing parties was a national pastime in Ireland. Everybody from the film showed up – except for Lean, who Sarah thought had stayed away because Mitchum was attending. Also there, it seemed to the hostess, was half of Ireland. All were let in on the basis that it was too early in the filming to recognise faces. With alcohol flowing, this was a recipe for trouble, and it wasn't long in arriving. Words were exchanged in the drawing room between Mitchum and a local man equal in bulk. What was said – or written – remains a matter of conjecture. Miles says that it started as a play fight before turning nasty. Others said that Mitchum, having been asked to sign something, had written an offensive message.

He had form in this regard, in Ireland. While making *The Night Fighters* (1960) near Dublin about ten years earlier, he was drinking with his fellow actor Richard Harris and their wives in Groomes Hotel, opposite the Gate Theatre, when he was hassled for an autograph by an irritating man who had called him 'Mr Douglas' and then 'Kirk'. Mitchum had written on a piece of paper 'kiss my ass' and signed it 'Kirk Douglas'. When he read it, the recipient of the insult had then thrown a punch, which struck Mitchum on the nose, and a rumpus had ensued with Harris at the centre of it and the Gardaí getting involved.

Now it was kicking off again in the house of *Ryan's Daughter*, with an argument between Mitchum and a local gate-crasher, but this was a more wicked act, as the assailant stuck his thumb into Mitchum's left eye. He then fled, with Mitchum chasing after him, loudly threatening revenge. Mitchum went to his Porsche and re-emerged with a large hunter's knife. The sight of Mitchum charging from room to room with the knife in his hand was the signal for Miles to deal with the situation. She summoned her most authoritative voice from deep within to announce that the party was over and everybody needed to leave immediately. Much to her surprise, people listened.

Back in Los Angeles, the story grew wings, with Mitchum's brother, John, telling everybody that Robert was slicing a piece of turkey at a lovely buffet and cocktail party when he was attacked and had responded by trying to pierce his assailant through with the carving knife. The knife that was actually used – or thankfully only brandished – was a seven-inch Puma White Hunter steel knife made in West Germany, which Mitchum had picked up when he was collecting his Porsche. Like the motor car, it was a Teutonic thing of beauty, and when the Spanish assistant director Pedro Vidal pointed this out, Mitchum sold him the knife for a penny. It was a wise move in the circumstances.

More wisdom was imparted when Mitchum went to see Dr Savage on the Easter Monday with his blood-shot eye.

'What did the doctor say?' Mitchum's driver asked him as he emerged, his big black eye still visible behind a large pair of sunglasses.

'Duck the next time.'

# 5. Five seasons in one day

Peter O'Toole found that working on *Lawrence of Arabia* after a while felt more like 'a way of life' than filmmaking. Sarah seemed to be singing off the same hymn sheet. *Ryan's Daughter* wasn't just a movie, she told the writer Stephen Silverman later. It was 'a way of life'. At least filming was underway and the days were lengthening as winter turned into spring. They hadn't quite got the storm they were looking for, but what was needed now was for the sun to shine, particularly so that they could film the many beach scenes. Instead, Kerry rain set in.

'It was terrible, terrible,' said Pedro Vidal, sucking on an untipped Camel as if to dispel the bad taste in his mouth. 'Every fucking day was raining and raining and raining. Never since I started in the business in 1955 had I fired anybody. I had a marvellous driver and he said to me, "Nice soft day, Mr Vidal" and I said, "Say that again and you are fired". I just couldn't stand it.'

Vidal had worked with Lean since *Lawrence of Arabia*, as had Roy Stevens, the associate producer, and they were both two of his very Dedicated Maniacs. It fell to Stevens to ring the meteorological office in Dublin each morning and evening to get an idea of the forecast, but only an idea. Half the time he would end up telling the weather people in Dublin what the conditions were like, and the reply he would get back would be along the lines of 'Well sure, it will probably be like that then for the rest of the day.'

'On *Lawrence*, I think David went two years over-budget,' says Stevens. 'The one that was more or less close to being on schedule was *Doctor Zhivago* and that was because there was always sun. One of the reasons why it took sixty or seventy weeks to do *Ryan's Daughter* was because the weather changed all the time. One minute it was fine, another minute it was cloudy, another minute it was rainy, then it was fine again. And David couldn't say, "We'll do the shot, end it there and make it work".'

On every other film the crew had worked on, there would be one daily call sheet, which was produced the previous evening and set out which actors were required for shooting the next day, the time and location, along with information about other requirements for shooting, such as transport, props, stand-ins and extras. On *Ryan's Daughter*, there would be four or five different call sheets, some internal, some external, like the one as follows for 8 April 1969:

1. If Sunny – Beach (Banna)
2. If Dull – Ext. (Village)
3. If Dull – Int. (Schoolhouse)
4. If cloudy and sunny – Ext. Schoolhouse
5. Standby – Ext. Schoolhouse.

'David would never take second best, the weather had to be right for that particular scene and that particular mood,' says assistant director Michael Stevenson. 'If the weather was that bad, we'd end up shooting in Ryan's pub and you could hear the wind howling and whistling around the pub and around the street.'

Sometimes one part of the film unit would be hastening to one location along a narrow country road only to run into a different part of the unit coming the other way, having been given instructions about a change of location for shooting. Or they would find one of the lorries stuck in the mud and nobody else able to move either. David ranted and raved, slamming his hand down on the horn of his Rolls-Royce, but a part of him really loved it. He was known as the last of the big spenders, but he saw it a slightly different way. 'I always say we are the last of the travelling circuses,' he remarked as he propped up the bar in Ryan's pub on another rain-swept day when no shooting was possible. 'We can hardly go anywhere without a great mass of vans and cranes and camera cars and all the rest of it.'

Everybody had to be ready to move and move fast, depending on the director's whim. 'You can't be prepared unless you take everything you've got with you every time. You [do] make up and now you have to place the camera, rehearse and by the time you're ready, it's pouring with rain,' says Havelock-Allan. The producer danced to Lean's tune, along with the rest of the crew and cast.

By this stage, Howard had settled in and kept his drinking more discreet. Besides the weather, in those early months it was really only Mitchum who was ornery. Lean had decided to shoot some sunny beach scenes early, while he was waiting for the village to be completed, so they were shooting in the cold Kerry spring, pretending it was summer. Even still, a lot more happened on the beaches in *Ryan's Daughter* than would have been the case in real life.

On a return trip from Dublin, Mitchum's schoolteacher character, Shaughnessy, walks from a bus stop to his home along a long, sandy beach where he is surprised to come across a former pupil, Rosy, who has contrived to meet him having decided that the nature of the relationship between them is going to change. Shooting from a nearby clifftop, Lean panned away to capture some of the glorious Atlantic landscapes around Dingle, with clouds scudding across the blue sky.

The shoot appeared to have gone well, but everyone was still anxiously waiting as the film had to be rushed to Los Angeles, developed and then returned, to be viewed by the director and his close circle, to check that they were happy with the images the camera had captured. Only when the director was happy could the instruction go out to 'strike the set' and the crew would dismantle the various props and screens before moving on to the next scene.

Viewing the rushes, or dailies as they were also called, was an extraordinarily tense occasion, especially on a David Lean film. At one point in early April, David was convinced that the rushes weren't sharp, and it caused an enormous hiatus as Freddie Young took David's claim as a personal insult. The rushes were viewed on a temporary screen erected in Dingle parish hall. Young said the lens on the projector needed changing, but Lean insisted on a weekend trip for the film's top brass up to Dublin, where the rushes were viewed at two different cinemas. Lean wasn't there for the second viewing, and Young swept by him as he was having coffee in the Shelbourne Hotel and declared, 'Pinpoint sharp'. Lean still wasn't happy, until he viewed them again back in Dingle on a new projector and declared them 'Bloody sharp'. Young was about to say, 'I told you so', but David had kept moving.

There was something clearly niggling at Lean, however. Having viewed the rushes from the beach scene, he was delighted with the way his cameraman had captured the wonderful panorama, but he wasn't happy with Mitchum's acting when it came to some of the dialogue. Mitchum was returning after a three-week lay-off necessitated by his unsightly black eye. Then Lean shot the scene in the living room of the schoolhouse, where Mitchum's character was putting plant cuttings in a scrapbook with the title *Flaura of the Parish of Kirrary. Collected by Charles Shaughnessy Dip. Ed.*, while his new bride was dutifully sewing his clothes. After seeing those rushes, Lean told Roy Stevens that he was finally getting the performances he wanted from Mitchum, and that he was going to reshoot everything that had been done so far involving the lead actor. Stevens was aghast, pointing out that they had been shooting for several weeks.

'What am I going to tell MGM?' Stevens protested.

'Tell them I didn't like his hat,' Lean replied.

The same excuse was trotted out to Mitchum, who snorted with contempt. Not to Lean's face, it has to be said, initially, for the director had despatched Stevens to relay the news. Mitchum asked the associate producer: why the reshoot? He was told, 'because you look like Charlie Chan'.

It was a common practice of directors to blame something else, like the bad performance of a minor actor, rather than tell a big star exactly what the problem was, and this was another case in point. The company had also received an insurance payout over Mitchum's blood-shot eye, which allowed Lean to shoot a number of scenes again. However, Mitchum was annoyed and bewildered that Lean hadn't spoken to him personally.

'If he can't tell me my performance was shit to my face, then fuck him,' Mitchum told Miles.

On another occasion, Miles complained that Lean had left Mitchum and herself waiting on the beach for over an hour, with the crew filming from the top of a nearby cliff, before the two actors discovered that the unit had actually moved on elsewhere. The sun was shining, but there was a biting spring wind off the sea, and Miles was starting to turn blue in her skimpy blouse. On another occasion he had her standing knee-deep in the freezing Atlantic. Miles claimed that the director was trying to break her spirit, which brought out the protective side in Mitchum's nature. The actor's mood began to darken and he started to misbehave, on the set more than off it.

A visit to the Betty Ford clinic back in Los Angeles wasn't far down the line, but here in Dingle there was nobody to pull him up, unless it was his wife during one of her visits, or the director himself.

David drank a glass of wine with his dinner and even a whisky, but he hated the sight or smell of alcohol around the set, which resulted in a lot of sneaking around. Pedro Vidal, who was from Madrid, had already tried to get Lean to relax a bit when it came to alcohol, but it was hard work. On *Zhivago*, Lean had even tried to stop the Spanish technicians having wine with their lunch, a sacrilegious prohibition in a Mediterranean country. Pedro had warned Lean: 'If you give hell to a Spaniard, because of their inferiority complex and hyper-sensitivity they won't work for you for the rest of the day. If you're right, they will have a guilty complex. So let them drink wine.'

David relented, but even his Dedicated Maniacs, such as Fowlie and Dukelow, who loved a drink, knew not to push it, and would get tanked up away from his company at lunchtime. Mitchum, however, wasn't in the mood to make Lean's life any easier.

Shooting at the schoolhouse, David got a shock. He needed to take a toilet break – the schoolhouse set had been built with a working bathroom – and when he returned, Vidal noticed the colour had drained from David's face. 'He was white and he says, "You know what a motherfucking nerve Mitchum has? I found him in the corridor gulping from a huge bottle of Courvoisier. I looked at him and he said, 'Do you want a gulp?'" David was horrified. "Motherfucking" wasn't a word David would normally use, but he used it that evening.'

'There was an almighty row in the office after that,' says the standby carpenter Fred Lane, 'but that was Robert.'

Drinking around the set was banned, before 6 p.m. When that hour was reached, Mitchum used to call out to Lean, across the set, raise his left arm and point to his own watch. Otherwise he hadn't lifted a finger all day. Lean even reasoned that the actors be called to the set early so as to control their imbibing, but the law was an ass. Hardened drinkers such as Howard and Mitchum would sip away in their caravans, but they didn't particularly like the subterfuge. Lean's assistants would bring Mitchum out from Milltown House, put him in his caravan so that he wouldn't drink, but then not call him. This annoyed Mitchum further, and he started acting up. He demanded Florida orange juice, freshly squeezed, in his caravan. Typically, when it arrived he was happy to share it around.

Liam Pike, the Irish set dresser, came back from one job about half a mile from the set, sporting a big grin. He was busy around the schoolhouse, planting vegetation to obscure something, when along saunters Mitchum, accompanied by Harold Sanderson, his personal assistant. Sanderson was carrying Mitchum's black leather bag, which contained a lot of his stuff; books, the Puma White Hunter knife (before he gave it to Vidal), Hershey chocolate bars and God knows what else. Mitchum knew Pike well from working in Ireland previously – he was one of those he invited around to Milltown House for a jar. The bottle of orange juice was produced.

'The very thing,' said Pike. 'I'm parched.'

Harold said: 'No, no, no.'

'Ah well, keep it then.'

And Mitchum said, 'Give him some of the orange juice.'

'I took some and I knew immediately it wasn't just orange juice,' says Pike, whose drink was heavily spiked with vodka. 'Mitchum said, "I know what's in it. Harold knows what's in it. Now you know what's in it. If *he* finds out what's in it, I'll kill ya".'

Even when Mitchum wasn't drinking, there was friction between himself and Lean on the set. Lean took his craft extremely seriously, and he took umbrage with those who didn't. Before the premiere of *Lawrence of Arabia*, the Duke of Edinburgh – the Queen's notoriously irreverent husband – made small talk by saying, 'Good evening. Good flick?' after David had spent two years baking in the desert suffering for his art. Wherever he went in the world, people had treated him with the respect he deserved, Lean felt, but in England movies were 'the flicks'.

Those who worked with David knew not to be flippant, and the atmosphere on a David Lean set was always very tense and reverential. Silence was required as Lean would pause, sometimes for hours, as his thoughts churned on how to shoot a particular scene. The American actor Rod Steiger once arrived on the hushed set of *Doctor Zhivago* and asked, 'What's the matter? Somebody's father just died?'

Mitchum liked to bring guests to the set, such as his occasional manager George 'Bullets' Durgom, who irritated Lean and Havelock-Allan. His Dingle landlady Margaret Sheehy was also invited to the schoolhouse. David was in one of his moods where he wanted all the 'wanderers and coughers', as he sometimes called visitors, out of the way. 'We were just sitting down and David Lean looked over and said "clear the set",' said Margaret. 'He was one of those men you felt his eyes were going through you. So we hopped up and Robert Mitchum said "sit".

'But he said we had to go.'

'You're my guests, sit there.'

'We sat there shivering for about two hours.' .

Like Lean, Mitchum had conflicts of his own. Another director, Sydney Pollack, detected in Mitchum,

the tension between his own sensitivity and delicacy and his cultural sense of what is macho, because you can feel those two elements at war ... Mitchum, like a lot of guys at the time he grew up had certain ideas about what masculinity is and what is appropriate behaviour for a man. Acting, like dancing – certain areas of the arts – seems inappropriate to men. It seemed to them like a slightly sissified profession. It certainly seemed that way to Mitchum.

Lean wasn't prepared to cut Mitchum quite so much slack, which probably only exacerbated the problem. Trevor Coop, the young clapper loader, who hadn't worked with either man before, found himself warming more to Mitchum than Lean.

David was intensely annoyed by people like Robert Mitchum who could turn it on and off. Robert loved being the centre of interest. He was a wonderful raconteur and he would be telling the crew a story about some film thirty years ago which would be extremely amusing, then he'd be called in front of the camera and he'd go and do his take. And as soon as the camera cut, he'd go back and continue telling the story.

It used to really get up David's nose that other people could concentrate and come up with the goods and then turn off and become their normal selves. He thought Mitchum was unprofessional, but I think it was based on the fact that he wasn't particularly capable of doing it himself and was jealous of people who could do it.

Michael Stevenson also marvelled at Mitchum's ability to switch on and off as he told stories in-between takes.

'Did I ever tell you the story about the girl from Milwaukee?'

'Ready, Robert?'

'You crack the whip and I'll take the trip.'

'Action.'

Mitchum does two-minute scene without any fluffs.

'Cut. Going again. Cameras reset.'

'About that girl from Milwaukee.'

'Action.'

Once the take was finished, Mitchum sometimes liked to act the pansy, skipping off the set, just in case anybody thought he was treating the whole thing anything other than frivolously.

Not everybody was enamoured with Mitchum for sending up the director, but his shtick did strike a powerful chord. While Mitchum was warm and genial, Lean came across as a bit of a cold fish. 'Lean was always very civil,' Niall Tóibín observed. 'He had an automatic smile which flashed on, teeth only, no eyes.'

With the exception of Mitchum, Lean would talk to his actors, but normally only to select members of the crew, his immediate subordinates, who would carry out his instructions. In all, he spoke to about six crew members when shooting: his cameramen Freddie Young and Ernie Day, his assistant directors Pedro Vidal and Michael Stevenson, the associate producer Roy Stevens, and Eddie Fowlie.

Leaning on one of the Brutes, shooting the breeze with Mitchum was another of the electricians, Bob Bremner:

David Lean didn't like chatting to us, so he sent Pedro and Pedro says, 'David wants you to stop talking to the electricians between takes'. So next shot, 'Action'. Mitchum goes, 'Oh I forgot my lines because the assistant director told me not to speak to the electricians'. David Lean was a bit of an old brigadier, very rigid like an old army type. The first time he spoke to me was on the set when I made a bit of a noise during a rehearsal or something and he said, 'You shut up or get out'. One night we were having a bit of a party in the Skelligs Hotel and he came and stood next to me at the urinal and I said to him, 'You've got to piss too, do you?' He did laugh.

The fact of it was that Lean didn't carry his responsibilities lightly. 'David took filmmaking very, very seriously, which of course he had to,' Havelock-Allan pointed out. 'He was handling vast sums of money and it depended on him. Mitchum's view of the film business was that it wasn't a serious business at all. It was just something that got you up, you played yourself and you got paid a ridiculous amount of money. His idea of a serious occupation was ranching, or Quarter Horse racing or boxing.'

For all that, however, it was widely felt that David himself was slacking on the film to some degree. Mitchum may have drank, smoked and womanised – not necessarily at the same time – but he was usually there on time and word perfect. It was not only Mitchum who felt that David was working at a pace that was considered decidedly leisurely. Lean was never a great morning person, and on *Ryan's Daughter* he found it particularly hard to get himself going. He had low blood pressure and hated the cold more than most.

Even when Lean arrived on the set, there were more delays as he spent another hour or so in his caravan, prepping the day ahead. Much to Havelock-Allan's dismay, David hadn't done a full shooting script, which was a technician's guide to the way the story is to be translated into the film and allows the director to know precisely what was going to happen before he went on the set. It contained a wealth of information about camera angles, sound effects and lighting. On a David Lean film, the shooting script was the blueprint and you deviated from it at your peril.

Although, without a shooting script, Lean had another crutch that he had relied on since teaming up with Bolt for *Lawrence of Arabia*. Lean regarded the writer as a wonderful reader of his own lines, and it would get to the point where he would ask Bolt to read the script as he wrote it and have it recorded. Over coffee and toast in the morning in his caravan, Lean would listen to Bolt's recording of the scene he was about to shoot, often with John Mills beside him to offer some suggestions. Only when he was finished listening would he feel ready to start shooting. 'That's what used to start Bob drinking,' says Trevor Coop.

> The actors would be called at 7.00 or 7.30 and David wouldn't turn up till 11.00 and then not come out of his caravan for an hour. It was more than impolite, it was bloody rude. Fair enough the oily rags like us, call us at 7.30 and we'll be sitting on the back of the van playing poker, but you don't do it to the Trevor Howards and Robert Mitchums of this world. In the village they don't take that long to make-up, so they could get that done quickly in the unlikely event of David turning up on time because he'd still spend an hour in his caravan.

From Coop's observation post, Lean's high-handedness was proving counterproductive. 'The production staff knew that unless everything worked, they would be out on their ear. So if that meant getting the actors there four hours early, they were going to be there. By the time God [David] said, "I want them on set", they were ready, even if they were a bit pissed at that stage. The one day they weren't ready, you'd lose your job. "You're the first assistant director. You're fired".'

There might be even further complications before shooting would start. First thing in the morning, Freddie Young would try to take the initiative and set up a scene for lighting and everything else, either trying to second-guess the director or carry out what had been agreed the night before.

'Freddie was a frustrated director really,' says Coop. 'Lean would come along and Freddie would say, "I've got it set up over there". David didn't like anybody telling him what to do so he would turn round completely, walk to the other end of the village and say, "We'll have the first set-up over here." So we'd have to move everything around. There was twice as much work as there should have been because they didn't get their act together.'

While Lean and Young poked around, Mitchum was determined to make his own life bearable. He figured that the time had come for the producers to come good on one of those promises that he could get away during a gap in his schedule. London, where he had many friends, beckoned, as did Los Angeles, while the spring rain fell on another soft day in Co. Kerry.

'He'd been on standby call for six weeks and I would go see him every night,' says Stevenson. 'Then one morning he drove his Porsche from Dingle to the set which took about thirty minutes. We were walking down the mountain together. I asked him, "Can I get you anything, Robert?" and he said, "I'm just going to grab a coffee."

"The coffee's this way, Robert."

"Not where I'm going."

'He got in his car, drove to Shannon airport, got on a plane and went and had a coffee in LA.'

Mitchum was concerned about the youngest of his three children, Petrine, who was in her adolescence and completing her schooling, which meant Dorothy was only able to visit fitfully. He also wanted to see his two grown-up sons, Jim and Chris. Hardly had Mitchum raised the cup, or glass more likely, to his mouth at his home in Bel Air when the phone rang. 'Don't answer it,' Chris said. 'It's them.'

However, Mitchum would answer the phone and then bitch about it. By Mitchum's reckoning, he was still mid-flight when the decision was made to haul him back because of a change in schedule. At least he enjoyed recounting what had happened, putting on the plummiest of plummy English accents on a trip to London:

> They said, 'There's no possibility of you being required for the next fortnight or possibly three weeks. You could go home, you know? As long as you are back within forty-eight hours' notice.' I'm like a trout at the bait. I flew off to Los Angeles and I could hear the phone ring at 39,000 feet. I landed. [Plummy English accent] 'We're awfully sorry about that.'
>
> I came back to Ireland. Didn't work for twenty-three days. Next time I went like a salmon for the fly. They said [plummy accent], 'Why don't you pop off somewhere more comfortable?' I came over here and got to the Dorchester Hotel. The phone was ringing when I walked in. [Plummy accent] 'Awfully sorry, Bob, but you are required.'

I flew back to Dublin, drove back down, didn't work for twenty-one days. So after that I gave up, just spent more and more time sitting round the joint [Milltown House]. I had guests. My bar tab was about 11,000 bucks.

He was, he would complain to anybody who would listen, 'stuck on Devil's Island'. When would it all end, he wondered? 'Can you imagine a picture which depends on a storm and we have got to stay here until it happens?' he asked Marjory Adams of the *Boston Globe*. Mitchum also came to the set relating amusing stories centred around what he described as his 'house arrest'. Eavesdroppers were amongst the audience. Direct dialling hadn't come to Dingle in 1969, and everything had to go through the local Dingle operator, Mrs Cummins, who wouldn't always patch the call through and at times sounded like his personal secretary, not to mention financial adviser. 'Mr Mitchum is out at the moment. Try again in about twenty minutes,' she would tell the caller.

One time he said he was on the phone to his accountant in Los Angeles discussing the sale of a property he owned. The figures were running into long-distance telephone numbers.

'What did we pay for it?' Mitchum asked his agent.

'A million, I think'.

'And what's the offer?'

'Three million.'

Mitchum says: 'Gee, I don't know.'

The operator couldn't help herself: 'Sell, sell.'

It turned out to be some house arrest. Booze was delivered up to Milltown House by the caseload as Mitchum did his entertaining. The drink would never run out, but Bob's hospitality then entered a new phase as everybody tried to settle in for the long haul. Eateries were few and far between in Dingle; in fact, there were no restaurants besides the one in the Skellig and another in Benners Hotel, which was more downmarket. Ashe's pub did an excellent Irish stew at lunch, but that service didn't stretch into the evening. Tom Long or another publican, Paddy Bawn Brosnan, would throw a big pot of seafood on the counter of the bar as though it were a bowl of peanuts, and the crab claws would be ankle-deep on the floor by the end of the night, but it wasn't exactly a four-course meal. Other than that, there was a takeaway chip shop that might or might not be open, depending on the whim of the owner. Into the breach stepped the Hollywood tough guy, who, if you believed the rumours, was brawling down in the pubs of Dingle every night. Having sat by the phone every day at Milltown House or returned early from another wasted journey to his caravan, Mitchum would don his apron and start cooking up a storm, with members of the crew, excluding the top brass, invited.

'The first time we met him he said, "How are you getting on for food? Kate [Ashe] looking after you? Come up to the house and I'll cook you a meal",' says Bob Bremner. 'We went up there. There he was. Bob Mitchum, big movie star, with an apron on, cooking a big spaghetti for the electricians. And maybe there might be a young lady there that he had brought in while his wife was away. He was a bit of a scallywag.'

Sarah Miles reckoned it was Mitchum's women friends who were bringing in his dope supply. Mitchum's euphemism for the girls was 'housekeepers'. 'Sure they're more decorative than flowers,' he told Kate Ashe, after she took him to task over the numbers when three young women in miniskirts came into her pub having been sent down from Milltown House by Mitchum and told to put everything on his tab. Even when cooking, Mitchum couldn't stop himself indulging in a bit of mischief. Not only did he make hash brownies, but hash burgers were a speciality too, and his sauces were often liberally sprinkled with the stuff. Many of his guests – grips, electricians, stand-ins, actors, good people of Dingle – had never heard, seen or tasted anything like it before.

One evening he held a special women's event and sent out delightful invitations to 'All the Esteemed and Venerable Ladies of Dingle to attend an evening of food and lively conversation'. Modesty didn't prevent him playing the album he had recorded, *Calypso – Is Like So...*, on the massive stereo system he had at Milltown House to get the ladies moving a little bit. He also had another surprise when it came to the cooking.

'I don't like gravy of any description. When I was in Mitch's house this one evening, Mitch was saying, "Have a bit, have a bit",' says the Irish actress Gladys Sheehan, employed as a 'special extra' on the film. 'He had put cannabis or something in the gravy, and he had all these highly respectable women high by the end of the night and I was the only one who wasn't. And they said, "You knew. You were in on the act", but I wasn't. He was a divil for doing that, but everybody loved him.'

Teetotal Gladys remained *compos mentis* and poured cold water on the outrageous womanising tales that were emerging on a daily basis from Milltown House. 'Mitchum used to bring in the call girls. They all said that Mitchum didn't have the call girls himself at all, but for everybody else. All the crew and everybody. I remember them all going up to the rooms and Mitch would sit there drinking. Maybe he was afraid of Dorothy. She was the boss.'

'She was very sweet. Very ladylike, very calm,' said Pedro Vidal of Dorothy Mitchum. 'There was the wild life of Mitchum and the family life of Mitchum. It was the sort of balance that he needed. And he was dedicated to her. We went out for a ride on a boat and he was like a tourist. He didn't make any of those cynical remarks. He was at ease, but then when she left: Boom! Everything went.'

Lean didn't get invites to Milltown House, but some of the mayhem arrived at his doorstep. In the film, the Rosy character is perceived as flighty and is chided by the priest for wanting 'wings', so Lean wanted plenty of seagulls hovering overhead in the beach shots to ram the point home. One of Eddie Fowlie's prop men, Mickey O'Toole, was employed with a bucket and spade, dumping dead fish on the beach to draw the gulls in. They arrived, in their hundreds. Raising his head from one shot, Lean was at his most exasperated. 'It's like an aviary, there is nothing but fucking seagulls.' Mitchum would watch on amused and up to mischief, using his own bait for the occasion, according to art director Roy Walker.

'There was a story that Mitchum made a cake and put the happy stuff in it and got the chief of police and the priest and all that weaving on their bikes. I know he did throw it up at the gulls because I saw the gulls take it and they were going potty up in the sky. He thought it was very funny, but not a lot of other people did.'

Still, for all the diversions, Mitchum hadn't forgotten that he could be back in California tending to his Quarter Horses and spending time with his family instead of making the best of a bad lot on location in Dingle. And for this he blamed Lean and Havelock-Allan. Mitchum frequently faced down producers because they cracked the whip a mite too ferociously. Now he wanted Havelock-Allan to do what he was paid to do, which was to push the production along.

Havelock-Allan had been an important influence on David's early career, championing him for a co-directing role in his first film, *In Which We Serve* (1942), and then working with him closely on *Brief Encounter*, which launched Lean's directorial career after he had spent years as an editor. Havelock-Allan had been a producer of what were known as quota-quickies, British films required by UK law to be shown alongside American imports. However, Havelock-Allan could turn his hand to quality as well, and it was through a company he co-founded, Cineguild, that David got the financing to make his two great Charles Dickens films, *Great Expectations* (1946) and *Oliver Twist* (1948). Their paths diverged, but Lean had never forgotten him when he started his collaboration with Hollywood for the blockbuster movies that defined the latter part of his career. For *Bridge on the River Kwai* and *Lawrence of Arabia*, Lean had Sam Spiegel calling the shots as producer and taking the glory, with odd visits to the remote locations accompanied by photographers and film crew. Lean claimed Spiegel had also taken the money, plenty more than what was owed to him, from *Lawrence*, and had vowed never to work with him again.

For the next big project, Lean had changed studios and producers, from Columbia to MGM, and from Spiegel to Carlo Ponti. The Italian was what David called an 'absentee producer', which is exactly what he wanted. The hands-off approach worked – or at least David produced another smash hit and one without any undue delays – so by the time *Ryan's Daughter* was conceived, Lean had as much control as any director in the history of Hollywood. MGM put up the money initially without even being told what the film was about, and David chose Havelock-Allan as the producer. The older man was a gregarious and charming individual who was happy to come along for the ride and gratefully accepted one of the gifts that Lean was bestowing, with another one going to Bolt.

'David was very grateful to Robert for the two very good scripts he had done for him, in *Lawrence of Arabia* and *Doctor Zhivago*, and it was really as a sort of present to Robert to make a story around Sarah,' says Havelock-Allan.

> In fact, his wife at the time explained that it was to show Robert that he could make a film out of very slight material. Whether that is true or not, I don't know. It was a present and it was a superb confidence in his ability as a film director that he could make a film in such difficult conditions. In a sense, asking me to produce it was a present to me too. We'd known each other for a long time and we hadn't worked together for twenty years or more. I didn't know how long it was going to take and how difficult it was going to be.

Havelock-Allan wasn't an absentee producer like Ponti. He was around all right. It was just that he didn't do much of what was needed, most of all to stand up to David as the director waited for the clouds to match or for the right number of seagulls to come into shot. In fact, soon the producer became known as Have-a-look-Allan.

'David didn't like anybody interfering, and if he had a producer who genuinely wielded the big stick, he wouldn't have been able to do what he wanted to do,' said Trevor Coop. 'So he employed somebody like Tony who basically did what he was told. He bustled around pretending to be a producer – sending memos to everybody, but he didn't have any power.'

This would have been an arrangement that Mitchum would have been quite happy with had he got on with the director and not wanted to be somewhere else. However, with Lean and Mitchum not talking to each other, the actor wanted the producer to flex his muscles and ensure that they could all get out of Dingle as soon as humanly possible. In a sense, Havelock-Allan was a fall guy. Mitchum knew he had to have some sort of relationship with David, so he blamed Havelock-Allan for the aborted shore leave that had resulted in him being confined to Milltown House, cooking more than acting.

Part of this routine was that at some point in the evening there would be a knock on the door of Milltown House and Pedro Vidal or Michael Stevenson would walk in, standing him down for the day and bearing news about the following day's shooting and other matters. Even Stevenson, who was the most emollient of Lean's Dedicated Maniacs, felt something was wrong.

I would see Bob and all the actors every night. Bob thought – and he was quite right – that the producer should have come to see him. He would ask, 'Why are they sending you all the time?' Somebody should have gone to see him, above me or Pedro. Whether you think Robert Mitchum was a good actor or a bad actor, Robert Mitchum was a big actor. He had worked with all these great directors and been in the business a long time. I don't think they showed him the respect that they should have, because you are talking about the ilk of Burt Lancaster or Kirk Douglas. Would you treat Kirk Douglas or Burt Lancaster like that? The answer is No. So you don't treat Bob like that. Bob's easy-going and rolls along with it, but he is the last person you want to upset. He's powerful. He wouldn't mince his words.

Mitchum would sit the assistant directors down for a drink and enjoy their company – he became particularly friendly with Pedro, whom he called the Cat from Castille – but Lean's lack of respect was noted nonetheless. 'Most of the time you would hang around till 5.30 in the evening when one of David's assistants would inform you there would be no call that day. I had surmised there would be no call. Outside, there was a 60mph gale and it was as black as the insides of a goat.'

At least publicly, Mitchum expressed his thoughts in a rather coded manner, as when he did an interview for Irish television, RTÉ, smoking a cigar and sipping from a wine glass outside Milltown House, within a dozen long strides of the telephone, should it ring. 'Working for Mr Lean is like being made to build the Taj Mahal out of toothpicks. I'm sure there are many people as devoted as he, but he really can't believe it. They also have other lives, but he is a man of no means really. He's like a gypsy. Like sleeping in a car, he dwells in the film for the two or three years it takes to make it.'

Mitchum did leave the house one night as John Mills was throwing a party at the house he had rented in Dingle. Mills supplied the venue, the electricians brought the food, curries and such like made by a Burmese woman in the area who they had gotten to know. Since Mills was such a close friend of David's, it wasn't clear whether Mitchum had actually been invited or not, but he showed up around midnight with the party already in full swing.

'The timing was unbelievable,' according to Roy Stevens.

We're getting our plates from the buffet when there's a knock on the door and it's Robert Mitchum, with a hat on the back of his head and his dark glasses on even though it's jet black outside. Bob is carrying this great big bowl with a napkin over it. And he stood at the end of the buffet. I said to [my wife] Jackie, 'Whatever you do, don't touch that stuff'. And with that David got up and left. Johnny [Mills] was all a dither.

Mitch was ladling the stuff out to all the crew that were going past. Everybody's laughing and joking. Mitch was totally uninvited. The make-up man Charlie Parker was there with his wife, a lovely woman. Rather large, very demur, very quiet. And suddenly she strips off, clothes going everywhere. Mary Bell [Mills's wife] went running to the bedroom. The whole party broke up. It was really, really the funniest evening.

What was in the bowl? Chili, according to one guest. Salad cream, according to another. And then something else. Whatever it was, one of the electricians, Bob Bremner – who was equal in size to Mitch and bowed down to nobody – took exception to the prank, even though he was on friendly terms with Mitchum. 'I didn't think it was funny. It wasn't a big confrontation. I just said, "You're out of order there" and he squared up to me. Big guy, but pissed I suppose. There was a sort of Mexican standoff.'

Roy Stevens reckoned the whole episode had much to do with Mitchum's stand-off with Lean. 'It was a gesture to the fact that, "You, David, don't talk to me. Everybody comes to the only social event of the week and I am not invited. Right, I'll fix the lot of you." Which is what he did. He must have been out there for hours waiting for people to go and eat. His timing was perfect.'

The actor felt that part of the problem he was having with Lean was that 'he speaks English and I speak American. And I understand English, but he doesn't understand American.' However, Mitchum was far from being Lean's biggest problem, as the director was about to find out.

# 6. Mrs Bolt

For all his frustrations and anger, Mitchum appreciated Lean's huge talent, which included an uncanny ability to discover talented actors and turn them into stars. It was something of which Lean was proud, and it contributed to his status as the Great British Director. He had given Trevor Howard his first big part, in *Brief Encounter* in 1945, and the following year had launched the film career of Alec Guinness, who was primarily regarded as a stage actor until he played Herbert Pocket in *Great Expectations*. The other most notable examples were Omar Sharif and Peter O'Toole in *Lawrence of Arabia* and Julie Christie in *Doctor Zhivago*. Part of what made Lean a star was that he was a star-maker. With *Ryan's Daughter*, he was about to do the same with Sarah Miles and Christopher Jones. All the two young actors had to do was reach out and take the opportunity they had been given, not bite the hand that feeds.

It was Sarah Miles's brother, Christopher, himself a rising star in the movie business, who said that his sister reminded him of the nursery rhyme: 'when she was good, she was very, very good and when she was bad, she was horrid'. Growing up, Christopher remarked, Sarah was a very naughty girl who loved to play pranks. Not everybody could see the good side of her, including, on occasion her mother Clarice, who beat her regularly with a silver hairbrush. Her pet name at home was Pusscat, and Pusscat, Pusscat claimed, got blamed for everything.

From her earliest memories, she 'fessed up to plenty of outrageous behaviour, like the time she tried to drown her second brother Martin in the pond at the bottom of the garden of their home in a well-to-do part of Essex after he had played a particularly unpleasant prank on her. It was an act of revenge, she later explained in her first autobiography, *A Right Royal Bastard*, that had brought up the 'evil we all have hidden away, if we really care to look'. Her mother was a strict conformist and Sarah rebelled, seemingly right from the first breath. She adored her father, a highly successful engineer, and it seemed at times she wanted to be a boy, for she behaved like a tomboy, climbing trees higher than any of her brothers. She was hopeless at school and found it difficult to read and write; much later she would be diagnosed as severely dyslexic. Indeed, she seemed to communicate better with animals than with humans and loved tending to the family's menagerie of domestic pets or helping the family's gardener. He called her 'Miss Sarah', and she addressed him by his surname, 'Brand'.

Sarah appeared to really go off the rails when she was sent to Roedean, an austere boarding school near Brighton that was devoid of trees, which Sarah had hugged from as early as she could remember. It was one of the most prestigious educational establishments in the country for girls, but Sarah hated it, a point she made to the Queen Mother when royalty came to the school, after curtseying respectfully. Sarah reckoned she was royalty herself, a lineage her family traced back to a bastard son of King George V. That didn't save her being expelled from Roedean over a number of offences. Likewise, she was kicked out of a number of other schools she attended, once gaining revenge by setting off fire extinguishers and tearing up the dreaded 'black book' into which her name had frequently been written.

She did have a talent, though, and it was brother Christopher who helped bring it out. He was a keen teenage film-maker and dramatist aided by some recording equipment his father had given him. During long holidays back in Essex, Sarah was on hand to provide animal noises and the like for her brother's home-made movies, but Christopher and their mother quickly realised she was a talented young actress as well. That was her route into the profession, via her studies at the Royal Academy of Dramatic Art (RADA) in London, which Clarice forced her into as another example of her tough love. Typical of Sarah, part of her research involved peeping out of a cupboard while her flatmate – a prostitute – was involved in a masochistic sex act with a client on the bed in front of her.

Sarah's career, and her personality, flourished. It was said of her – by the *Daily Mail* writer Lynda Lee-Potter – that 'she both ensnared and alienated people with her wanton exhibitionism'. No surprise, then, that the newspaper was obsessed with charting every twist and turn in the life of this extraordinary young woman and actress. She landed prime parts alongside Laurence Olivier in *Term of Trial* (1962) and then in Joe Losey's film *The Servant* (1963). Lean had considered her for the role of Zhivago's sweet and understanding wife, Tonya, but Bolt thought she was 'too hard, too sure of herself' and the director cast Geraldine Chaplin instead.

Soon after, she met Bolt for the first time at a party in London where her agent planned to introduce her to Warren Beatty, the actor/producer who wanted a leading lady for his film *Kaleidoscope* (1966). Miles was a successful actress in her own right who already had a house in Chelsea, west London. Bolt was seventeen years older than Sarah and had a son about the same age as her from his first marriage, Ben, who considered her a 'gorgeous, wild girl'. His three daughters with Jo weren't quite so enamoured, and neither were others close to Bolt. His influential agent, Margaret Ramsay, disliked Sarah intensely, and thought she was a corrupting influence on her client, whom she believed could be a great playwright if his head wasn't being turned by Hollywood and his flaky new girlfriend. Some of Bolt's friends were alarmed when the couple then got married. The joke went around that Bolt had found his nut.

Bolt's older brother Sydney, an academic at Cambridge University and an author, told the writer Adrian Turner that:

> Bob's attitude to Sarah was indulgent. I don't mean to say that he wasn't very attached to her, for he was very deeply attached, but in the sense that she could be forgiven or allowed almost anything because she was only a child. He thought she was madly amusing. She'd say the most ridiculous things and Bob's shoulders would heave and he'd say: 'There she goes again! Isn't she marvellous!?' She was Rousseauesque,

a child of nature, not a Pygmalion figure since he wasn't trying to fashion her into something else.

In one of her interviews after she met Bolt, she had told people that her mother had encouraged her to have numerous lovers at the age of 16, a comment that Clarice described as 'pure fantasy'; Clarice had merely pointed out that she shouldn't date someone just to marry them. What titillated some people further, and offended others, was that Sarah could be very stiff-upper-lip one moment, reflecting her wealthy background, and the next be cursing like a Billingsgate fish wife in her cut-glass accent. She was considered a 1960s swinger, but reckons that was because she had taken her clothes off in most of her movies rather than what people read in the gossip columns, for she preferred the company of her dogs and horses at home rather than venturing out. When she was in unfamiliar company she tended to blurt out things from a sense of nervousness then carry on, leading to Bolt's description of her on first sight as a 'debauched Alice in Wonderland'.

She had also gained a reputation for being a bit difficult over quitting the avant-garde Michelangelo Antonioni movie *Blow Up* (1968) after she asked the director, 'Who is this man lying on top of me?' and was told, 'Just do the shot'. Miles was trained to give her characters motives and create an inner life for them, whereas Antonioni didn't think this was important. Bolt had encouraged this act of rebelliousness when he should have been cautioning against it, for Miles was discredited to some degree after that. Having moved back out to the countryside to start a family and breed horses, Miles said she didn't care, and she was somewhat bemused when, as she put it, Bolt 'took his love for me to his study' in trying to resurrect her career and make her a star. She was never far from the public eye, however, with her coquettish behaviour and attacks on the Women's Liberation Movement. Lean was wary of Sarah, but he admired her acting ability and was happy to give her the part of Rosy after a screen test, which she says she had insisted upon, though nobody else was afforded the same opportunity. The fact that she would generally only work in the UK because she wanted to be with her dogs was typical of Miles's eccentricity. It meant that making the step over to Ireland came very comfortably to her, and she enjoyed being lady of the manor at Fermoyle House, when she wasn't stuck in her caravan.

The swinger label followed Miles to Dingle, and there were double standards at work on *Ryan's Daughter*. While Miles was frowned upon by some for her behaviour and language, Mitchum was 'a bit of a lad' or 'a rascal'. However, Sarah's behaviour was probably more outrageous than anybody's and she seemed to enjoy scandalising the neighbourhood, even if they weren't trying to peep through her keyhole. Addo, the biggest of her dogs, was free to run around the fields worrying sheep, until one local farmer threatened to shoot him. In the meantime, Sarah was trying to load one sheep, paralysed by fear, into the boot of her Lamborghini in order to bring it to the vet. She was accused of sheep-rustling. All the while, of course, the farmer was flirting with her.

The gaffer Bernie Prentice nipped into Mitchum's for a drink only to find John and Mary Mills playing darts at the back, along with Mills's stand-in, Freddie Clarke, and Sarah. Prentice suggested they play a game called Bullseyes.

'What's that?' they asked.

'You throw for the bullseye. Every time you miss, you undo a button. She was game for anything, old Sarah. Game for a laugh whatever you done.

Another game was called 'goosing the grips' and the rules were simple. 'Men would be standing with their back to her and she'd grab them from behind,' explained the production secretary Maureen Whitty. 'The men didn't know how to behave with her.'

The unit nurse, Noreen Curran, a Dingle woman who had served for years around the world in the Queen Alexandra's Royal Army Nursing Corps, wasn't easily shocked: 'I remember the twilight scenes at the schoolhouse. She was absolutely flying that night. She was in with the electricians and you really have to get rough to play with them. There was no better woman for it.'

The electrician Bob Bremner also remembered being grabbed by Sarah, as did Trevor Coop. 'Yeah, from behind,' Coop said. 'We all suffered that, or not suffered that, when you were least expecting it, particularly if you were standing behind the camera.'

Miles responded firmly: 'At the most I might, out of fun, pinch somebody's bum, but grab their balls? No thank you.' Much worse had been done to her, as she pointed out herself. On a number of occasions she had to apply a 'knee in the balls' to keep lecherous producers at bay and she spoke of a famous theatre director who fired her because 'I wouldn't open my legs'.

For all her gallivanting, she worked tirelessly on *Ryan's Daughter*, even when Christopher Jones was on top of her. It was like *Blow Up* all over again, except this time it was Jones being told 'just do the shot'.

# 7. The Jones Gang

One of Lean's favourite scenes in any of the sixteen movies he directed was the first meeting between Rosy and Major Randolph in her father's pub, which marks the start of her sexual awakening. With Rosy's husband a dud in bed, she longs for the type of love she has read about in romantic novels when mooning around the beach. Fr Collins is on to her, and advises her to quell her desires, but she finds that impossible. As soon as the handsome, clean-cut British major appears, we know that Rosy is going to fall in love with him. Bolt and Lean were desperate to think of an idea that would get them together as quickly as possible so that the audience wouldn't be ahead of them. They threw around various ideas, such as the pair bumping into each other on the street, but all of them were predictable.

The light went on in Lean's head as he lay in his bed with Sandy at around 4 a.m. Half awake, and with his mind freed for some fantasy, he thought of the idiot Michael sitting in the deserted village pub one afternoon, swinging his hobnail boot against the bench as he is happy to see the major entering to provide him with some company. This creates a loud banging sound, which upsets the shell-shocked major as he stands at the bar, and causes him to have flashbacks to his time in the trenches on the Western

Front and the bombardment from German artillery. The major, having ordered a whiskey from Rosy, who is standing in behind her father's bar, suffers a severe bout of the shakes, which sees Michael flee the pub in terror. Rosy comes off her chair to offer comfort to the major in his moment of need. Bang! The explosion of Brock's Benefit that Bolt and Lean had been seeking. 'They look into each other's eyes, kiss and we're home,' said Lean. 'I leapt out of bed, grabbed hold of an envelope and a pencil, terrified of it evaporating like a dream.'

The idea was a good one, and the execution of it should have been simple enough, but it presented Lean with one of the most difficult directorial moments in his long and distinguished career. Enter Christopher Jones, the rising young American actor cast as Major Randolph Doryan, who by the end of *Ryan's Daughter* would be in a kind of shell-shock of his own. Forget the dream. 'I'm trapped in my own casting nightmare,' Lean told Bolt as the enormity of his error in giving Jones the part dawned on him.

David's relationship with actors was a strange one. Trevor Howard said he regarded them as no more than 'puppets'. Yet he presented them in such a wonderful manner that actors were more than willing to submit to his regime. He had given Sharif one of the most wonderful entrances in movie history, when the actor was first presented to the world emerging from a mirage in the desert on a camel, from which he shoots an enemy who is drawing water from his well. When filming *Kwai*, Lean had argued fiercely over the portrayal of Colonel Nicholson with Alec Guinness, who wanted to play the part for laughs, then collected a Best Actor Oscar when he was forced to follow the director's instructions to the contrary. Nominated for Best Supporting Actor was the Japanese commander of the concentration camp, Sessue Hayakawa, who had torn all the pages out of the script except those that contained his own lines, and didn't even know that his character would be killed at the end of the film.

David could, however, come across as intensely cold and humourless, and some detected a strong sadistic streak in the way he insisted on take after take. Havelock-Allan reckoned that Lean wanted to be all the actors, the writer and the director rolled up in one, and have the same relationship to a film as an author to a book. Havelock-Allan's first wife, the actress Valerie Hobson, found Lean 'such a cold director, he gave me nothing at all as an actress'. Lean was conscious of his lack of warmth, and put it down to his strict Quaker upbringing. That coldness explained why Lean needed to work with actors who were secure; if they were nervous or needed their confidence built up, then there could be problems.

For all the trouble with Howard and Mitchum, at least they were established actors who knew when they needed to switch on and produce the goods. Mills hardly needed any directing, and tried to make life as easy as possible for everybody, while Miles was a fine technical actress. It wasn't the actors who were holding up the film; it was the weather and the director. Asked by a local reporter during an open day on the set what type of director Lean was, Mitchum replied: 'He's a tall director.'

'Is he not a genius?' the reporter replied.

'Yeah, sure. Give me fifty-four takes of any shot and I'm a genius.'

Originally, the part of Major Doryan was to go to Marlon Brando, who had long admired Lean's work and had struck up a friendship with the director; he had been one of a handful of guests at the wedding of David and Leila in Paris in July 1960. Brando had subsequently been pencilled in to play Lawrence, but had withdrawn to play Fletcher Christian in *Mutiny on the Bounty* (1962). He had also rejected the part of the corrupt lawyer, Victor Komarovsky, in *Zhivago*. Finally, for *Ryan's Daughter*, he had accepted the part of Major Doryan, but doubts were creeping in.

Doryan was originally conceived as a war hero who had lost an arm but won the Victoria Cross. Brando would call Lean about attempts to make the loss of an arm look real. He couldn't turn from his front to his back and make it look convincing. To accommodate him, Lean and Bolt decided to drop the missing arm and give Doryan a limping leg instead. But Brando continued to prevaricate and Lean could feel him slipping away. During pre-production, Lean sent Pedro Vidal, a friend of Brando's, to the actor's home in Beverly Hills to see if he could talk him around. Vidal found the pony-tailed Brando pacing the lounge wearing a kimono. With him for company were a racoon and a St Bernard, the smaller animal terrifying the giant dog.

Brando was agitated, as he made plain, not least by his son Christian's burgeoning drug addiction. Lean despatching one of his minions also didn't help, as Vidal himself made plain. 'Marlon said to me, "Pedro, I was very unlucky. I married several bitches and my kids need me now. They've got problems. And I can't do the film." One night in Dingle I was a little bit tipsy – I got along so well with the Irish that they made me little presents of bottles of poteen – we were having dinner together and I said to David, "Brando did not do the film because you didn't go to see him. You sent me; you should have gone yourself".'

Brando would have been quite capable of causing Lean problems. With Jones, however, Lean was entering a new type of pain. Knocked off track by Brando's rejection, Lean needed to find a replacement quickly. An arm-twisting letter from Havelock-Allan to the London-based casting director Bob Lennard, dated 29 November 1968, showed that the situation was becoming critical:

I told David of your concern that we might end up with an old picture if we cast the principal parts with actors of the same vintage as Trevor and Johnny Mills and it is entirely on the strength of your comment and your suggestion which I have passed on to David that we might find and make some new stars that we have held up our negotiations with some big names. So I am relying on you to save your reputation and my blushes by having a few new faces to show David, either on screen or in person over the course of the next week. David arrives on Sunday and I would like to be able to talk to him about some of these people as soon as he arrives because as you may imagine both of us are a bit het up by the situation. We start shooting in two months' time.

Lennard had cast a film called *The Looking Glass War* (1970), based on a book of the same title by John le Carré, and he arranged a viewing for Lean of the rough edit when the director arrived in London the following week. He thought the young Welsh actor Anthony Hopkins might be suitable for the part of Major Doryan. Instead, Lean's eye was drawn to Jones, who had looks that reminded everyone of James Dean, and a rather doom-laden but sensuous appearance that suited requirements.

In *The Looking Glass War*, Jones played the part of a defector from behind the Iron Curtain who spoke English with a Polish inflection. The accent was important. MGM wanted American actors cast for obvious reasons, but for Lean and Bolt it was important that they, as the writer put it, 'can speak English'. Mitchum fit into that category, and he spoke 'Irish' too, as well as American, as he had made clear. Jones was a risk, but watching the rough cut of *The Looking Glass War*, Lean was struck by an extraordinary screen presence that he found difficult to articulate. Out of the blue, Lean shouted 'hire the bugger'. The schedule was too tight for a screen test to be organised, and a deal was quickly done in London between the agents.

It turned out that Jones was an American, from Tennessee, who had wound up in jail in New York after skipping out of the army. On his release he had pursued a career first as a gigolo – successfully, as word spread that he was quite a swordsman – and then as an actor attached to the famous Lee Strasberg school of method acting in the city.

Jones had modelled himself on Dean having seen *Rebel Without a Cause* (1955), and was married, turbulently, to Strasberg's daughter, Susan. As his career progressed, he was given a lead in a television series playing the part of Jesse James, and starred in a couple of low-budget but popular counter-culture movies, *Wild in the Streets* (1968) and *Three in the Attic* (1968), the latter telling the story of a frat boy who is locked in the top of a house and treated as a sex slave by three college girls. He had then come to Europe, where he made the more arty *Brief Season* (1969) in Rome, before doing *The Looking Glass War*.

Had Lean sought a reference from Anthony Hopkins, he wouldn't have received a glowing one. Hopkins described Jones as a 'silly fucker' who was doing a 'heavy number' on all around him during the making of *The Looking Glass War*, trying to get various members of the crew sacked even for looking at him the wrong way. Accompanying Jones were his agents and minders, Rudi Altobelli and Stuart Cohen, a homosexual couple who had rented out their Los Angeles home to Roman Polanski and his wife, Sharon Tate, while they went on a European sojourn. Altobelli and Cohen had built up a respectable stable of clients, which included John Savage and the *M*A*S*H* actress Sally Kellerman.

Also in the colourful Jones entourage was the beautiful 18-year-old actress Olivia Hussey, fresh from playing the female lead in Franco Zeffirelli's smash hit, *Romeo and Juliet* (1968), and now his new girlfriend as he completed a messy divorce with Strasberg. Jones was the last of the actors to arrive, in April 1969. Welcome to Dingle – though the *Ryan's Daughter* soundman John Bramall was gobsmacked to see Jones cast in the role of an upper-class British officer.

Mitchum, as ever, had his finger on the pulse as he lolled around, shooting the breeze with members of the crew. 'I was sitting with the soundman, Bram, and he said, "How did he [Jones] get that job?"' Mitch explained to Bramall that Lean had seen an edit of *The Looking Glass War* and had picked him out as his new star. Lean was particularly impressed that the young American actor could do such a good British accent. 'Bram said: "Young Tony Walbrook dubbed all that. I worked on that film. We couldn't get a squeak out of him, let alone a sentence, a full bloody sentence".' Mitch replied, sardonically: 'Come on now, we're working with a genius, he has to know this.'

Mitchum continued this extraordinary tale over drinks with film writers Harlan Kennedy and Nigel Andrews: 'So anyway Robert [Bolt] and Sarah came over to the house that evening and I told Robert and Sarah what Bram had told me. And Robert looks like he's just messed his pants. He said, "Doesn't David know?" I said, "I'm not going to tell him." Sarah, of course, was furious.'

Freddie Young saw a long-haired, pale-faced, sad-looking actor, and over the period of several days and tests they gradually cut Jones's hair shorter and shorter till it was a reasonable length for a British army major in the First World War. Jones, according to Havelock-Allan, 'had hardly heard that there was a thing called World War One, let alone knew anything about it.'

Despite playing such an important role in the film, Jones hadn't many lines to deliver, but as soon as he opened his mouth, the problems started. His character, Major Doryan, is replacing Captain Smith, who is heading over to continental Europe and the same battlefields where the major was injured. Captain Smith assures Doryan that he will get all the rest he needs in this Irish backwater, and is then anxious to know how bad it really is on the battle-front, as he is clearly a worried man who admits to possessing none of Doryan's bravery. Young watched as Lean rehearsed the actors and then said, 'All right, let's try it. Action.' The camera started turning and Jones sat there, motionless and mute, just staring ahead. Finally, David exclaimed, 'For Christ's sake, Christopher, what's the matter with you?'

'I ain't that kind of actor,' Jones replied.

'There was a stony silence,' Young recalled. 'We all wondered what we were going to do, with a leading man on our hands who couldn't act. David took me aside and said, "Throw him in silhouette as much as you can".'

Young changed the lighting to make Jones's face dark, with a little slit across his eyes, and Lean played the scene with the camera mainly on the other actor, an old trouper by the name of Gerald Sim. Jones sat there trembling as Sim paced up and down, doing all the work.

Voice lessons were stepped up. Jones even moved in with Johnny Mills for a few days. Mills had the modulated tones obligatory for all British actors at the time, as a result of having elocution lessons that had smoothed out the Norfolk accent of his youth. Lean himself had managed something similar. According to Mitchum, Lean was 'a perfect example of the British self-made man. When he was young, he used to speak with a Cockney accent. He worked very hard at acquiring the poshest English accent he could.' If even David could do it, why couldn't Christopher? An aristocratic friend of Havelock-Allan's, Lord Dunraven, was taped and presented to Jones as a model, but all Chris had to do was listen to Lean.

Shooting moved to the village for the scene in the pub – that first passionate clinch between Rosy and Doryan, which Lean had dreamed up and which was so close to his heart. Jones had decided that for this scene he was going to 'work small', an approach that didn't tally with Lean's vision. Lean wanted the shell-shocked Jones character to get the shakes real bad, but the actor didn't want to over-emote. There was a stand-off. Exasperated, Lean called over his prop man, Eddie Fowlie, who could turn his hand to anything, even acting lessons. 'Jones was supposed to have one of his flashbacks and he couldn't do it,' Fowlie said. 'So David said to me, "Show him". The pub had a fireplace with big lumps of peat in it. I flung myself into the fireplace, covering myself with peat. And David said: "There you are. Why can't you fucking do that?"'

When Rosy comes to the major's aid and her kind gesture suddenly turns into a passionate clinch, Lean wanted Jones to virtually dry hump her against the wall of the pub. Lean kept putting his hand on Jones's ass, saying, 'That part, Chris, push that part.'

Havelock-Allan watched on, worried.

> David had hell's own job. It wasn't that the boy was a bad actor, or couldn't act, but he was an actor who needed to be told exactly how to do it. He needed a director who loved actors, had infinite patience and could see where the boy was going wrong. David doesn't like to have to struggle to do that, so that was rather unfortunate. Then the boy, when he knew that David was getting impatient with him, got scared; his nerve went. So that was rather difficult.

Lean was quick to threaten Jones with breach of contract, and it was clear that the actor was in the same dangerous territory Trevor Howard had vacated. After a week of shooting in the pub, Lean was coming to the end of his tether. The illicit lovers' clinch in the bar is ended by the noise of Rosy's father and a group of hangers-on returning merrily from the local fair, ready to have one for the road. They gather around the major in the bar, gawking. Jones was having problems with the basics, hitting his mark and delivering his lines at the same time.

'Take two steps, put your cap on the table and say your line,' Lean would instruct him.

Jones would take two steps and say his line.

'Christopher, you forgot to put your cap on the table.'

The next time Jones would take the two steps, put the cap down and forget the line.

'I don't know how many times we had to do it,' said Gladys Sheehan, who was in the scene. 'He could not take three sets of direction. And the two managers [Altobelli and Cohen] would come down and say, "You're doing fine, Chris. Take your time." And they would calm him down and make a terrible fuss about him.'

MGM were also concerned, and over to Dingle from their New York headquarters came their new vice president of worldwide motion pictures, 38-year-old Herb Solow. 'It was a move I shouldn't have made, but we all make mistakes,' said Solow of his new job. 'I should have realised that MGM was a politically dead company and was financially almost broke.'

Solow took the obligatory tour of Kirrary, marvelled at the authenticity of the grim make-believe and had dinner with David in the Skellig. 'He was a bit stand-offish because he didn't know who the hell I was and what the hell I wanted,' said Solow, a gregarious fellow who managed to disarm David by the time dessert was served.

He was very frustrated with Christopher Jones. His line was, 'The man can't limp and talk at the same time' and he was very put out by it. I got the impression that the New York office had leaned on him to put in American leads. Mitchum at least was a tried and true actor, though I think miscast for the part. Jones was best known in the US for playing Jesse James on television and all of a sudden he is playing a British army officer. David talked about the fact that he could depend on Johnny Mills and he picked off all his travelling company of magnificent actors and suddenly the crux of the movie was handed over to two Americans, one who could act and one who could not.

It was a time of huge shifts in the movie industry, and at MGM the changes were particularly seismic. Lean's great backer at MGM, the studio president Robert O'Brien, had been eased out as a new cost-cutting regime moved in to stem heavy financial losses. Lean was alarmed at the imminent closure of the MGM studio at Borehamwood, North London, but O'Brien's demise was a far more pressing matter. It was O'Brien who had read *Doctor Zhivago* when it was a little-known book and had contacted Lean to say he was the only man to direct it. O'Brien regarded Lean 'as one of the great jewels of the motion picture industry'. Just the sort of sentiments David loved to hear when backed with hard cash and cast-iron guarantees of artistic independence, after years of mind games and arguments over money with Sam Spiegel.

When O'Brien hired Lean for *Doctor Zhivago*, it was he and the MGM hierarchy who flew to Rome to meet the itinerant director. O'Brien thought he was vying with rival executives at Columbia for Lean's business – not knowing

On the village set of *Ryan's Daughter*, David Lean directs Robert Mitchum, but for much of the time they weren't talking to each other.

Kirrary, the village built for the film on a small mountain outside the town of Dingle, looking out to the Atlantic Ocean and the Blasket Islands.

Local tradesmen and labourers worked on the construction of the village through the winter of 1968/69, often in appalling weather conditions.

Robert Bolt, who wrote the screenplay, visits his wife Sarah Miles during shooting at Inch Strand, with restless costume designer Jocelyn Rickards in the background.

John Mills rows out to sea at Dunquin, while crew and director keep a wary eye on the incoming tide.

Everybody was nervous about the love scene involving Sarah Miles and Christopher Jones in the bluebell wood (*right*) and with good reason. It was the first instance of nudity in a Lean film and a heavily medicated Jones was barely able to undress Miles (*below*).

Jones, in 1960s finery, with girlfriend Olivia Hussey, the teenage star of *Romeo and Juliet* (1968). Their relationship foundered in the cloistered conditions of Dingle

Actor Leo McKern, who played the part of the British informant, Thomas Ryan, in deep discussion with Lean at the schoolhouse set.

[L-R] Lean, Miles and Eddie Fowlie (holding seagull prop over his shoulder) watch while cinematographer Freddie Young demonstrates how Sarah should hold her umbrella.

Trevor Howard, as Fr Collins, warns bride-to-be Rosy Ryan about setting her expectations too high, while one of the giant Brute lamps shines down on them.

David Lean's assistants rush to rescue John Mills and Trevor Howard after their boat overturns during filming in rough seas at Coumeenoole Cove.

Bearded assistant director Pedro Vidal (*far left*) and Nurse Curran (*far right*) join in rescuing the unconscious Mills (*being carried*) and barefooted Howard.

David had vowed never to work with Spiegel again – and had agreed to pay him the highest salary ever for a director, as well as a high percentage of the profits. Lean's stipulations, such as the hiring of Robert Bolt to write the screenplay, were agreed to readily.

O'Brien was largely a benign presence. He had presented a box of cigars to the first cinematographer on *Zhivago*, Nicolas Roeg, after viewing some outstanding early rushes, only for Roeg to be then sacked by Lean, with whom he had a clash of personalities and styles, and replaced by Freddie Young. When *Zhivago* was running $3 million over budget, Lean had expected to be reined in, but instead O'Brien remained enchanted by his work, and told him so when they met. Lean had never experienced anything like it, and pronounced himself O'Brien's 'slave' from then on. Heavy losses on *Mutiny on the Bounty* had cost O'Brien's predecessor his job, but *Doctor Zhivago* proved to be a successful rescue mission for the studio, only after O'Brien had backed the film with a huge advertising campaign, which countered some awful reviews. In his gratitude for the money-spinner *Zhivago* became, O'Brien had been even more willing to cater to Lean's every whim when it came to *Ryan's Daughter*. That Lean had chosen an Irish locale for his new project only increased O'Brien's devotion.

Another Irishman, John Trehy, was employed by MGM as the accountant on *Ryan's Daughter*, effectively making him the movie studio's eyes and ears on the ground. A Tipperary man normally based in London, he soon made himself at home in Dingle. 'Nobody told Lean what to do,' Trehy says. 'He was in complete charge. After *Doctor Zhivago*, Robert O'Brien said to David, "Here's a blank cheque. Go and make your movie".'

However, too many of O'Brien's and MGM's other projects hadn't been successful, as the studio failed to capture the 1960s 'zeitgeist'. MGM's problems were shared, though to a lesser degree, by the other six major studios, four of which were also heavily in debt. Television was king, and movie theatres had lost more than half their customers since the Second World War. Debts at MGM had risen to $80 million, with net losses of $2.5 million for the final quarter of the fiscal year in 1968. The studio was about to default on its bank loans, and was pondering a write-off of $45 million because of a lack of confidence in a slate of new pictures.

Edgar Bronfman, the 40-year-old scion of the Seagram drinks dynasty, had purchased MGM in 1968. O'Brien, who had been on sick leave, was replaced by Louis 'Bo' Polk as president. Polk came from a job running the giant food company General Mills, and had an MBA from Harvard. Appointing an outsider to such an important position was virtually unheard of in the movie industry, but Bronfman wanted the company run along more conventional business lines. With Polk came what one former MGM executive, Peter Bart, described in his book *Fade Out* as 'squeaky-clean business-school types who spouted statistics'. Solow, who had a solid CV in the creative field, albeit in television, with series such as *Star Trek* and *Mission Impossible*, wasn't impressed by Polk. 'I took Bo Polk to see the cut on [the Antonioni movie] *Zabriski Point* in Rome. I don't think Bo knew what a rough cut was, but then there was no reason why he should have. I didn't know anything about the cereal business.'

Solow had reservations, too, about some of the content commissioned by O'Brien that had now fallen into his lap.

They were more the old-school films. Tastes had changed because of television and we weren't doing films that audiences wanted. One of the films I inherited was *Ryan's Daughter*. All I heard about it when on the outside looking in from television was that David spent a lot of money, he was a perfectionist and nobody on the [US] west coast was involved in it because it was all being done out of New York City. Then I learned that New York had made certain recommendations for casting on David's films because they had to have an American, otherwise Americans won't go to see it.

Of course, if you have good actors, the picture works, right? *Lawrence of Arabia* was a pretty good film and that only had Anthony Quinn, who's Mexican. The whole thing was kind of ludicrous, but it was an example of a frightened management who were saying, 'These are our last few dollars, let's protect them wisely'.

In Dingle, Mitchum enjoyed it immensely when he got chatting to one of Bronfman's entourage in Ashe's pub who asked him where all the money was going. 'Just look around you,' Mitchum answered as the place heaved. Bronfman didn't get po-faced about it. How could he? His diversification into the movie industry helped explain the crates of booze that were arriving in Dingle, much of which ended up in Mitchum's place. At one point somebody worked out that there was more of Seagram's premium Scotch, Chivas Regal, going into Dingle than the rest of Ireland put together. 'Seagram's used to send me a case of whiskey and a case of Chivas Regal every week which my stand-in, Harold Sanderson, promptly drank,' the actor claimed.

Bronfman himself then came to visit, and spent a day on the set, which helped reassure the director. Lean was also happier after he viewed the rushes from the barroom scene with Jones and Sarah that had proved so difficult and destructive. 'He called me over after the dailies [rushes] got back from Hollywood,' Jones says. 'After he saw them, he apologised up and down. He said, "I'm sorry, I couldn't see what you were doing." And I said I wasn't acting for the crew, I was acting for the camera.'

Jones didn't particularly help himself by locking himself away in his room at the Skellig Hotel and not mixing either with his fellow actors, the crew or the local people of Dingle, who were getting on with their lives while this madness swirled amongst them.

> Robert Mitchum came to my room once. I guess he had been drunk or something, for about a week. He hadn't shaved and he knocks on my door. I didn't know who the hell it was. I was sitting there talking to Olivia. I go to the door and open it and there's Mitchum standing in the hallway with these two girls. He said, 'Chris, I've brought these two girls from New York, let's have a party.' I looked over at Olivia and I said, 'I can't have a party. No. Sorry about that.' I think he got upset about that and he never talked to me after that.

If Jones was aloof, Messrs Altobelli and Cohen – the agents cum managers cum minders who took turns to accompany him and frequently overlapped – didn't endear themselves to others either. In fact, they made a virtue out of getting up people's noses. On *The Looking Glass War* they had annoyed a lot of people with their behaviour. Anthony Hopkins was convinced that Stuart Cohen was a drug addict and was feeding Jones on the stuff, though he didn't specify what stuff it might have been. Also, they had been making diva-like demands of *The Looking Glass War* producers – for instance, that they open an account for Jones at the designer store Hermès in London's West End, otherwise Christopher might have problems turning up for work the next morning. When they got to Dingle, they had made a big fuss about the car and the driver they had been given.

'Nobody had ever seen Christopher Jones; a lot of people didn't even know who he was because he hadn't done anything really,' said Altobelli.

They immediately disliked me because I was the manager, but I won them over. I won everybody over. I ended up taking the publicity car because the Irish didn't smell that well. You had to leave the windows open and it was cold. So I said I wanted the car that the MGM publicity people had. That didn't go down too well with them, but, hey, I didn't have to freeze and I didn't have to smell the driver, because the driver was nice and clean. And don't go saying that I said the Irish are all dirty, just 90 per cent of them.

Altobelli and Cohen quickly made it clear that they weren't interested in making an effort in Dingle, which explained why Jones was so aloof. Communications breakdowns and dietary preferences didn't help either.

'He was [aloof],' said Altobelli.

> Come on! There was no place to go. All you could do was walk around the atrium of the hotel. There was nothing. The food was hideous and the Skellig Hotel was all you had. I once ordered a roast beef sandwich with tomatoes. I took a bite out of it and it was awful. I opened it up and it had greasy mashed potato on it. When I called the waiter he said, 'Well, you said you wanted potatoes. If you wanted tomatoes, why didn't you say tomatoes?' They served chicken with gravy over the feathers. You think English food is terrible, but the Irish food is really bad.

Cohen and Altobelli were clearly intent on doing another heavy number on *Ryan's Daughter*. 'They were flanking him, guarding him,' according to Sarah. 'Nobody could get near him to embrace his fears.'

With Jones separated from the rest of the crew, gossip and conjecture quickly spread, with Sarah at the forefront of much of it. 'Although they were pretty camp, it still took quite a leap of the imagination to visualize Christopher getting up to any hanky-panky with either of them,' Miles wrote in her autobiography, *Serves Me Right*. 'But when I shared my doubts with Mitchum, he gave me a withering look. Was it because I was such a romantic that when Olivia Hussey came out to join him I experienced a sense of relief? She would come out for weeks on end just to be with him. What a beautiful pair they made or would have made, if one ever saw them together. She was always alone at the hotel, never once did anyone see them doing what normal lovers do.'

Trevor Coop, the young assistant cameraman, had film-star looks himself, and ended up getting enmeshed in some of Chris's paranoia. Coop had developed a cyst on his back, and was given three weeks off to have an operation done in London. Coop's absence from the set coincided with Jones's arrival.

Chris had been there for about two weeks when I came back. He was a very inexperienced actor, very nervous. He was working with all these big names and he had a huge part in a huge movie and David was swearing and cursing at him all the time. I came back on the Friday and we weren't shooting again till Monday. I was young, tall, lean. We were swanning about the Skellig Hotel. He thought I had come to replace him as major. He was so frightened of David for those two weeks. On Monday, when we started filming, he realised he was mistaken.

Or so Olivia must have told him. 'Chris was almost reclusive. Olivia was drop-dead gorgeous. She used to spend more time with us than Chris.'

Bayley Silleck, the MGM publicist on site in Dingle for the entirety of the shoot, was as mystified as everybody else by Jones. 'Olivia Hussey came over supposedly to be with Chris, but she spent most of the time hanging out in the bar talking to us. I don't think I saw her once with Chris. I don't know what that was about. Because she seemed to spend no time with Chris, naturally tongues were wagging that it was a put-up job.'

If anybody was putting it up, it was Cohen, who had a reputation for being manipulative, even by the standards of Hollywood talent managers. 'Stuart was one of those big Hollywood huggers,' says Silleck. 'He'd put his arm around you and say, "There's no goddamn way in hell you're going to get an interview with Chris today." And then he would slap you on the back and buy you a drink. I don't think I got more than three interviews with Chris in the six months he was there, and Stuart was impossible. I don't know whether he wanted to do it or not, or whether they didn't want him embarrassed in the press.'

Jones was sociable to the extent that he made it to the only room in the Skellig with a television set, which in turn had only one channel, the Irish state broadcaster RTÉ. One of his fellow guests in the Skellig was the Irish actor Niall O'Brien.

'You would get a pint of Smithwicks and go to the TV room. There was Christopher Jones, watching the farming programme *Mart and Market*, in black-and-white,' says O'Brien. 'RTÉ went on air at 5 p.m. with kids' programmes. Then you had the Angelus and the news, then *Mart and Market*, then *Broadsheet*, then *Bewitched* or something like that.'

RTÉ News was screening pictures of British troops being deployed on the streets of Northern Ireland as civil rights marches had turned into violence. Dressed in his British army uniform, Jones didn't have a clue what was going on, but he felt safe sitting in the hotel, self-isolating.

# 8. Dingle '69

It was a shame that Dingle couldn't get more out of Chris Jones and Chris Jones couldn't get more out of Dingle, for that was how the rest of the cast coped. There were clauses in many of the contracts that cast and crew couldn't travel more than twenty-five miles from Dingle without the permission of the production manager, and while those were widely flouted, nonetheless there existed in Dingle what Niall Tóibín described as 'cloistral conditions'. While the Jones contingent ruffled a few feathers, the *Ryan's Daughter* people had already built up plenty of goodwill in Kerry. They were big spenders, huge spenders in fact, and they made sure that the money stuck in the area. Hundreds of local people were hired at multiples of five or even ten times their normal weekly salary, not just in building that village on top of the mountain, but in ferrying the cast and crew around the place, and as assistants, stand-ins, extras, cleaners and caterers on the film. Tom Fitzgerald, the owner of the Dingle hardware store, which was besieged with orders during the construction of Kirrary, even found a job as a stand-in for one of the minor actors once he had hired sufficient staff to deal with the unglamorous side of his business.

The natural charm, warmth and humour of the Kerry folk was appreciated by Lean, even if at times he appeared even more remote than young Jones. Many of the Dingle shops had a little bar in the corner where you could take the weight off your legs and have a swift drink. A visit to the baker's, the bike shop or the ironmongers wouldn't be complete without a refreshment and an enquiry about Greg Peck, who was related to most people in the town, it seemed.

'There was nowhere to go, nothing to do,' said the associate producer Roy Stevens. 'There were only the pubs, something like forty-seven of them. There's a butcher's and it's a pub. You go in there and get your pork sausages or whatever and it would be, "Oh will you be having a drink?" It was hilarious really.'

Leo McKern was much loved, and adjusted better than most to what was a different way of life. 'The first month or so in an Irish community of this kind can be sometimes infuriating, until you realise that they've got it right and you, with imported ideas of attitudes and behaviour, have not; you simply have to change gear,' he wrote in his autobiography, *Just Resting*. McKern learned the history of the area and the fact that most people survived on a subsistence level through farming and other odd jobs. 'I felt, all the time I was there, despite the warmth and friendliness, a sense of apathy, or a patient, patent disbelief in any possibility of betterment, a passive acceptance that tomorrow, next month, next year, would hold the same as today ... not much of anything.'

The *Ryan's Daughter* crew were starting to feel the same, except on better rates. McKern had all his family with him, and would sail his boat around the Dingle Peninsula on his time off, or he would jump in his Volkswagen camper van and go hunting and fishing around Mount Eagle. By night he could be found in Ashe's or Tom Long's, drinking pink gins, and he might even be persuaded to perform his party trick, which involved his glass left eye, the real one having been lost in an industrial accident back in his native Australia when he was a teenager. McKern, after a few glasses of Chianti, was known in London circles to take out his false eye and half submerge it in a bowl of spaghetti bolognese, before complaining to the waitress, tongue firmly in cheek. Pasta and Chianti weren't readily available in Dingle in 1969, but McKern would improvise, placing his glass eye on the bar to watch over his drink when he went to the bathroom.

The good vibes weren't confined to the pubs, which were busy not just with the crew but with visitors who were attracted to Dingle by the extraordinary tales emerging in the local newspapers about the construction of the village, in particular, and the various injuries the actors had picked up, either on or off the set. Away from all the boozing, acts of generosity were quietly made, without any expectation that the favour would be returned. The gaffer, Bernie Prentice, was a particularly sociable and friendly fellow, who would return to his car to hear scuttling in the boot, where somebody had placed live lobsters in a bucket for his consumption, or there might be a couple of fresh bass wrapped in a newspaper with some langoustine.

Gaffer Prentice reciprocated. Bernie found time off from running a team of fourteen electricians to stand in when O'Connor's Undertakers were stuck for a hearse driver. 'I'd just come off location, I was all shitted up, but I didn't have to get out of the hearse when they were collecting the coffin from a cottage, so it didn't matter.'

When it came to matters of life and death, Dr Donal Savage was never too far away. The unit doctor had a fondness for the drink, but he was widely respected, and he may have even saved the lives of one of the actor's daughters, by spotting early symptoms of meningitis. Other than that, he entertained the unit with outrageous stories told over a drink or two in the bar. One concerned a woman who was a teetotaller all her life and had terrible diarrhoea. Dr Savage told her the only thing for it was a glass of brandy and port, for he had nothing else.

'No, no,' the patient replied. 'If I was to die, I wouldn't like to go before my maker with the smell of drink off me.'

'Well would you rather have the smell of shite off you?'

'He was savage by name and by nature,' says Tóibín. 'But he was a brilliant doctor. Jim Brosnan, the other local doctor, used to say: "Life's very easy for me. They go down to Savage for the diagnosis and come to me for the treatment".'

Laws, as they related to alcohol, were widely flouted and ignored. Pubs were supposed to shut at 11.30 p.m., but Bob Bremner, busy spending his money in Ashe's, claims that the local constabulary turned a blind eye most of the time: 'The Gardaí used to come around about midnight and one of them would say, "Anybody in there?" Somebody would say, "No" and he'd walk away. This is no joke. We'd be there till two o'clock.'

Likewise, the crew enjoyed the laxity when it came to the drinking and driving. Two of the electricians were pulled in by the Gardaí driving back from Tralee. Dr Savage was called out to test them, getting them to pick a coin off the floor without falling over and then pronouncing them sober. 'He was drunker than anybody, and he gave the police a bollicking for getting him out of bed,' Bremner says.

The only unit member to have a serious brush with the law was Eddie Fowlie, or Foul Eddie, as Mitchum called him.

Eddie had found himself a place well outside Dingle, out in the hamlet of Ballydavid, which meant he could come and go pretty much as he wanted without people noticing. He was, after all, a loner, except when it came to Lean. While Lean and Fowlie were devoted to each other, Eddie was regarded with suspicion by other crew members. 'He was a complete fucking monster really,' says Bremner. 'We had an expression for them – the upper-class twit and the thug, or something like that. Lean was so aloof and gentlemanly and there was Eddie, the foul-mouthed pikey. A very clever man, though, Eddie.'

Fowlie's deviousness knew no bounds. Stealing credit and props in equal measure were all part of his make-up. His rivals, as they became, in the art department were particularly incensed. Josie McAvin had somehow found original tyres for the Ford Model T used in the film, loaned to her after she swore on her life that they would be safely returned. 'They got into Eddie's hands,' she complained. 'He wouldn't give them back.'

'I got to know the locals,' McAvin said. 'I would buy off them or from the Travellers. They would also go and find stuff for me and I might take it or not. Then Eddie was off scorching the countryside too. When you're dressing a set, Eddie would be there if there wasn't something more exciting happening with David Lean. That was one good thing. He always wanted to be with David Lean. So he got out of your hair quite a bit, but meanwhile he had his brother working, he had his nephew working. They were all saying, "We'll have to ask Eddie".'

The locals didn't warm to him much either, except for a pretty *cailín* called Kathleen O'Connor, who was all of 18 years of age. Having been partly responsible for bringing *Ryan's Daughter* to Dingle, Fowlie should have been fêted by the locals, but his manner dictated otherwise, virtually from the get-go, when he had been too forceful in moving on some old rubber-neckers who were sitting on the currachs, watching the unit shooting out to sea. Niall Tóibín was also there. 'Fowlie arrives and he says, "Get off those fuckin', boats, you fuckin' cunts. Fuckin' local bastards. You're fucking up the whole continuity of the film. Those boats are put there and the continuity of the film has to be maintained." The following morning, we came along and the boats were in smithereens because there had been a storm during the night. Somebody said: "Where's your continuity now?"'

Tóibín, from the neighbouring county of Cork and well versed in country ways, was wise to what was going on. 'I'm sure that the tide did some of the damage, but the question is: did it do all the damage? I'm sure somebody said, "Fuck him" and when the tide came in maybe they helped.'

When Fowlie was in and around the Holyground in the centre of Dingle, his behaviour became no more reverential, especially when he had been drinking, as the local chemist Vera O'Keeffe noticed. 'He used to stand out there at the cross at about five in the morning and he'd start shouting, "Did you hear about Mrs so and so? She robbed the church box. And the chemist, Jim O'Keeffe. He's in bed all day. He never gets up." He was up, so he thought we should all be.'

Fowlie was also chucking litter about the place and generally making a bit of a mess. It prompted the production liaison officer, Lt Col Bill O'Kelly, to warn Lean and Havelock-Allan: 'You'd better tell your people that it would be a grave error to mistake the innate courtesy of these people for weakness or stupidity.'

With Foul Eddie, it was always fucking this, cunting that ... and bugger the consequences. 'He was a man who got things done, no matter what,' says Bronco McLoughlin, who worked as a stuntman, wrangler and occasional second assistant director on the film. 'There was a big rock in Dingle Bay. David would say, "Eddie, wouldn't it be wonderful if that rock wasn't there? The view we could have."

"Don't worry, guvnor. I'll get some local cunts to move it, blast it out of the water. Dig out the fucking thing." Movie companies had power. That was Eddie, if David said it's got to be done.'

Fowlie's energy and resourcefulness seemingly knew no bounds. Not content with doing David's biding from dawn to dusk, he also set up a late-night drinking club at the office of the props department on Main Street, as if there weren't enough liquor houses already in the town. 'I had two rooms there. One was my office, the other I turned into a pub for the boys, the technicians and the grips and such like when they got chucked out of Ashe's. One of the things I found was that there were a lot of chamber pots, which I bought. In the beams on the roof I put some nails in and hung the chamber pots off them and put the guys' names on them. And that is what they drank out of. Piss pots.'

This might explain why Eddie's imbibing emporium wasn't the most popular spot in town. However, he was differentiating himself in another way, by showing blue movies in one of the upstairs rooms, according to one or two of his select clients who were let in on the secret. This wasn't the side vivacious young Kathleen O'Connor saw. Kathleen worked in Atkins, the agricultural store, and on a break one day was perusing books in another shop around the corner, Garveys on the Holyground, when she got chatting to Fowlie. He then delivered to her some of his own favourite works of fiction to read. They started dating, in the Rolls, with Eddie driving Kathleen to some of the movie location sites as he mixed a bit of business with pleasure. Word had spread like wildfire about Fowlie's rough manner, but Kathleen also found a kinder, gentler side and quickly became 'overwhelmed' by his personality. Her parents didn't and his Spanish wife, Conchita, wasn't impressed either. Fowlie had met Conchita through her brothers, who worked on *Zhivago*. The ink on their marriage certificate was hardly dry as Conchita's family wouldn't let her join Fowlie in Dingle unless their union was formalised. In matters of the heart, Fowlie was unusually discreet, perhaps because in tying the knot with Conchita he was actually committing bigamy. He was technically still married to his first wife, Doris, since the time he lived in England. It made David's sneaking about pale in comparison, but secrets weren't going to stay that way for long in Dingle. Kathleen's mother tried to protect her, but Cupid's arrow was too powerful.

Fowlie called on the assistance of Roy Walker, the art director. 'He asked me to go with him to a hotel in Tralee (Ballyseedy Castle) when he first took Kathy out of town with her friend, who was her chaperone. We stayed in the bar. And that was the start of that romance. I drove back with him in the car the next morning and he was fine. I never thought it would carry on, but it did. And Kathy turned out to be a really sweet girl. Very intelligent. Amazing, actually.'

This was not a view that Conchita shared, as the truth dawned on her when she came to see her husband.

Conchita spoke no English, and became known locally as *Maquillaje* – the Spanish for make-up – as that is what she used to ask for in O'Keeffe's chemists. She gravitated towards her compatriot, Pedro Vidal, who was prepared to take up the cudgel on Conchita's behalf when it came to her errant husband, once he had a few drinks inside him and another member of the crew had wound him up about Spain's national pride being offended. Con Cremins, one of the production accountants on the film, was having a drink in Benners Hotel when he was alerted to trouble across the road at Eddie's props office.

> Somebody spotted Conchita and Pedro Vidal marching down the road trying to get access to the prop shop. Pedro was trying to kick the door down, but he couldn't because it was a strong front door. '*Hijo de puta*. Come out you white-haired so and so,' he was shouting. At about 3 a.m., I wasn't around at that stage, Eddie was seen opening the door, his white head poking out low to the ground. And then he scarpered. If Conchita had caught him, she would have done him an injury.

When the local glaziers were called to Fowlie's remote residence out in the hamlet of Ballydavid, it would seem that Conchita had eventually caught up with Eddie and her Latin blood had boiled over. 'We used the club a bit, but we liked the pubs for the crack,' said Bob Bremner. 'I was in the bar one night. Kathleen was there, a beautiful girl. And Conchita came in, screaming and shouting. And we were all sitting there, wondering what was going to happen. And

Eddie says to her, "If you don't like it, fuck off". That's what he was like. He was a lout really.'

Conchita didn't give up without a good fight, which finally got the Gardaí involved, who in turn put a call through to Pedro Vidal. 'Each time there was a problem they [the Gardaí] were calling me,' says Vidal, who had earlier sorted out a problem with some late-night drinking at one of the hotels during Holy Week. Now there was an incident at the Holyground. 'Fowlie was having a problem with his wife in his Rolls-Royce. She wanted to get out of the car and he didn't want to stop the car. She grabbed the steering wheel and the car was going round and round in circles in the middle of Dingle. Then she jumped from the car and he stopped to see what happened to her. Two priests were coming and they said, "Since this motion picture arrived, everything is different" and Eddie said, "You two cunts, fuck off". That was so Eddie.'

The local Gardaí on this occasion weren't so forgiving; one of those insulted was, after all, the parish priest, Canon Padraig Lynch. Fowlie was arrested and was facing possible charges. This meant potentially more delays on set, as Fowlie was the gatekeeper to some important properties, such as the schoolhouse, and had the keys in safe keeping at his house in Ballydavid.

The clergy in Dingle were powerful and worth keeping onside. They had originally been hostile to the film, in part because of the fact that some work was done on Sunday, which meant that numbers were down at Mass. There was also a fire-and-brimstone sermon from Canon Lynch on the moral fabric of the town being torn apart by the devil's work in the form of Hollywood. Kathleen wanted the wooden floor of St Mary's Church on Green Street to open up and swallow her as she absorbed what Canon Lynch was saying. It was also an uncomfortable moment for others. 'The parish priest certainly didn't like us around the place,' says Cremins, a regular churchgoer back up in his home town of Dublin. 'Some of his sermons from the pulpit, "The ruination of the young girls from the area. They mustn't be allowed out with the film crew." There I was in the middle of the church and everybody staring at me. I only came to Mass to say a prayer.'

Furthermore, there was a suspicion amongst the local priests and nuns about the promiscuous content of the film, and that Lean was engaging in a 'stage Irish' production, where the villagers would be portrayed as ignorant and stupid. Rumours abounded. 'Somebody who has never seen the film, for the simple reason that it has not been made, decides that the morals of the community are being threatened,' remarked Niall Tóibín. 'The fair name of Ireland is being sullied by all this carry-on and the nation is being made a mockery of and brought into ridicule.'

That wasn't Tóibín just exercising his considerable wit. 'The nuns got a bit annoyed with me when I asked them for help,' said Fowlie. 'They wouldn't be very helpful because they would say [puts on an Irish accent], "Oh you're making a fillum about keeping the pigs under the table and the chickens flying in and out the window". They thought we were making a film that was going to demean the local people.'

Why did they think that?

'It's Ireland. That excuses a lot, but I liked it.'

Nonetheless, there was no desire to alienate the film people either, for obvious reasons, and the Gardaí knew that as much as anybody when it came to Eddie Fowlie cussin' the clergy in public. It was made clear to Pedro the peacemaker that Lean's henchman would just have to eat humble pie, being made to knock on doors where his language may have caused offence and apologise to the residents, who may or may not have been upset by his behaviour. One or two older residents, it is said, couldn't understand him, as they spoke only Irish. However, honour was saved on all sides, and he could get back to his work.

A less abrasive figure around Dingle, Bolt was watching and listening as he continued to fine-tune the script, surprised by how sensitive people were to the 'stage Irish' question, but not entirely emollient: 'If you dared to write down some of the dialogue you hear in the pubs round here every day, you would be laughed out of court,' he told Adrian Cronin of RTÉ. 'Certainly any English critic would say "but nobody talks like that". I do assure you that you, the Irish, do talk like that.'

# 9. The bluebell wood conspiracy

It was Jocelyn Rickards who was the first to say, 'I've had enough'. Her travails were multifaceted. For one, her reservations about doing a second film in a row on the West of Ireland were proving well-founded. As Josie McAvin put it: 'When you thought of Jocelyn, you thought of "style". She wouldn't do a farmyard or anything.' Rickards had delighted in discovering the black Kinsale cloaks worn by Irish peasant women in the eighteenth and nineteenth centuries, which she purchased from a toothless Traveller who would arrive on a horse and cart laden with goodies outside No. 2 The Holyground and ring his bell. Rickards would come out and haggle, but nonetheless she found all the peasant stuff hard work.

Rickards went to the first crowd fitting having sprayed herself head to toe with insecticide and holding in her hand a bunch of Kleenex soaked in the Christian Dior perfume, Diorissimo. At the end of the day, Jocelyn was bite-free due to these precautions, but when she looked at her assistants – Diane Jones and Johnny Briggs – she thought they both had German measles. Not all the extras wore underwear. 'God, two hundred shitty crotches again tomorrow,' said Briggs, signing off for the day as wardrobe master.

Once a day, religiously, the marquees on the Holyground where the crowd fittings took place were fumigated with DDT, but Jocelyn reckoned the fleas bred faster than they could be killed. Eventually, the smell in the marquees got so bad that Jocelyn, despite her scented tissues, insisted on doing the fittings outdoors. 'I do believe our Irish crowd, all raised from nearby villages, were inured against such pests, for they never complained,' Rickards, an Australian, asserted in her autobiography, *The Painted Banquet*. This was not the kind of banquet she had in mind. 'It seemed to be only British blood the fleas chose to suck on.'

The other thing that was getting Jocelyn down was the weather and what it meant for her job. She didn't believe in the forecasts that came from the Dublin meteorological office, pointing out that Dingle was in such a distinctive and isolated position geographically, on a peninsula jutting out into the Atlantic with a range of mountains between it and the rest of Ireland. Like others, she would listen to the associate producer phoning the weather people in the morning and she would then stick her head out the window looking onto the Holyground and relay to Roy Stevens what she could see.

For the first time in her long career she longed for a normal call sheet, instead of the one with four or five alternative weather calls. This meant that the costume department had to go everywhere with one giant wardrobe van equipped to shoot in five different locations with five different sets of actors.

She could cope with this, but it was Lean himself who was the biggest problem. The decision by David to blame Mitchum's hat and suit for having to reshoot the first two or three weeks' filming didn't reflect well on Jocelyn. Rickards didn't appreciate the subterfuge and contrived reasoning, even if the schoolteacher did look more suited to a fedora rather than the bowler hat he originally wore. There were other skirmishes over Mitchum's nightshirt and whether he should wear his shirt inside or outside his trousers.

Mitchum had also given Lean a piece of his mind over the way he was treating Rickards. Having originally approved the drawings for Sarah's costumes, Lean started having second thoughts. 'What no one had told me was that he [Lean] couldn't read a costume drawing,' Rickards claimed in *The Painted Banquet*. 'I might as well have shown him blank sheets of paper. Stephen Grimes [the production designer] said later that he always got David to initial every set design sketch he approved. I don't think that would have helped me though. A lot of the drawings of mine that he liked clearly wouldn't have produced the clothes he had locked somewhere in his mind, but was incapable of describing to me.'

The tricky negotiations continued for several months in Dingle. Lean came to the conclusion that Jocelyn wasn't fully onside, and was, in fact, in the Mitchum camp, which only made him dig his heels in further. This reflected an insecurity in David, which even young Sandy had identified in her much older boyfriend: 'He very much had the feeling that you were either with him or against him. With David, there was no middle ground,' she later observed. Rickards detected that David was pining for his regular costume designer, Phyllis Dalton, who had done so well for him on both *Lawrence* and *Zhivago*.

'I certainly wished she was there instead of me,' Jocelyn concluded. 'It got to the point where nothing I did pleased him. This was aggravated by Robert Mitchum coming to my rescue and telling him that he didn't deserve such a talented, hard-working designer anyway and why didn't he pull himself together to try to help rather than hinder me.'

In despair early one morning, Rickards went to the production office and was drafting a letter of resignation when she was interrupted by Grimes's assistant, Josie McAvin. When McAvin learned of Rickards's intentions, she sped off in her Ford Cortina to bring Grimes to No. 2 Holyground, and there he pleaded with Rickards not to leave them in the lurch.

'What's the point of working your guts out to please a man who's determined to be displeased?' Rickards asked him. Grimes, who tended to mumble through his luxuriant beard, said he couldn't disagree. Nor could he see Lean apologising, he said, but he asked Rickards not to do anything before that night's fitting, and Rickards said she would hold off.

The costume in dispute this time was for a particularly important scene, namely Rosy's assignation with Major Randolph after their clinch in the pub had left them both yearning for more. The lovers-to-be also share a passion for horse riding and illicitly arrange to meet on horseback near a local castle. Rosy, despite her relatively humble background, would be wearing what felt right and proper for a lady's riding habit. In preparation for the scene, Rickards had arranged for the mare to be brought to the yard at the back of the production office on the Holyground, so that Lean could see horse and rider together.

Rickards had decided to go completely over the top, as her fine description made clear. She presented Lean with three choices. The first offering was a beige skirt with a silk taffeta petticoat and Liberty lawn blouse. The second offering she described as a dark-green riding skirt over a crimson silk taffeta flounced petticoat, a vermilion blouse with matching silk scarf, a heavy fringed black chenille shawl and a black bowler hat. There was a third offering which she couldn't quite remember. Lean chose the second costume, which Rickards thought was unsuitable, because the petticoat would have been too expensive for Sarah's character in Ireland at that time, but she had gone beyond caring. Rickards also noted that the blouse originally had a period cut and collar, but Lean wanted it to open down the front, which in the designer's opinion made it look like an expensive, modern shirt. David was going for 'poetic truth', but it jarred with Rickards to be so 'flagrantly out of period in a period film'.

The fittings for Sarah and others on the Holyground had become what Rickards considered a 'nightly cabaret' for the department heads, where everybody came in after the day's shooting and started to wind down over a drink while watching the fitting. As Sarah went out to mount the horse and ride past the production office window, David turned to Jocelyn in front of his Dedicated Maniacs and said: 'Jocelyn, I owe you an apology.' Rickards's mouth dropped open; like so many women before her, her resolve melted in front of Lean, and she knew that she couldn't walk away. Caught off-guard and suddenly disarmed, it was only some time later that Jocelyn realised that Grimes had stage-managed the whole thing.

Rickards may have been beyond caring, but for everyone else the 'tryst' between Rosy and Randolph was one of the most important scenes in the movie, and the tension and nervousness over its shooting was cranked up accordingly. The scene would feature nudity in a Lean film for the first time – once Major Doryan had removed all those expensive garments – and Lean fretted over whether he could shed his 'old-fashioned' ways without being seen to be gratuitous and crude. It was also important for the film-makers that the audience empathised with Rosy as she seeks sexual and emotional fulfilment, even though she is committing adultery and betraying not just her husband but her community in so doing. As Havelock-Allan put it: 'It was a lovely warm day, full of all sorts of stimulating sounds and feelings, and for two people who were excited by each other nothing could be better than that they rip off their clothes and start creating another human being.'

Fowlie – who else? – had to find the place in the great outdoors for them to 'fuck', as he put it rather less eloquently. He had been recommended a spot near the Castleross Hotel on the banks of one of the lakes of Killarney, where a reclusive and forbidding English lady lived. Fowlie realised this called for special treatment:

> I got the Rolls out and I opened the gate and I drove through bloody miles of wonderful trees and there were masses of bluebells with wild garlic mixed in with them. It was glorious. And you are never going to believe this, but it's the truth. There was a fox running along with a salmon in its mouth. You wouldn't put it in a script because it's too corny. And the atmosphere was incredible, full of dappled light. I drove up to the front of the house. A big woman

with a horsewhip came to the door and I said, 'I'm just admiring your beautiful forestry around here. I'm from Metro-Goldwyn-Mayer'.

Many would have liked to have seen the woman put the whip to good use. Instead, she invited Fowlie inside and offered him a drink.

'I said I'd like a whisky and she thought that was an excellent idea. So we had whisky at 9 a.m. and by the time I'd finished, I'd got all the permission I needed to film. She even invited us to film inside the house. That beautiful bluebell wood. I have to admit that I cut down some trees to make a track through the middle for the big crane to go through.'

The acclaimed Hollywood celebrity photographer Bob Willoughby also tried to help David when it came to narrowing down the spot where the tryst would take place. Willoughby had arrived in Dingle to do a photo feature for *Life* magazine on Christopher Jones, and also some work for MGM. He came from working on *Catch-22* (1970) in Rome and drove up to the set in his Maserati sports car, far too close for David's liking.

The assistant director came over to me and said, 'Is that your car with the Rome licence plates on it? You're going to have to move it.' I thought the car, for whatever reason, was in the shot. I went over and there were cars parked all around me and right next to me was Lean's car with Rome licence plates. So I moved my car, which was a problem because there was a lot of equipment which I had to carry, lugging it up hills and stuff. So I went to the AD and I said,

'What's the deal?' He was embarrassed to tell me that Lean didn't want another Rome licence plate anywhere near his car.

Willoughby then spotted David walking around the bluebell wood, uncertain about where to start filming.

> I had been looking myself and I felt that I had the perfect spot, and when he caught my eye, with only the best intentions, I made the big mistake of forming my hands in the shape of a camera frame to indicate that I thought this would be a good spot. He looked at me with such anger in his face that I just faded away, having committed the terrible sin of suggesting to the master where to put his camera. Lunch was called right then, an hour early. I realised too late just how neurotic Lean had become. When we returned from lunch there was the camera in exactly the spot I had indicated, and Lean totally failed to even look at me for days.

It was here that the establishing shots for the love scene were completed, with the couple meeting by the weir of a river where the salmon leap, and then nudging their horses deeper and deeper through the bluebell wood towards a spot where they were sure they could be seen by nobody. This was Lean in his element, shooting down on the players from atop of the giant Chapman crane, which had seats for two people at the top and had to be driven into the forest once Fowlie had blazed a trail. Unfortunately for David, the skies darkened and the rain started to fall as the expectant couple picked a route through the bluebells, but at least he had got something in the can. Once the rain stopped, the couple could return and get down to business.

The rain poured from the skies for days and the bluebells were washed away, with seeds of doubt sown in their place.

David was determined to keep his upper lip stiff, but his Dedicated Maniacs were growing increasingly concerned. After three-and-a-half months of shooting, on 11 June the film was officially forty days over schedule and $940,000 over budget. The following five weeks were a disaster because of unsuitable weather, and by 15 July the film was sixty days behind schedule and $1.5 million over budget.

It was supposed to be summertime, but it rained for days on end, and when the sun shone, it was frequently through a light mist that had descended on the peninsula in those summer months for no particular reason. Cinematographer Freddie Young had terrible difficulties matching shots because of the different cloud formations. Then the crew would arrive and set up the equipment, only for the weather to change again. 'We had four seasons in one day, sometimes five,' Bob Bremner remarked. Lean didn't see the funny side of it. 'You could start shooting at ten o'clock and not a cloud in the sky and by half-past it's pouring with rain. You can't guarantee it. It's sort of heart-breaking, and we wasted so much time waiting for the weather.'

Everyone reckoned that David was having awfully bad luck with all the rain, but that wasn't really the case. By local standards it was actually a reasonably good summer, with the local *Kerryman* newspaper reporting bumper crops and large numbers of tourists coming to the Dingle Peninsula. As the annual report for the Irish Meteorological Service noted, rainfall for the whole of the country in 1969 was 85 per cent of normal, and 'the year was notable for the exceptionally dry spell experienced over most of the country from July to October'. However, getting two dry sunny days in a row was always difficult. As Niall Tóibín put it in his autobiography, *Smile and Be a Villain*, 'The Irish weather, notoriously uncooperative, scuttered around in its usual way. It conjured up mist, fog, rain, sunshine, sleet, hailstones and permutations in eternity of these.'

All this shouldn't have been news to Lean or Bolt. However, as Leo McKern noted, there was 'a confident expectation that circumstances will conform to the projected intention'. Now it was the projected intention that might have to change rather than the circumstances, a realisation that dawned with the drowning and dying of the bluebell blooms. There were also beach scenes in sunny conditions that needed to be shot. The Dedicated Maniacs got themselves in a conspiratorial huddle – the production accountant John Trehy, production manager Doug Twiddy, associate producer Roy Stevens and art director Roy Walker. Going into autumn, the production was running out of time, light and leaves. Moving the whole production out of Ireland to sunnier climes was suddenly becoming a serious option.

'We knew what was going to happen,' said Walker. 'He hasn't shot the scene in the woods. We didn't even think about the bloody beaches. So secretly, Roy, Doug and John Trehy arranged for me to go to London. I went to Kew Gardens and asked them where in the world around Christmastime would there be trees that you would believe were in Ireland. The people at Kew got their heads together and came up with Chile, Japan, New Zealand and South Africa.'

Next stop for Walker was the South African embassy on Trafalgar Square.

I went to South Africa House, which in those days was very unfriendly. It was like going into Gestapo headquarters. They were very, very rude and then directed me to their tourist shop. I went to the shop in Piccadilly and they finally showed me these 16mm shots of woods which I thought were good. And I kept seeing these beaches and I thought, 'Christ, they do look like Ireland. They had light reeds and everything. So that was in the back of my mind. I go back and nobody tells David a thing. We carried on shooting.

Lean still refused to let his upper lip quaver.

'David didn't want to discuss openly that we wouldn't be able to finish filming in Ireland because it would be admitting defeat,' says Trehy. 'He may have known, but not wanted to know. He closed his eyes to it. We were all forbidden to talk.'

That conversation with David would only take place on a 'needs-must' basis, but in wrestling with the Irish elements Lean had clearly met his match. A reconnaissance mission along Inch Strand, one of the glories of the Dingle Peninsula, graphically illustrated the point. Early one Sunday morning, David arrived in his Rolls-Royce and drove onto the hard sand, like so many day-trippers before and after him. He then transferred into a Land Rover, sensibly as it turned out, and his party drove out down the magnificent stretch of sand.

A local driver was at the wheel, with Lean, Roy Walker and Freddie Young as passengers. About three miles down, the Land Rover went around the elbow of the beach, where the sand was at its narrowest, and David told the driver to head towards the dunes. The driver urged caution, and so did Roy Walker. 'I said, "No, David, it's too soft, it will go down", but David wouldn't hear of it. Sure enough, the Land Rover got stuck in the soft sand.'

The tide was coming in, fast. Walker, being the youngest and most athletic member of the party, traipsed all the way back along the beach and got a local farmer, Jack Bowler, to leave Mass and drive his tractor down the beach, with the promise of a £20 reward if he could rescue the Land Rover. The farmer, who had a couple of his children with him, got to within about twenty-five yards of the Land Rover and promptly announced, 'I am not getting my new tractor stuck in there'. He did a U-turn and started driving away, to the clear frustration of David, whom Walker could see gesticulating wildly on the dunes, but on this occasion his directions were to be ignored.

Walker argued with the tractor driver all the way back to the car park, but to no avail. So Walker hopped in his rented Fiat 124 and drove back down the beach as a last desperate measure. 'If you hit a bloody puddle in this thing, it would conk out. At this stage the tide is really coming in. The next thing a wave comes in and my car stalled about fifty feet from the Land Rover.'

He rejoined his colleagues on foot. David was incandescent with anger. 'What happened to that idiot? What are we going to do?'

'I told him I was going to empty my boot and he better empty his, because there was no way we were going to save those vehicles. By this time the water is beginning to lap round the wheels. And then we had to walk back. David was never too good on his old legs; he was slipping and sliding, until the tractor picked us up and we drove back with all the children. Then there was the most awful drive back to Dingle in the Rolls-Royce. Absolute stony silence.'

Word reached Mitchum, who was highly amused and decided to blame Eddie Fowlie, whom he regarded as a Lean lickspittle. 'I don't know how many vehicles we lost,' Mitchum reflected. 'He'd say, "I've checked the tidal table, guv, it's alright". They'd park the Land Rover down, the sea would come in, because it's like the Straits of Gibraltar, that bay in Dingle. The sea rushes in, it builds up like this and suddenly it comes in in a big flood. You'd park the car there and suddenly there's an eight-foot tide and it would be rolling out to sea. We lost half a dozen cars. And David had great faith in Foul Eddie.'

The Land Rover was eventually retrieved once the tide retreated, and afterwards it was placed for a few days in the stream that runs through the centre of Dingle to try to wash out all the salt, but it became a rust heap nonetheless. The Fiat was never seen again.

# 10. Dangerous occupation

*Ryan's Daughter* was a difficult and dangerous film, but at least nobody died. Or did they? Fatal accidents were something David had learned to live with on his films. On the first film he directed, *In Which We Serve*, the chief electrician, Jock Dymore, had died in agony from burns suffered when a film can containing a substance called lycopodium, used in studios to create explosions, had blown up in his face. David packed up shooting for the day, despite the protestations of his co-director, Noël Coward. On *Bridge on the River Kwai*, the stuntman Frankie Howard died after being swept downstream in a current during rehearsals, and an assistant director, John Kerrison, was killed in a car crash on a jungle road near Colombo. Filmmaking was a dangerous business, especially in the wild, out-of-the-way locations David favoured, such as the jungle, the desert or the North Atlantic shoreline.

David was prepared to take risks on *Ryan's Daughter*, particularly when it came to Johnny and Trevor in the currach, when the locals had warned him not to put them out to sea. Leo McKern also complained of being bullied by Lean, and of almost being drowned at Coumeenoole when they dumped water tanks on top of him while filming close-ups of the storm scene there. The director had hissed, 'Leave him, leave him' when McKern, a highly accomplished swimmer, had raised his arm, which signalled he wanted to be rescued. Then, when they tried to haul him in, they only succeeded in dragging him under, and he had swallowed a bellyful of salt water before he was finally rescued. In the process, his beloved false eye also fell out, but he didn't cause a fuss.

'Leo was just wonderful,' Lean said. 'I would go and do mad things – anybody will go and do mad things if they are excited enough. And I suppose we were excited. Everybody was insured, nobody got hurt. You get cut cheeks and that sort of thing, but that's all part of my boy-scout background.'

Nobody killed, nobody seriously hurt. Yet *Ryan's Daughter* took its toll in a rather tragic way. 'No names, no pack drill,' says Niall Tóibín. 'But there were certainly three people that I am absolutely convinced died as a result of their drinking within five or six years.'

Hardly the fault of David Lean. Yet for all the Sarahs and the Mitchums, the glamour and the girls, the Lamborghinis and the Rolls-Royces, arguably the most incredible story about that crazy year-and-a-bit in Dingle and beyond concerns the 'Hard Lads' who came down from Dublin. And at least a handful of them remained around long enough to tell the tale.

The Hard Lads was a group of Irish actors hired to play the parts of the rebels who are trying to land a shipment of German arms on the Atlantic coast, a plot line inspired by real-life events leading up to the Easter Rising in Dublin in 1916. In Bolt's script, their work is made near-impossible by a storm that blows up, forcing the German cargo ship to curtail the mission and send the arms towards the coast in giant inflatable rafts. However, since they are Hard Lads, they are determined that nothing will get in their way, even if Rosy's British lover is waiting just around the corner to nab them, having been tipped off by a traitor in the village.

Casting for the Hard Lads was done mostly in Dublin. Tóibín himself arrived in Lean's suite in the Shelbourne Hotel, where the Irish casting director Don Geraghty and assistant director Michael Stevenson were also in situ. Tóibín had been doing work in his garden in South Dublin, wearing Wellington boots and an oilskin coat, and hadn't bothered to change. 'You look as though you are dressed for the film,' they laughed, and he got the part.

Another was Niall O'Brien, who was part of the Abbey Theatre company performing the John B. Keane play *Big Maggie* on tour. O'Brien met Lean at the Great Southern Hotel in Killarney, landing the part of Hard Lad Bernard. 'My contract ran for nine weeks and then it was extended to thirteen and then it was never extended. It was never specified. I ended up being on the film for fifty-three weeks.'

When the Hard Lads and the other Irish actors first got to Dingle, in January 1969, they gathered in the local parish hall and Lean showed them *Man of Aran* (1934), the drama documentary shot by Robert Flaherty about the desolate life of Irish peasants, which features a famous storm scene. Lean was strongly influenced by the work of Flaherty, an Irish-American, since watching *Nanook of the North* (1922), a study of the Inuit, decades earlier. The storm in *Man of Aran* was something of a benchmark, which he presented to the Irish actors who had come on board. 'There's some jolly good stuff in it,' Lean said. 'Funny, after a bit it's not quite as good as one thought it was originally, but bloody good, for God's sake. I'm not trying to run it down, but it's a curious thing when you see a film several times, generally the most effective time is the first.'

The tempest in *Ryan's Daughter*, Lean told his Irish actors, would make what Flaherty shot look like a storm in a teacup. Or, as Tóibín wrote, 'this film would contain the storm to dwarf all storms. The storm in *Man of Aran*, till then Ireland's most celebrated celluloid tempest, would be as a linnet pissing in the breeze, compared to the seething deluge which would crease the cliffs of Kerry, like the Crack of Doom itself … if it came, like.'

Most of the storm sequence was supposed to be in the can before the likes of Mitchum and Miles even arrived in Dingle and got their faces in front of a camera. From the time Lean first landed in Ireland, in November 1968, he was on the lookout for a storm to film – great panoramic shots in 70mm that would fill the wide frame. The closer stuff with the lead actors could be added later and faked, if necessary. He even followed Flaherty's trail to the Aran Islands off the coast of Galway to see what they had to offer, but was convinced he could obtain more dramatic footage elsewhere.

The cameraman Bob Huke then came over in January 1969, weeks before the main unit, and good material was shot in rough weather with stand-ins running in the distance. One particular spot, the Bridges of Ross near Kilkee in Co. Clare – about seventy miles north of Dingle as the crow flies – was particularly susceptible to storms, and excellent footage was caught there of 80mph winds blowing in mighty rollers that crashed against the black cliffs. They managed to get dramatic footage there, not just of stormy seas but of Lean himself, hair blown back by the gale, facial features stretched and energised, which the unit stills photographer, Ken Bray, captured, with Bayley Silleck holding on to the photographer's back to steady him. The gusts were so strong that the front door of the Land Rover was bent when it flew open. What was needed was more of the same.

As the crew tried to tap into local knowledge in the Dingle pubs, the talk was not encouraging, and Tóibín's cutting wit was again being sharpened. 'Veterans of filming tornadoes in Florida dismissed the Kingdom's [Kerry's] best as mild flatulence. Old folk in chimney corners and pub snugs donned the mantle of an extra half-century to reminisce about the "night of the big wind" but held out little promise of a repeat in the foreseeable future.'

Lean looked at the storm footage he had shot from the winter and early spring and realised that it wasn't enough. This begged the question about what to do with the dozen or so Irish actors who featured in the storm scene and whose contracts were already running out. The answer was to hang on to them in Dingle and get them in front of a camera as and when the weather deteriorated to such a degree that the storm scene could be finished off.

Niall O'Brien's wages had gone from £18 a week on the stage to £100 a week in Dingle, so he and the other Irish actors weren't entirely dismayed to learn that they would have to hang on longer than they expected. They were also prepared to live with a term in their contract that said they couldn't travel more than twenty-five miles from base without permission, in case a storm unexpectedly manifested itself. Even Havelock-Allan could see the danger involved in this: 'It's a terrible trap, Ireland. It can be the dullest place in the world and there is nothing to do but drink. All the actors had long periods of not working but they couldn't go away. There are seventy-two pubs in a town of 2,000 people and we patronised them quite a lot.'

Seventy-two pubs – or fifty depending on whether the butcher or baker serving gargle could be classified as a pub – but no gymnasia or pottery classes. Had there been, what do you think the Hard Lads would have done? The answer had even been put to verse:

> A producer named Havelock-Allan
> Watched the actors drink pints by the gallon
> David, he said
> They're drinking our bread
> And none of them have any talent

'While we were all waiting for the storm, we tried to drink ourselves to death,' said Tóibín. 'And some, it must be said, succeeded.'

Tom Long's pub at No. 1 The Holyground was where the Irish actors waited, and waited and waited. The story that their names were carved on the bar stools is not entirely fictional, though the real story is probably a better one. 'They were just ordinary bar stools with a foam rubber top,' says Niall O'Brien. 'Tom [Long] noticed that somebody was picking the foam rubber out of the inside of it. He didn't say anything, but he was keeping a watch out. It was me. I was having a pint and was picking the inside out of it and he said to me, "You, you fucker. You're picking the insides out of the seats. Here, I have one especially for you." And he brought one out, with the foam taken off it and just the plywood top and my name written on it.'

The Hard Lads would sometimes jump behind the counter and serve other customers, or else one of them might go for a nap in Liam Long's bed upstairs while the youngster was out at school. They groused along with the crew of Welsh desperadoes who were trying to recover Spanish gold from the wreckage of the *Santa Maria de la Rosa* in Blasket Sound, but who had only retrieved a few cannon balls and a couple of barnacle-encrusted shopping trolleys. The leader of that venture, Syd Wignall, was threatening to scuttle his own boat in the Sound, such was his frustration. Would Lean's expedition be any more fruitful?

At least for the film people there were also solid professional reasons for colonising Tom Long's, even if some people had forgotten what they were. Altered scripts would be dropped in there from the production office at No. 2 The Holyground. 'Tom Long's was the office for everything,' said Gladys Sheehan, who was much in demand as a special extra as a result of coming to Dingle with a black Kinsale cloak which Lean liked to shoot as often as possible. 'A crowd of us used to knit while on the set because we'd have nothing else to do. Mrs O'Sullivan had the wool shop. She would bring the wool up to the pub and leave it there, because by the time we were coming off the set she would be closed.'

What were most eagerly awaited were the call sheets for shooting the next day, to see who was needed and where they would be shooting. Inevitably, the Hard Lads would be left behind in the pub while everyone else went out on location for the day. The crew worked hard and played hard, but the same couldn't be said of the Hard Lads, for there was no work for them to do. 'Doing nothing's a dangerous occupation,' roars Fr Collins about his feckless, beaten-down villagers at the start of *Ryan's Daughter*. Somebody should have roared the same at the Hard Lads.

'Lean would come out in the morning and look at the sky and say, "No, nothing today", so we would go to the pub and we'd be there all day from ten in the morning to midnight,' says Eoin O'Súilleabháin, a well-known actor from the Dingle Peninsula who was also employed as a consultant and dialogue coach. Most of the consulting he did in Tom Long's. Even when a fellow actor dragged him out of the pub and they borrowed a boat and went fishing, he brought a crate of Macardle's ale. 'I was getting £10,000 a year from it. I had to get a loan of £30 to get there and £30 to get back.'

There were some legitimate gripes, some of them concerning O'Súilleabháin, who was a tremendously good-looking fellow and dashing to boot. No Irish actors were cast in any of the principal parts; even the prominent roles amongst the Hard Lads – who were as Irish as they come – were given to English actors and not very suitable ones at that, namely Barry Foster and Doug Sheldon. Foster was playing the Michael Collins-type character, but didn't have the physical stature; Sheldon was regarded as too much of a pretty boy who wasn't up for the rigours of the shoot, and Lean punished him by pushing him further and further to the periphery as the movie went on.

In order to get themselves out of the pub, the Irish actors would go on the set and watch the shooting. To Niall O'Brien's ear, it wasn't just Jones who was having problems with his accent; all the foreigners playing Irish parts were struggling as well. 'They were surrounded by the real McCoy. Eoin O'Súilleabháin was actually from the Blasket Islands and was a wonderful actor but didn't have one word to say in the film. And he was fifty-three weeks there as well.'

O'Súilleabháin was a star in his own right down in Dingle, who would be recognised in the street before the likes of Trevor Howard or Tóibín, much to their amusement. Irish television had started in June 1960, and had quickly swept the country. 'We were out on the street with Trevor', said Tóibín. 'All these local convent girls rushed towards us. Trevor said, "Oh fucking hell, I can't put up with this, not in Dingle." And they all rushed by him and surrounded Eoin, who had an Irish-language programme on RTÉ TV. He was the pin-up boy. He was so good-looking. And Trevor said, "Oh it's him they want. Fuck old Trevor, they have never heard of him." And he pissed himself laughing.'

Even when they did get out with the rest of the crew, O'Brien and the rest of the Hard Lads were left twiddling their thumbs. 'They had us on set in wet suits and over those woollen trousers and a woollen sweater and you would be baked alive, in the middle of a field. The idea was that they might be shooting a mile away from the sea and then if the weather broke, we would rush to the sea. We were there on David Lean's whim, if he saw an opportunity. He felt, "Well I am paying them, they may as well be here."'

There was nothing to do, but there was plenty to see, especially for a young sports car nut like O'Brien, who could barely believe his eyes when he saw what was being paraded before him. 'I was staring at Robert Bolt's Lamborghini in Dingle. Lean had bought it for him as a kind of tax dodge. Bolt came up to me and said, "Here's the keys, have a spin". He was a lovely man. The producer had a Lotus. He was far too old for that car.'

There were the Hard Lads and then there were the dozens of extras, a tough crew in their own right. David had demanded 'wild faces' to go with the wild landscape, and had been directed by the Irish casting director, Don Geraghty, to a settled Traveller community in Tralee called The Bullring, from where busloads of extras were brought to the set on a daily basis. Michael Stevenson encouraged and cajoled them and there was plenty of fun and games on No. 2 The Holyground. 'It was a job getting them out of Tom Long's and back on to the coach in the evening. At one point the banisters in the production office were smashed in a fight, but they were marvellous.' Sean Moran, the Dingle transport manager and garage owner who supplied the unit with vehicles and drivers, feared the worst when one of the doors burst open as the coach was speeding along the road from Dingle back to The Bullring and one of the passengers had fallen out of the bus and onto the road. The poor man was covered in cuts and bruises, and his lovely white Aran sweater, which he had purchased that day with his wages, was ripped to shreds, but all he asked for was money enough to buy a new one.

Bloodied faces were commonplace as a result of the odd stone being thrown, in anger or in jest. When there was nothing to do, the Bullring's burliest played tug of war with the electricians on the beach, but eventually even the Travellers grew restless. Roy Stevens told Lean they would have to shoot the big crowd scenes quickly, as the Travellers wouldn't be around for much longer, because they were leaving for England. 'I said, "What do you mean leave for England?" Roy said they come over to England and during the winter get the insurance pay or whatever it is. You can come over to England, do nothing and get paid for doing nothing and that's what these extras used to do,' Lean later remarked.

While their compatriots living in Dingle accepted the good fortune that had come their way without question, the Irish actors had a slightly more jaundiced eye. They were irritated that the company, and Fowlie in particular, had changed some of the place names around the peninsula, because they wouldn't make the effort to pronounce the existing Irish ones. Coumeenoole became Conchita Bay, named after Fowlie's wife. Clogher Head looking out onto the Blaskets became known as The Puddles. Then there was Brennan's Corner, where the speeding electrician had overturned his Land Rover and the trailing generator.

'We had never seen the likes of them,' says O'Brien. 'They were all these kind of uneducated English people who had so much money. They were all dripping with gold nuggets around their neck and they had flash cars. And they really knew nothing, except how to jump to David Lean and do whatever he wanted.'

However, the most outlandish stories told by the Irish actors were about each other, in the absence of anything meaningful to do. Dingle was a town of about 1,400 people, but with the passing weeks and months, it started to shrink. As O'Brien put it, 'We were all stuck in this little village. Anybody you could get a laugh out of was fair game.'

A cement block had dropped onto Niall Tóibín's toe and it had become infected. On the insistence of Dr Savage, he had to take a bed in the small infirmary run by the Presentation nuns from their convent at the top of the town. Savage had remarked that 'the nuns will like nothing better than injecting a load of penicillin into your illustrious backside'. The nuns did fuss over Tóibín, and in return they were keen to hear all the news from the set. Was the priest really carrying on with Rosy? What was happening with Mitchum and Miles? Then a present arrived for Tóibín, carefully wrapped in beautiful gift paper and tied up with a big red ribbon. 'Your friends sent it up. Be careful, it's very heavy,' one of the nuns remarked as she carried it in with some difficulty. Tóibín took one look at the package and roared 'Take that away', having realised without even having to open it that the Hard Lads had amused themselves by sending him up a present of a cement block.

O'Brien on Tóibín:

Did you hear about Tóibín going into the Skellig? Pissed. Shouting and roaring. Last orders were about 8.45 and Tóibín came in at ten past nine and sat down at the table to eat. Then he falls asleep. The waiter goes up to him and he is wondering what to do with him. The waiter went off and he got a dirty plate, with a few pieces of fat and a bit of mashed potato and vegetables and put it on the table in front of him. And he shakes Tóibín and says, 'Are you finished, Mr Tóibín? Can I take your plate?' And Tóibín wakes up, 'Oh yeah, yeah. Thanks very much.'

Tóibín on O'Brien:

Myself and O'Brien were staying in a lady's place on the waterfront there and we were in one room and there were two truck drivers who stayed there every week in the other room and two tourists in the third room. O'Brien said to me at breakfast, 'Where does the landlady sleep?' I said, 'I don't know, I suppose she sleeps down in the kitchen or the living room.' He was coming home one night, pissed, and there was a built-in wardrobe on the landing and he opened it thinking it was the bedroom. There's yer one, asleep in the wardrobe.

Tóibín managed to get himself barred from the Skellig for a while, but being a fluent Irish speaker himself (his father refused to speak English), the actor got on particularly well with the locals, especially the guys who owned the pubs, like Tom Long and Paddy Bawn Brosnan. Leaning over the bar and jawing away *as Gaeilge*, Paddy Bawn served Tóibín a tasty morsel. The hotel was happy to arrange for food to be imported from Harrods in London, such as Iranian beluga caviar and Indian water buffalo. Tóibín recounted Paddy's story:

David Lean was having guests over from London, he was having them for dinner, and he ordered black caviar from Fortnum & Mason or some fuckin' place, and it was flown over. He was having the dinner party for six or whatever. Anyway, the chef, or a chef – we can't use his name unfortunately – woke up one morning after being on the piss the night before. 'There's an awful taste of caviar. Where the fuck would I have got caviar last night? They don't have any caviar in Paddy Bawn's, you know.' Anyway, he goes to work and opens the fridge and there's the big tin, open. 'Oh Jesus Christ, I must have been really pissed.' He'd opened the tin and eaten half the caviar. So he goes back down to Paddy Bawn's.

'I must have been very pissed last night.'

'You were, you were.'

'Jesus, Paddy, I'm in an awful fuckin' pickle. Lean is having a dinner party tonight and the caviar was sent over from London and I ate most of it last night. What the fuck am I going to do?'

The Bawn, who was a fisherman as well as a publican, says, 'I'll think about it.' He came back to him afterwards, 'Have you any vegetable dye?'

'Yeah.'

'Black?'

'Yeah.'

'Get some cod's roe and soak it in the black dye.'

'Ah for fuck sake, these people will know the fuckin' difference between cod's roe and caviar.'

'Now hang on. You make a bit of this phoney stuff and mix the caviar through it. Have it all ready on the plate. Do the big fuckin' act. Come in in your chef's hat and the white apron and the whole lot. You serve out the thing. Take out the lid and serve David Lean first. Give him the real caviar and give the others any shit you like. Because when David turns around and says, "How do you like the caviar?" They're his guests. They're not going to say 'tis shite. They're going to say, "It's lovely, David."' And yer man did exactly that. Old country man's savvy.

As it happened, the complaints department at the Skellig became less and less busy as the teething problems were overcome. The hotel, following representations from the production company and a possible threat of a move into one of the big hotels in Killarney, had upped its game considerably halfway through the shoot under a new manager, Sean Kerry. They were now doing fashionable fondue dishes and the like, which met with approval from the film people rather than the usual dismay. Those high standards were maintained thereafter under the stewardship of Kerry and others. Lean even asked Kerry to work with him on his next film, *Gandhi*, where he would run the hotel owned by Sandy's parents. Whenever that would be.

# 11. World's first hippie

Mitchum had hunkered down and was employing his own survival strategies. The occasional American tourist would call at Milltown House looking for an autograph. 'Come back at four,' Mitchum would tell them. 'The zoo's closed'. If they were too persistent, he would lower his trousers and moon them.

He tried to remain light-hearted. He had boxes shipped over from the States, full of toys. Local kids were given a plastic device, shaped like a flying saucer, called a Frisbee. There was something for older folks as well. The Irish carpenter Denis Butler, who knew Mitchum from a previous film, was invited to drop by and pick up stuff for his eight kids back up in Dublin. 'I drove up to where he was living and he was coming out with Harold. He walked back in with me and there were all these cardboard boxes on the floor in the room, with all sorts of funny things for kids. He told me to take what I wanted and pointed out where the bar was and then he left. There were a lot of sex aids and all that as well. This was Bob's scene to an extent. He'd bring them on to the set the next morning.'

Mitchum, to get up David's nose and generally lower the tone, would blow up life-size plastic dolls and fly them from his caravan, as though they were flags. 'He would have a big plastic dick hanging out of his caravan, or a dildo, or an artificial fanny or something with a dick in it. Harold probably got it for him. He was a bit of a lad. The girls on the unit used to walk by and say, "Oh my God",' says Bob Bremner.

Sarah was the exception, along with Mills's wife, Mary Hayley Bell, who enjoyed fooling around with Mitchum's full-size Playboy doll.

Another import that Mitchum popularised was the Americanism 'No way'. No wonder he was described in the *Chicago Tribune* that year as the 'world's first hippie', even though he hadn't grown his hair long in decades and would pontificate, to stave off the ennui, about how Britain had corrupted his own country by importing the sexual revolution. He also brought over and displayed douchebags – popular amongst American women for washing their genitalia after sex, but little used in the British Isles.

The actor had to come up with other ways to pass the day. For the interiors shot in the schoolhouse and the pub, smoked plexi-glass panels were placed over the windows to control the amount of light entering the building. When a sheet was scratched, it had to be replaced. Rather than throw them away, Mitchum asked Bremner and his electrician mates to put to one side any damaged panels. Mitchum was recycling them for use in building a greenhouse somewhere around the back of Milltown House. 'I didn't know what he was doing with them,' the associate producer Roy Stevens remarked, and nor did he want to know.

What Mitchum was doing was taking matters into his own hands as the weather refused to improve and his marijuana crop struggled. When the well-known film critic Roger Ebert visited at what was supposed to be the height of summer, he slipped in a question about Mitchum's drug-taking. 'What about pot?' Ebert asked, and in answer Mitchum had picked up a flowerpot at the side of the house that contained what Ebert described as a 'sickly spindle of twig'.

'I sit here and weep and wait for the weather to change, waiting for my crop to grow. In my hands I hold the hopes of the Dingle Botanical Society,' he told his bemused visitor from the *Chicago Sun-Times*. However, once his makeshift greenhouse was up and running – a resourceful member of the production team who lived around the corner had enthusiastically helped in the construction – and his crop started sprouting after a couple of weeks, Mitchum was a little happier.

Still, with Mitchum you had to choose your moments, and if you camped in Bayley Silleck's publicity office on Dingle's Main Street, it also helped. Silleck's role was evolving in ways he could never have imagined. While Mitchum had his minder, stand-in and bouncer with the Popeye forearms – Harold – Silleck's office, across the road from Ashe's pub, became the reception room for much of what was going on at Milltown House. Silleck was St Peter and his office was the Pearly Gates. 'He had a lot of friends coming, from Dublin, from London. A steady stream of girlfriends, former girlfriends, present girlfriends. A lot of people came to my office because they couldn't find Mitchum's place. He'd say, "Go to Bayley's and he'll bring you over here".'

Although her 'lewd' books were banned in her native land, the Irish novelist Edna O'Brien was a welcome guest, fresh from a one-night stand with Mitchum in London when he had been making *Secret Ceremony* (1968) the previous year, a fling she said had brought a 'sparkle' to her half-empty life at the time. Other times, Milltown House was out of bounds – Mitchum 'treasured' sleep but was something of an insomniac, and found it extremely difficult to come by. At times, the closest even Bayley could get to Mitchum would be Harold, who would inform him whether or not his boss was receiving guests. Flout the traffic signal and you were asking for trouble, as the London *Evening Standard* film critic Alexander Walker discovered.

Walker didn't get the red-carpet treatment in Dingle when he arrived with a BBC crew to make a documentary. Lean snubbed him as a result of a review Walker had written about *Doctor Zhivago*, in which he had borrowed the line, 'when a director dies he becomes a photographer'. Lean had stored the insult and declared himself officially 'dead' to Walker when the scribbler arrived in Dingle; incapable, therefore, of being interviewed. Silleck faced this kind of problem constantly, but found a way around it. Off camera, Walker's producer, David Wickes, put the questions to Lean in his place, so neither side lost face.

Getting the actors to talk was also difficult. Walker sensed that tempers were frayed by the perfectionism Lean imposed on the actors, and that it was better for them to say nothing than speak their mind. Even Walker's long-time friend, Trevor Howard, offered no more than a few guarded words, and then suggested, 'Have you seen Bob yet? He'll talk.'

Walker had heard that Mitchum wasn't approachable.

'Bloody nonsense,' roared Howard, reminding the critic of a cannon firing at the Light Brigade. 'He'd love to see you.'

Walker sensed mischief in Howard's voice, but tagged along nonetheless. In Howard's small rented Fiat, they drove across the bridge to Milltown House, 'as ominously isolated as any Hollywood mansion on a *film noir* set,' Walker noted. Howard braked sharply and noisily at the front of the house, strode to the door and thumped the door knocker. Stand-in Sanderson answered, stony-faced.

'Bob's asleep, Trev,' said Harold.

'Well, wake him up. Tell him I have a friend who insists on meeting him.'

According to Walker, Howard marched into the hallway at Milltown House and hollered up the stairs: 'Bob, Bob, BOB.'

Rather than come to the top of the stairs ready to put on his apron and get cracking in the kitchen, a different Mitchum emerged, wrapping around him a black yukata bathrobe and looking 'like the Minotaur on day release from the maze', as Walker recounted in *It's Only a Movie, Ingrid*. Without saying a word, Mitchum glided down the stairs and then straight across the hallway towards the visiting party. Harold spotted the warning signs, and leapt in-between his boss and the endangered film critic. Virtually in the same movement, Harold had spun Walker and Howard out of the house with his giant arm and then slammed the door shut with his boot.

An American journalist who had gone through the proper channels conducted his interview with Mitchum in his trailer on the set, as the actor lay on the bed with a wide-brimmed floppy hat over his face. When the interviewer remarked, 'this is the first time I ever interviewed anyone who really talked through his hat', Mitchum afforded him more respect, and rose to a sitting position, remarking, 'Until I got to Dingle my life was all downhill and shady, but this is the most joyless period of my life – except for working at Lockheed and being in the Army. I have put away more Scotch since I got here than I have in my whole goddamned life.'

MGM were flying over showbiz writers and television crews by the dozen – first class – as they ramped up the hype about what their star director and actors were doing. The tone of the reports back was generally upbeat, but the influential entertainment trade newspaper *Variety*, in its edition of 13 August 1969, reflected the uncertainty that was starting to surround the film. 'Is it MGM's Tenderest Hour?' ran the punning headline on efforts by the Las Vegas hotelier, Kirk Kerkorian, to take over the film studio, reportedly with the support of Howard Hughes. Flip over the page and there was 'Report of $20-Mil budget for "Ryan" disturbs MGM, Brings Correction', which dismissed a column by Leonard Lyons in the *New York Post* on 2 August about the spiralling costs associated with the film. Lyons had written that the film would now cost $20 million – more than *Cleopatra* – 'but MGM doesn't mind' as Lean's previous three films had amassed $200 million. It wasn't what the MGM top brass wanted their stockholders to read, especially with Kerkorian looming. As the *Variety* article put it,

In an era when so many big budget epics, after disappointing at the b.o. [box office] have brought financial grief to major companies, it is deemed neither business-like or promotion-worthy to have budget figures in excess of $15,000,000 in general circulation – especially when, as in this case, completely erroneous.

There is no question, however, that the Lean picture has gone way over schedule, if not so much over-budget. Almost every visitor to the set comes back with gruesome tales of tension within the unit, a result of the prospect of filming until Christmas in Dingle, which is described as one of the most remote towns in Europe. Cloudy weather when sun is needed has plagued the production and there was one 10-day period when only a minute of film was put in the can.

No wonder such tales emerged when Mitchum was telling Bob Ellison of the *Chicago Tribune* that 'this film was originally budgeted at around four and a half million [dollars]. Well, David has already spent 10 million on hay for the horses.'

MGM president Bo Polk corrected Lyons's report, saying the film would cost about $9,200,000, or only $700,000 more than had been expected, which was due, he said to 'the weather conditions'. Another of Lyons's assertions, concerning the first moon landing that had just taken place, was also striking: 'On the day Armstrong and Aldrin walked on the moon, the men of Dingle were cutting grass with scythes and horse-drawn wagons were delivering cans of milk.' That was a familiar theme. Paine Knickerbocker of the *San Francisco Chronicle* and others noted that on the maiden solo transatlantic flight back in 1927, the Dingle Peninsula was the first piece of European land that Charles Lindbergh flew over, exchanging greetings through hand signals with the folks below as he flew by, and that not much had changed in the intervening forty-two years. Knickerbocker found it difficult to separate fact from fiction when he visited the village set and found a small peat fire burning in the fireplace of the police station at Kirrary.

Joseph Gelmis, the *Newsday* critic, came to Dingle researching his forthcoming book, *The Film Director as*

*Superstar*, and he wrote that the cast would sit around 'watching the moths die on light bulbs for excitement. Some of those who have worked on *Ryan's Daughter* tell apocryphal stories of Lean's working habits. They claim the moody Englishman sometimes wanders away from the set when he's unable to find precisely the right solution to a shooting problem. And then he keeps on walking and meditating over the heather and out of sight, while the crew waits a couple of hours and finally packs up and quits for the day.'

Sarah Miles had claimed that Lean used to wake up in the Skellig Hotel, take one look out the window at the rain and go back to bed, while everybody waited in their caravans or in the back of a Land Rover at the set.

Gelmis continued: 'Over dinner at the Dingle hotel's modest dining room, Lean vehemently denied the rumours. "If I don't feel like working one day, I've got to be damned ill before I knock off – let alone walking over the hills looking for inspiration." He was irritated because he knows there was just enough plausibility in the stories to worry the financiers in America, who have watched with some concern as the initial budget of under $5,000,000 has spiralled up a couple of million since shooting began.'

Amongst the visiting scribes was the famous Hollywood gossip columnist Sheilah Graham, who had caused some scandal of her own back in the day as the long-time paramour of F. Scott Fitzgerald. Graham had her own reservations about Ireland as she travelled the 100 miles down from Shannon Airport in a studio car to meet the actors. 'We passed farmers driving small donkey-propelled carts with eight-gallon milk cans on the way to the dairies,' she wrote. 'Oh the rich cream of Ireland! It was well that I was only staying a couple of days. We passed Limerick, which I had not expected to be drab. I have listened to an ecstatic Richard Harris praise by the hour his native city, so I was disappointed.'

It was worth it all to see Robert Mitchum. Graham was a sassy broad who had known the actor for decades and was well able for anything he would throw at her.

'I see you're not wearing any underwear today, Sheilah,' Mitchum ventured in front of the publicity people.

'No, I am not,' came the straight reply.

'She and Mitchum got along famously because they were both very feisty and told each other all the latest dirty stories from Hollywood,' says Silleck.

Graham ended up conducting her interview with Mitchum in Sarah's caravan, with the actress in attendance as well. Mitchum was grousing endlessly: 'I've never eaten so many potatoes in my life… in Ireland they make the rain a national monument … I told them I planned suicide …. He has the only prop man who drives a Rolls-Royce. Nothing like stretching it out … He shoots the film then he reshoots it. Then he looks at it all and shoots it again. The rehearsals take the budget.' Miles snapped: 'Shut up! I'm sick to death of your complaints. You knew when you signed on for a David Lean film that it would take a long time and no one can help the fucking weather.'

When he wasn't complaining, Mitchum liked to shock for a moment of amusement. The gentleman from *Christian Science Monitor* almost dropped his notebook when he asked a bored Mitchum why he liked working with Deborah Kerr. 'Well, the best thing about Deborah was that she loved to take it in the ass,' Mitchum said.

In reality, Kerr was one of those actresses who Mitchum worked with closely, but admired from a distance, Jane Russell being another. The arrival to the set in Dingle of a nun from the Catholic League of Decency in New York revived fond memories for Mitchum of working with Kerr in the Caribbean a dozen years previously. On the island of Tobago, they were shooting *Heaven Knows Mr Allison* (1957), the story of a nun and a US marine stuck on a desert island together during the Second World War. The Catholic Church was concerned and sent a representative to keep an eye on the content, a relatively common practice, especially for films concerning the clergy. John Huston, the director, had organised a spoof shoot, where the marine and the nun suddenly go into a passionate clinch, groping each other through their uniforms, all for the purposes of shocking the observer from the League of Decency, who spluttered his indignation on cue.

Unlike Huston, David wasn't one to lighten the mood and bring some levity to proceedings, but others on *Ryan's Daughter* had a little surprise in store for the visiting nun, which helped relieve their own boredom in the process. The nun in question from the League of Decency was a movie buff and difficult to shock. She was offended by Roman Polanski's horror film *Rosemary's Baby* (1968), which was condemned by the Church principally because of a scene where the female lead has a nightmare in which she is raped by the devil. While the storyline of the Irish film was slightly risqué, the nun had no difficulties with what the makers of *Ryan's Daughter* were serving up, and decided she could clear off.

Before she returned to New York, she gave her 8mm Canon movie camera to the dedicated MGM stills photographer on the set, Ken Bray, to take a few shots of her in the company of Lean. Bray put the camera aside for one moment. The chief electrician Bernie Prentice was really a frustrated cameraman, and he loved a laugh and a joke. 'They picked up her camera,' says Bray, 'went round the back of the huts, dropped their trousers, took some shots and then replaced the camera back where it was. I never did know what happened, but what she thought of me I don't know.'

Finally, clear summer skies and hothouse conditions helped grow Mitchum's marijuana crop, and David was also able to shoot some of those beach scenes that had fallen so heavily behind schedule – in this case the one where the schoolteacher starts to suspect all is not right in his marriage when he spots Rosy and Randolph's footprints in the sand and then discovers a seashell amongst his wife's possessions. David approached Pedro Vidal and said: 'I can't direct Bob. I have no connection with him whatsoever. Would you mind directing him?'

Vidal knocked on the door of Mitchum's caravan.

'Who is it?'

'Pedro.'

'Come in, Pedro.'

'He was smoking his sailor's pipe. He passes me the pipe and I take a drag. Wowww! Then I pass the pipe back to him and I say, "We're going to do the scene with the shell." That was my direction. He comes out and I say, "Ok, here we go. Ready to shoot." David says "Action". It went like a dream. Mitchum went back to his caravan and David was following me and he says, "I still can't understand that." And I didn't do anything. Mitchum knew it. He'd read the script. He knew the script by heart.'

David Lean was later asked by his official biographer, Kevin Brownlow, what his relationship with Mitchum was like, and he wasn't particularly forthcoming. 'Bad. It was an unfortunate story, the making of *Ryan's Daughter* with Mitchum. I don't want to go into details because it's extremely personal.'

Havelock-Allan, the producer, said the problems with Mitchum stretched Lean to breaking point: 'He never hit it off with Mitchum from the word go. We had to stop shooting twice because he got David so upset that he couldn't go on.'

While he remained aloof, Lean was always keen to hear any gossip from the set.

Even on *Zhivago* he would ask, 'Who's going with who?' said assistant director Michael Stevenson. 'I used to say, "I don't know, David."'

'Yes, you do.'

'David, it's not really my business, is it?'

Perhaps Lean should have been less curious, for one titbit going around appeared to really upset him: the whispering that Mitchum and Sarah Miles were having an affair. Bayley Silleck saw Lean's dismay. 'Lean would just sit very quietly in the dining room of the Skellig Hotel and smoke and have dinner and watch everybody. He loved gossip, but Mitchum was all about provoking, making hash brownies and inviting everybody over and getting them stoned, really causing lots of trouble. So I think you had a problem. And there was this thing with Sarah. That infuriated Lean. He was really pissed off about that for Robert Bolt.'

David expressed his frustrations over dinner with the Canadian photographer Douglas Kirkland and his beautiful French wife, Françoise. A serial adulterer himself down the years, all Lean saw was potential problems in the making of the film when word reached him about Sarah and Mitchum's alleged antics.

'David said to me, "It's terrible the way she behaves because Robert is really a gentleman; the way he just waits and lets it burn out." I didn't take much notice of it. These things happen,' Eddie Fowlie remarked.

However, Fowlie said it contributed to the difficulties between Lean and Mitchum, whom he argued had been an even worse casting decision than Christopher Jones. 'He was not only unconvincing in the role of sexually repressed school teacher, but proved to be a behind-the-scenes troublemaker from start to finish,' Fowlie claimed in his autobiography, *David Lean's Dedicated Maniac: Memoirs of a Film Specialist.* 'Sometimes he would lock himself up in the caravan, refusing to come out for a scene. On another occasion he would vanish, mostly to spend time with four or five young women he had especially flown over to take part in one of the many private parties he often threw, although that wasn't enough to keep him satisfied and he ended up having an affair with Sarah Miles.'

What evidence was there of this alleged affair? To those around her, Miles was clearly infatuated by Mitchum and his aura but, as Fowlie admitted, 'I never saw them in bed together.'

That didn't stop people talking, however.

'This topped everything for everybody on the unit,' Silleck says.

It was all that anybody ever talked about in the pub for days. You know, 'Look at this. She has no interest in this Hollywood hunk [Jones]. What she is really interested in is the guy who plays the cuckold.' And right there, of course, though they didn't say it out loud, a lot of people said the film was badly cast for that reason. Mitchum still had a lot going for him as a sexy movie star, and he really had more oomph, more erotic power than Chris did.

The storyline had Mitchum's character, Mr Shaughnessy, as a dud in bed, unable to meet the expectations of the virgin Rosy, who wanted her new husband to do what she had surreptitiously been reading about in bodice-rippers. We share Shaughnessy's awkwardness and Rosy's disappointment on their wedding night. Shooting the scene in a barn that had been skilfully dressed up as the marital bedroom, it was soon clear to anybody in attendance, including Robert Bolt, that the mutual attraction between Mitchum and Miles was strong. Lean was nervous shooting this bedroom scene, even if the love-making was taking place underneath heavy blankets and was all over very quickly. Bolt, sucking on his pipe, picked up on the general mood and excused himself from the room.

Mitchum had sensed Lean's discomfort and preyed on it, suggesting that the lovemaking scene be played with Miles on top, which had the director spluttering indignantly. Under the covers he was also behaving badly. Mitchum had pulled up Miles's nightdress and had strayed drastically from what was in the script, grabbing her by the 'lower cheeks'. Mitchum, Sarah concluded in her autobiography, *Serves Me Right*, 'knew that any woman who had an ounce of lust within her would find it hard to resist his bearlike proximity and I was, after all, apart from being the writer's wife, also a woman'. If that suggested Sarah enjoyed the sense of frisson surrounding herself and Mitchum, she said otherwise; gossip about the alleged affair she found 'tacky'.

When it came to Mitchum, in some ways Lean himself was responsible for what was going on. On set, Sarah's modest caravan usually stood between the much larger ones designated to Lean and Mitchum. Having distanced himself from Mitchum, he used Sarah as a go-between and message-giver.

'Tell Robert he's got to wear his shirt outside his trousers.'

'Tell David I'm not going to wear my shirt out.'

'Tell him he's got to.'

'I was pig in the middle, because the mountain would not go to Mohammed and Mohammed would not go to the mountain.'

Sarah was frequently in Mitchum's caravan during all the downtime. She had also taken to spending much of her time around at Milltown House. Working away at Fermoyle House, about an hour's drive from the set, Bolt got to hear about the rumours pretty quickly, even though he was somewhat isolated. He went to Milltown House, seemingly intent on getting an explanation. Perhaps this was the time he called around when Mitchum had given Miles a cube, claiming it contained LSD given to him by another actor, Barry Foster. In fact, it was just a lump of sugar, but so susceptible was Miles to the power of suggestion, particularly from Mitchum it seemed, that she says she started hallucinating anyway. Mitchum did give Miles her first experience of pot, but LSD wasn't his bag. As for Bolt, Miles said, all he wanted was a large whisky, which Mitchum duly served up.

The landlady, Margaret Sheehy, also cleaned Milltown House and washed the dishes after Mitchum on a daily basis. 'Sarah was very fond of him,' said Sheehy. 'She used to come nearly every evening. She would breeze up the stairs to him. I just closed my eyes to these things.'

Mitchum, quoted in George Eells's book, *Robert Mitchum: A Biography*, thought Sarah was 'wild', and said she would call around to the house in the middle of the night, come into his room and ask, 'Bob, can I procure a woman for you?'

Dorothy Mitchum came and went, sometimes accompanied by their youngest child, 15-year-old Petrine. She had heard similar stories, and worse, virtually since they were first married thirty years earlier. On at least one occasion, the local driver bringing Dorothy from Shannon Airport would give a knowing wave as a driver from Dingle came the other way, carrying one or two of Mitchum's lady friends who were about to hop on the same aircraft from which Mrs Mitchum had just emerged. 'The quality of most wasn't particularly appetizing, some of them being no more than scrubbers,' Miles remarked in her autobiography *Serves Me Right*. 'Did Mitchum, like he'd have us all believe, really sleep with a different girl every night, or was it bravura PR?'

Regardless of whether Mitchum and herself shared a bed together in Dingle, Miles felt the attraction was mutual, and there was plenty of evidence that she was right. 'Robert Mitchum really liked Sarah and why shouldn't he?' asked Michael Stevenson, who took the relationship on face value. 'Sarah was a very attractive woman. Lots of energy. Funny. Witty. Clever. Strong. Strong personality. And I always thought she was a good actress. She worked extremely hard on *Ryan's Daughter*, was always up for it and never complained.'

Mitchum turned 52 on 6 August 1969 – 'I was a young man of 26 when I arrived here,' he told one bemused visitor – and his birthday party was held a few days later at

Milltown House, a pretty raucous occasion, even without the gate-crashers who had spoilt Sarah's earlier effort over at Fermoyle House. Lean and Havelock-Allan weren't there – not invited – and everybody else really let their hair down. Sarah spotted John Mills's wife, Mary Hayley Bell, cuddling an inflatable full-size Playboy doll and then disappearing upstairs with it before she could have a go. Miles danced with Mitchum in the sitting room to Marty Robbins records, while her husband was stuck into a darts game in the back room with Trevor Howard. Trevor was neglecting his wife, Helen, which upset her. Tearfully, Mrs Howard left the party with her pet poodle Mathieu, but fell on rough ground outside the house and then dragged her way back inside Milltown House from the darkness, *sans* Mathieu. She had to be brought to hospital in Tralee forty miles away, having damaged her coccyx, which concerned Mitchum.

Husband Trevor stayed at the party, reasoning that there was no point in two people having to suffer the bumping and banging over the rough roads. Howard's knowledge of anatomy was nothing like as good as Mitchum's. 'Coccyx?' Howard roared, 'trust me, she hasn't got one.' Had he made the trip, he would have noticed that Helen ended up in the same bed where he had been convalescing after his riding accident all those months ago.

Sarah then spent an hour or two looking for Mathieu and, having found the dog, brought him along to the hospital. Such was her empathy for living beings that when Miles later found herself alone again in Mitchum's house, she was taken by the sight of two live lobsters that had been placed in a pot of cold water on the stove in Mitchum's kitchen as he prepared for another evening entertaining his guests. Miles had stared into the lobsters' eyes and found herself with no alternative but to return them to the sea. She clambered with the pot across the slippery rocks outside Mitchum's house – the same where Mrs Howard had come a cropper – and then waded out to her waist before releasing the two lobsters. According to Miles, they 'gave each other a smug sideways glance' before swimming to the seabed. Mitchum was furious with her, and swore revenge. He got his own back by revealing to anybody who would listen, including the press, that Miles drank her own urine, for medicinal purposes.

# 12. Bloody murder

Mitchum and his birthday party guests were still nursing hangovers in Dingle when terrible news came through from Los Angeles. Sharon Tate, the actress and wife of director Roman Polanski, and four of her house guests had been brutally murdered at the couple's home, 10050 Cielo Drive, by a gang that was on the loose. For a moment, Mitchum lost his permanent cool. His oldest boy, Jim, and his wife, Wendi Wagner, were friends of Sharon's, and occasionally hung out at her place. At first, Mitchum and Dorothy couldn't get in contact with Jim, but eventually Mrs Cummins at the Dingle switchboard plugged them through and Mitchum went back to being his old cynical self.

'On the set, everybody was speculating for the longest time on who had done it,' says Jones, who recalled Mitchum saying he thought the killings were the work of the Black Panthers, a popular theory until members of the Manson Family were arrested. 'He thought it had to do with drugs and all that. I had no opinion. I was in a state of shock. I didn't know what the hell was going on.'

For Jones and his entourage, it was more than just a matter of idle speculation. The house at 10050 Cielo Drive was, after all, the home of Rudi Altobelli and Stuart Cohen, who had rented it out while they went on a long European sojourn. Sharon was one of their clients, which was how she and Polanski had ended up living there. After his potato sandwich experience, Rudi was in Rome at the time with Olivia Hussey on a gastronomic break – 'I was just dying to eat some garlic and pasta and to see those wonderful Italians in their fitted shirts'. Hussey was also collecting the Donatello Award for her work on *Romeo and Juliet*. Cohen had drawn the short straw. He was at the Skellig, having dinner with Chris and the actress Susan Strasberg, Jones's former wife, who was wearing a see-through blouse that was the talk of the restaurant. Strasberg had declined the offer of a cardigan from the manager Sean Kerry, saying she was 'warm enough, thank you'. Michael Stevenson was also there. A waiter came to the table: 'Sorry to disturb you, Mr Cohen, there is a long-distance call from Los Angeles.' The actress Sally Kellerman, who had spent many a pleasant day in Cielo Drive looking out on the view over Beverly Hills, was on the phone in tears. Cohen returned to the table to relay the awful news: 'Sharon Tate and some others have been murdered in my house. They are blaming the house boy.'

It was decided that Rudi would return to Los Angeles from Rome, and Stuart would stay in Dingle with Chris. Jones was deeply upset by Sharon's murder. Before coming to Dingle six months previously, he had done post-production work on a movie called *Brief Season* he had made with Renato Castellani in Rome, where he had been joined by Rudi and Sharon. Sharon had been married to Polanski for about a year, but made a beeline for Jones, perhaps as a form of revenge because she was hurt that Roman hadn't curbed his womanising despite taking wedding vows.

Floating around the most romantic city in the world with one of the most beautiful women in the world probably also explained why Jones still had strong feelings towards Sharon, even though he had moved on to Dingle and Olivia, both also beautiful in their own ways. 'I went there with high hopes,' said Chris of his journey to that strange place and starting his first big-budget movie. 'And once I got there, it was fine. I was a little intimidated at first by Mitchum and Trevor Howard and John Mills. They were seasoned actors. I wasn't in the same calibre as them, but I was young and I figured that would get me through my youth.'

From Jones's perspective, Mitchum's relationship with Lean was as much a problem as his own relationship with Lean.

He and Lean didn't seem to get along at all. He was always making jokes. Lean would come over and whisper in your ear, you know, and Mitchum would jerk away from him and say, 'David, I told you not to kiss me on my ear.' He was trying to get a laugh out of the crew, but they wouldn't laugh because they were all English and cronies of David Lean. They had all worked on *Lawrence of Arabia*. And when David and I were fighting, you know, I was just minding my own business, but they took it badly.

Miles was particularly put out that Jones was so aloof. Had Jones reached out more, or been allowed to do so, the problems he suffered might not have been so acute, but he was a strange young man. For one thing, with the start of the violence in Northern Ireland that year – and Chris stuck in the hotel watching the trouble unfold on Irish television – he became paranoid about being assassinated: 'That thing in Belfast started. I was scared to walk around the set in an English uniform. I thought they were going to shoot my ass or something.'

Lean wouldn't have shed too many tears, nor would other members of the crew. Asked to give his reasons for all the delays, Pedro Vidal was unequivocal. 'The weather and Christopher Jones. David could have strangled Christopher Jones. Everything was a problem and with my temper, I felt like hitting him. Every scene we did. He didn't do anything. He was a piece of wood.'

'An idiot boy,' was Eddie Fowlie's unusually restrained description.

Still, Lean was able to work with Jones initially, until the actor's mental state started to deteriorate sharply. There were problems with Olivia, who Jones wanted to marry, but was talked out of doing so by Cohen. Manipulative in the extreme, Cohen had other plans for Hussey and for Christopher, which didn't involve them remaining a couple.

Cohen and Rudi were trying to fix Hussey up with Dean Martin's son, Dino, who was infatuated with the actress and kept phoning her from Los Angeles, something Chris also fumed about. The relationship deteriorated, with Hussey starting to wonder what she was doing stuck in Dingle, wandering up and down the desolate beaches, when she was a hot property in Hollywood in the aftermath of *Romeo and Juliet*. Had David spotted the doe-eyed beauty on those solitary beach walks, he might have been tempted to recast the female lead as well. Just like Rosy, Olivia was alone with her fears and frustrations; the cameraman Bob Willoughby reckoned she was the only person he ever saw smoke, chew gum and bite her fingernails all at the same time.

It wasn't going to take much to tip Chris's relationship with Olivia over the edge, and the Tate murders and a series of other bizarre events that followed certainly did that. 'It really got heavy on the set. They really crucified my butt,' Jones says. 'After all that happened in America, it started getting rough. Hell on earth. I was disorientated, you know.'

Since his affair with Tate wasn't known about, Jones wasn't cut any slack – Lean probably wouldn't have cared anyway – and in the days that followed Chris almost lost his own life. Jones was waiting on call in the production office, listening to one of the riggers describing being driven back at high speed to the office in Bernie Prentice's six-litre Jaguar E-type. Prentice had given it the gun on a lovely stretch of straight road that ran out of Dingle to Ballyferriter and was lined with tall trees on both sides, which gave the impression, at very high speed, of driving through a long, green tunnel. Much to his passenger's astonishment, Bernie had got to 115mph in third gear coming down the straight, before common-sense intervened. 'Christopher Jones – I forget what motor he had – must have said to himself, "I can give it the gun along there". He was driving up there,' Prentice noted and just like one of his idiot electricians, he 'never made the corner'.

The Jones car in question was a Ferrari 365 GT, a grey four-seater. It was the two seats at the back that saved the actor's life. The producers of *Brief Season* had originally given him a classic red two-seater Ferrari, but Chris was giving it the big one again. 'I said I wanted a brand-new one, right out of the factory,' said Jones, who was another car nut. Jones brought the car to Ireland and parked it outside the Skellig Hotel, but he was barred from driving it by the production company on insurance grounds, and was instead driven around in a Ford Zephyr by a local man, Walter Sheehy. Having viewed one particularly disappointing set of dailies – the scene where his character, Major Doryan, shoots the Irish rebel who is trying to escape across a field – Jones hurried back to his hotel in a rage and jumped in his Ferrari. He blared The Animals on his eight-track and took off as though, according to Michael Stevenson, 'he had just robbed a bank'.

'I was really mad at Lean, that he would print something like that, and I was mad at myself.' Jones was unhappy that his girlfriend had left him to go to the awards ceremony in Italy with their agent, and Altobelli said that his client had warned him he would crash his car if Altobelli didn't return with Olivia to join him in Dingle. 'Christopher was a great stuntman and he had the body of a young stallion. He could roll a car and walk right out. And he did it on purpose. He told me. He called me and said, "You're not going to come back so I'm going to roll the car." So I said, "Go ahead and do it." And he did. And he was fine. There wasn't a mark on him.'

Miles and others were convinced that the crash was a suicide attempt, and that Jones was playing out his James Dean fantasy to its ultimate conclusion, by attempting to drive the car over a cliff and into the Atlantic Ocean.

'She's fucking crazy. She's fucking nuts,' says Chris of that theory, but how else did he explain his self-destructive behaviour?

What was really weird about it, it was like a coast road, I didn't know where the fuck I was, I was just driving around. They were very narrow roads, and I came one side of a village. It looked like a convent or something and I saw this nun walking towards me, a young nun, right? And as I got closer, I saw that she was really beautiful, she had a really beautiful face. And our eyes connected for a second, we were looking directly in each other's eyes. Then she bowed her head and she had this crucifix round her neck and she touched it and it sort of glinted. She held onto it and she bowed her head and I went past her like a shot – *SSSHHOONNN!* – and I went into a dip and I came out of that. And I saw the road made a big left like an 'L'. There was a big pole or a tree or something right at the end of it and I knew that if I ploughed into that, it would kill me, definitely. So I hit the brakes, man. I must have laid ninety feet of rubber. The wheels blew out on me and you couldn't even see the car for the smoke. And I looked out to my right and I could see I was skidding sideways and I was going to go over into – God, it was so far into the ocean – but there was a green slope right before that, a field or something, and I felt the car go over and start to roll. I tried to open the door and jump out, but I said, 'No, no, it will roll over on me.' So as it rolled, I pushed myself off the steering wheel and jumped into the back seat. And it kept rolling. And I was watching the windows crash out and I said to myself, 'This is it.' And I'm looking down at the ocean to my right and I just yelled as loud as I could: '*STOP!* And the car sort of went up on its side one more time and then it sort of teetered and then – *BOOOM!*

– it went back down and stopped. I don't know how I
did it. It was, like, amazing.

The car had come to rest a few yards from the cliff face and
the waves crashing on the rocks below. The roof at the front
had been crushed so badly that the gear stick had pierced
a hole and was poking out through it. Jones kicked open
the passenger door, jumped out and ran away. 'I was afraid
it was going to blow up or catch fire. The funny thing was
that everything else shut down except the eight-track, so I
couldn't hear anything except Eric Burdon [the vocalist for
The Animals] singing "Monterey".'

Jones saw headlights approaching, and then a Jeep from
the company driving along the road. He waved it down and
hopped in and was driven back to the Skellig.

At Jones's behest, the unit's roving photographer, Ken
Danvers, went along and had the scene filmed; the skid
marks, the wreck itself. He gave the pictures to Christopher,
who had them blown up and displayed all over his caravan.

Jones enjoyed the notoriety and was rather proud of
his role in the prevention of his own death, but he clearly
needed help, and there was one Dedicated Maniac amongst
David's team who was able to provide it. It was in the
weeks that followed that Pedro Vidal left Dingle and the
production for good and returned to his home in Madrid.
His wife was heavily pregnant, the weather was seriously
getting him down and with his Latin temper he knew
anything could happen. In his stead came a Londoner,
David Tringham, who was familiar with Chris's ways, and
with Lean's. Tringham had worked on *The Looking Glass War*
with Jones and Anthony Hopkins and was dismissive of the

Welsh actor's claims that Jones was a drug addict. 'He broke Tony Hopkins's wrist on *The Looking Glass War* when they were staging a fight,' Tringham pointed out. 'He was strong, he used to be a boxer, had great coordination. There was nothing wrong with Chris. Go and see Chris Jones in *Wild in the Streets* doing his Jim Morrison imitation. It's brilliant. He gave my wife Annette those leather trousers after *Wild in the Streets* and there were big stretch marks in the trousers where they had a cucumber in place.'

Tringham had also worked for months with David on *Lawrence of Arabia* as second assistant director. Working again under the same director almost a decade on, Tringham noticed a huge difference:

> On *Lawrence* there was something vital and wonderful about what was happening. David, burnt almost as black as the volcanic buttes in the Jordanian desert, directing thousands of extras in heat which radiated from the desert floor like a furnace and with a production crew of 200 people behind him. Eddie Fowlie, stripped to the waist and wearing the shortest of shorts, beside him, like a magnificent lion, roaring out his master's instructions. David was the leader, nobody questioned him, stuck in the middle of the desert for six months, working weeks on end with those enormous crowds. Again and again and again. You felt that the director thought it was good and everybody thought it was going to be good and somehow everybody was on the same wavelength. By the time he got to *Ryan's Daughter*, he was being questioned – no actor would question

him on *Lawrence*, not even Anthony Quinn. On this one, it was as though he had self-doubt in a way. The actors questioned him, particularly Sarah, and she had Robert [Bolt] so she had strength and she had infiltrated herself in with Robert Mitchum. And Trevor Howard.

Tringham loved Lean, and even eulogised him in poetry:

A true romantic
He made us believe
In what lay concealed
Compassion and passion
Is what he revealed

On *Ryan's Daughter*, however, Tringham suggested David was getting delusions of grandeur.

David thought he was King Canute and could beat the elements. And they had this great big circus going and five different call sheets every day. It would be sunny and they would rush down to the beach, get set up and then the clouds would come. They were forever chasing the weather. It's all very well saying an actor needs to be prepared for everything – Robert Mitchum, 'You crack the whip, I'll make the trip.' They have to get in the mood and in the end, they just got cheesed off with it. The thing that drove Chris and all the actors crazy was that they were all up first thing in the morning on call, on tenterhooks, and they were never used. Or they would be on their way and then sent back. Then called again at 4 p.m. and by the time they got there and were made up, it was too late. So they were never shooting anything. It was a shambles. A complete and utter shambles.

On the beach, David wanted Sarah to walk with the umbrella behind her. She kept holding it in front of her and it was being blown inside out. 'I can't David. I can't. The wind is blowing it.' And walking with that silly pigeon-toed walk of hers. So David would say, 'Okay, that's a wrap. Send her home. She can't do it. She won't do it.' I'd say, 'David, it's 10 a.m., we have got the whole day.'

'No, I can't work like this.'

That would never have happened before. It would have been, 'Do it my way. I am the director.' David had lost that aura. You could see the power draining away from him. And there was no producer person. AHA [Havelock-Allan] was hopeless. He didn't do anything.

Mitchum was about to send a warning shot across the bows. His resentment had been building with the delays and, in particular, the two false alarms when it came to the need for him to hurry back to Dingle from wherever he was. He was also in a mood because the production team had overlooked an agreement to provide a driver for twenty-four hours a day, to cater for the nefarious needs of Mitchum and his guests. At one point he had to place one of his young women in the house of Jack Redshaw from the special effects department late at night because he couldn't get her out of Dingle at short notice. The twenty-four-hour transport perk was restored after Mitchum pointed out that it was contained in his contract, but it was another black mark in his book against Havelock-Allan. He decided that it was time for revenge, which led to two of the most unpleasant incidents between himself and David.

'He gets a little testy with high-minded directors or producers, especially if they are trying to push around other actors or the crew,' his long-time friend and acting partner Jane Russell once remarked. 'He will very calmly go out of his way to plan something to make them fall on their face.' There was a certain logic to this, Russell explained, as it was a way of letting off a little steam. 'It's very difficult to get him angry. He doesn't like to get angry because if and when he does get angry, it is going to be terrible.'

An example of what Russell believed to be terrible was what Mitchum did going into the third year, on and off, shooting *His Kind of Woman* (1951), a project started in 1949 and finished in 1951, delayed repeatedly by the erratic behaviour of studio boss Howard Hughes. Mitchum had taken to drink and was stashing vodka in water glasses all over the set, meaning he could start a scene sober and finish it much less so. A staged fight with stuntmen had turned into something far more serious, and after being rebuked by the director Mitchum destroyed the set, smashing chairs, lamps, windows, plywood walls and doors.

As a virile 40-year-old filming *The Night Fighters* (1960; originally called *A Terrible Beauty*) in Dublin, Mitchum had got into an argument with the producer, Raymond Stross, apparently over the competence or otherwise of the female lead, Anne Heywood, who also happened to be Stross's fiancée. Mitchum had refused to work if Stross came on the set, and when the producer did appear, he hanged him upside down from a lamppost after tying a noose around his ankles.

A dozen years later, on *Ryan's Daughter*, Mitchum was tired, and the anger didn't burn like before, but he was again intent on humiliating the producer.

'You heard the "cunt" story?' Tringham asks, slightly tremulously.

Yes, from several different people.

The associate producer, Roy Stevens, had been dismayed at how Lean and Mitchum hadn't patched up their differences as the movie progressed. 'It went from bad to worse because of the complete distance that they had created for themselves,' Stevens said. Mitchum knew he had to work with David, no matter how much he complained. He didn't have to deal with Havelock-Allan, however. Mitchum had reached an agreement with Lean whereby the producer wasn't supposed to be around when they were shooting, a sensible arrangement, as the actor was so annoyed with Havelock-Allan that he had taken to abusing him verbally. Then he could switch in a flash to the gentle schoolteacher who only saw the good side of everyone.

The scene in question was at the schoolhouse as the sun set, with the Blasket Islands in the background. Mitchum's character, Charles, is soulful as he discovers that his wife has left him for the night to be with her British major, even though her affair has already scandalised the priest and the village. As usual, Lean was being high-handed.

'David had sent me into the schoolhouse to tell Robert what he wanted,' Stevens said.

> Bob was just sort of nodding: 'Why doesn't he talk to me? Christ, it's only half a dozen paces.' So he was really

upset about that. As we were doing the shot, Havelock-
Allan was walking down the pathway towards the
schoolhouse. And the door opened and Robert came
out and took a deep breath. And we were going to
cut to the sunset over the Blaskets and so forth. Then
Robert breathes out and says, 'I smell cunt.' David
said, 'Cut, cut, what did he say?' I pretended that I
hadn't heard what he said. Then I went back inside and
said, 'Robert, for God's sake, don't mess around. We've
got only about five minutes to get this shot with the
sunset. Don't Bob. Don't, please.'

'OK.'

By this time Anthony Havelock[-Allan] had
come down and was standing behind David. 'Action.'
And Bob came out and was doing it perfectly. Then
he looked up and said, 'Ahh, I still smell a cunt.'

That was that. We didn't get the shot.

Mitchum was still supposed to be heartbroken as he
traipsed along the beach in his nightdress, his character
having half lost his mind because of his wife's infidelity.
Mitchum wasn't comfortable with the scene, nor with
having to wear a nightshirt while walking along the beach.
Also irritating Mitchum was that Eddie Fowlie – whom he
disliked almost as much as Havelock-Allan – had persuaded
Lean to shoot, even though it was dark and cold. Mitchum
was this time clearly drunk, so much so that he wasn't able
to hide it, but in the context it could still work if he was
staggering somewhat.

As Mitchum's friend, Roy Stevens had to be on the set as
mediator for any scenes involving the actor.

When we went to do the shot, he should have been there first thing in the morning. About 2 p.m. he turned up absolutely pissed out of his brain. He was just like a dummy. And David said, 'Tell him to walk to the edge of the water and walk slowly in.' So I said to Robert, 'Walk straight into the sea.' Robert didn't say a word. On 'Action' he went into the sea and got up to his waist. I said to David, 'If you don't cut he is going to keep walking.'

'Let him fucking keep walking.'

Then we got him to turn left.

Finally back out of the water, Mitchum had his own surprise. As the cameras rolled, he looked around mournfully, then raised his nightdress and started urinating on the sand. Eddie said that Mitchum tried to piss on him as he made a few adjustments to props that were scattered on the beach, but the prop man dodged out of the way. Nurse Curran, unshockable after so many years in the army, remarked: 'We got a big pee. Eventually somebody persuaded him to turn out to sea. "Up yours" was the message.'

It was some pee all right. Sarah says that he urinated on a camera lens. Thankfully, Havelock-Allan wasn't there, but he still rejected Sarah's claim, saying that 'that would have ended the film'.

Christopher Jones. Sarah and Mitchum. Trevor and the horse. The weather. MGM. The food in the Skellig. His own damn stupidity. David had had enough. A piece of camera equipment that failed to work as he attempted to set up a scene in the village on 16 September was the straw that broke the camel's back.

'Report Lean Quitting MGM's Ryan's Daughter' ran the headline on the front page of the *Hollywood Reporter*. Their man in Europe reported: 'David Lean has quit MGM's marathon *Ryan's Daughter* in differences with Robert Mitchum, *The Reporter* has learned here from a source close to the director. Film has been locating in Dingle, Ireland since Jan 24 and is not slated to finish, even under normal circumstances, until November. Lean could not be reached last night, although he still was registered at a hotel in Dingle.'

Lean retreated with Sandy to the more salubrious Great Southern Hotel in Killarney to lick his wounds. A plane was chartered to bring fifty of the crew back to England on a few hours' notice. Trevor Howard would have joined them, if somebody had bothered to tell him the time of the flight: 'The administration side has no consideration for anybody,' he complained to *The Kerryman* newspaper. 'There is no communication. People like Robert Mitchum and myself like to feel we are contributing something to the film, but here we are just like puppets. However, I must say that I have no grumbles with David Lean on set. I am totally happy working with him.'

Adding to the confusion was a power struggle back at MGM that had left the company rudderless. On the day that the *Hollywood Reporter* ran its story, Kirk Kerkorian, the Las Vegas hotelier and the largest individual stockholder in MGM, had moved to take over working control of the company, and had travelled to New York to sack the chief executive, Bo Polk. That process was slightly delayed by Kerkorian having to secure a majority share in the company, but Polk was a dead man walking at MGM, and Lean was left in limbo back in Killarney.

While Havelock-Allan blamed Mitchum for Lean's walkout, the actor was not prepared to take sole responsibility for upsetting Lean so much. By Mitchum's reckoning, Chris Jones was more culpable in that regard, while his own behaviour was more like the tipping point. In a few pithy sentences over cocktails with the film writers Nigel Andrews and Harlan Kennedy, he later condensed nine months of torture for David into one very colourful episode, with as much skill as Robert Bolt had shown cramming *Doctor Zhivago* into a three-hour film. 'We had a crane which we hauled over County Kerry and all over Ireland, those little roads,' sighed Mitchum over his martini. 'Not a prayer of using it. The scene is me in the phone booth, or something like that. What are you going to do with the SAM Mighty [crane]?' Mitchum asked, with some justification.

So finally comes the day when we are going to use the crane, down the centre of the main street of the village. So they lay the tracks on this. Coincidentally this is the day Christopher Jones speaks.

So they crank up the SAM Mighty, it goes [here Mitchum makes a horrible noise] and just claps out there in the middle of the street. David raises his eyes. So they pull it back and get a hand dolly and a normal crane, and they crank it up and down they go. And they get to Chris Jones and he says, 'I can't talk like that.' He spoke no known tongue. The Choctaw or something. And that was lunch.

And David was, he holds a cigarette like this [between his thumb and index finger], he was standing at the edge of the cliff, gazing out to sea, seething. I walked by him and said, 'I adore you when you're angry.' And that was it. He quit.

He sent a cable to MGM announcing his resignation. And Bo Polk was running the studio at the time, and he was on his way out. He was leaving. So the cable and Bo Polk passed each other in the hallway and there was no one to whom to resign.

And David took off and went to Killarney or someplace like that. And I said, 'Wait until I quit, because that is established precedent. Anybody could quit.' I said, 'I'm going all the way to Tipperary', which is about sixty miles away. Killarney was about forty miles. So anyway, I hung around.

The British crew chartered a plane which took them back to London, most of them who wished to go. And David came back in two weeks and he resumed.

Finally, Havelock-Allan was able to earn his money by sorting out the mess. Back on the ground in Dingle he fronted up to rubbish the *Hollywood Reporter* story – describing it as 'entirely false' – and to smooth over what was really going on. 'At this very moment,' Havelock-Allan told the *Hollywood Reporter* for its edition of 24 September, 'David Lean is on set directing Robert Mitchum very happily in a scene and I simply don't know where you got such a rumour. They're getting on perfectly harmoniously and with a great deal of mutual admiration.'

Lean himself was keeping his counsel.

'I don't suggest you contact him,' said Havelock. 'You'll get a very curt answer. I'm the producer. You can take it from me there is nothing in it.'

# 13. The Smiling Cobra

While David pouted in the Great Southern Hotel in Killarney for a week, at least one good thing came of the hiatus. He decided that when the film was finished – he was optimistic in that respect – he would take over a wing of the hotel and convert the rooms into editing suites. Editing the film in the hotel would allow him to continue his sojourn in Ireland, for reasons that had more to do with keeping ahead of the remittance man than his love of the country and its six-seasons-in-a-day weather.

Sandy did a great job pampering David and restoring his spirits so that he could muster the energy to get the film over the line. It probably helped that Mitchum and Sarah Miles appeared to be keeping more of a distance. The actress was still a law unto herself around at Milltown House – banging on the doors and galloping up and down the stairs, according to the landlord Margaret Sheehy who lived next door – but Mitchum was laying low.

They were all becoming big-stick producers now. David moved back into his suite in the Skellig Hotel and the various heads of department were summoned. This was a crisis meeting in all but name. Three vital elements of the film – the love scene in the woods, several of the beach sequences and virtually the entire storm scene – had yet to be completed going into October, and with the filming of *Ryan's Daughter* rapidly approaching its second winter, David finally had to accept that he was going to have to cheat if he wanted to finish his movie. God forbid a studio would be used, but David knew that he needed to suspend filming for the winter and return for the Irish spring, or over the winter months take the circus to sunnier climes where good weather, golden beaches and leaf-bearing trees would be guaranteed, and could be passed off as the West of Ireland.

The Dedicated Maniacs decided that now was the right time to brief David about Roy Walker's surreptitious visit to the consulate of New Zealand and the South African embassy in London. 'David was absolutely furious that somebody had gone behind his back for a start,' says Walker. The associate producer then helped to concentrate David's mind. 'We have been sitting here for eight days now in our caravans unable to work because of the constant rain,' Roy Stevens pointed out. 'Do you realise that the money that we've spent could have taken the whole unit to anywhere you like in the world?'

'Oh, don't be ridiculous,' David replied.

Lean was genuinely surprised when he saw the figures, but he shouldn't have been. When shooting *Lawrence of Arabia*, he had after all been uprooted out of Jordan by Sam Spiegel. The producer, suspecting that Lean had started to love the desert too much, closed down the production without consulting the director and moved it to southern Spain, where costs were lower. Mitchum's claim that David had been carried out of the desert on his director's chair as a war raged about him was an exaggeration, but it made the point succinctly. Later, David had planned to shoot the entirety of the Russian Revolution as featured in *Doctor Zhivago* in Spain, but was forced to relocate to Finland when the snow on the mountains of Soria, north of Madrid, failed to fall in sufficient quantity.

However, the idea that he would have to complete his little gem anywhere other than the Emerald Isle was anathema to him, because, as Robert Bolt had put it, the Atlantic locale, was 'the star of the film'. One of the reasons for trying to change this small-scale film into an epic was because of the beauty of the landscape they had discovered. Mitchum had also mused on the subject, saying that David 'hissed at me like a cobra' when he suggested to the director that he go away on his own and paint rather than drag the circus around with him. Perhaps not in Ireland, the actor remarked, for while it was a beautiful country, 'you can rarely see it'.

Now, with a heavy heart and his director's spirit dampened by the continual rain, Lean had to relent. It was agreed that Eddie Fowlie would go on a recce to Cape Town, where sun was guaranteed but it would be necessary to check whether the beaches and vegetation could pass for the west coast of Ireland.

'When are you going?' he asked Eddie.

'When do you want me to go?'

'Now.'

Eddie was wearing a wetsuit at the time, and he started to rip it off.

'Not now, tomorrow,' said Lean. 'Do you want somebody from the art department with you?'

'Not the bloody art department. I want somebody from the money department,' Fowlie replied, as he anticipated having to set up bank accounts, book hotels and gain permissions if the sites were as good as he thought they were. So Eddie went to South Africa, along with the one-eyed production manager Doug Twiddy, another ex-British army man, to scout the beaches near Cape Town.

It was also decided to send Roy Walker to Spain to check out the coast around Seville, where some of *Lawrence of Arabia* had been shot. Walker put the miles in along the Spanish coast, but he already had the feeling that he was on a fool's errand. 'Eddie went to South Africa, asking me where to go, which I had already marked on the map. I went to Spain and you couldn't tell the difference at all. The beaches were fantastic. I drove for 24km along the sand and never saw anything, just these beautiful dunes, with the same type of reeds. And the sea was the same. Anyway, Eddie comes back from South Africa, he's hailed a hero. He has found the beaches that are going to save us, blah, blah, blah.'

The sense of urgency was heightened by developments in New York, where Kirk Kerkorian had decided who was going to run the company following his dismissal of Bo Polk. It was an appointment that alarmed film-makers not just in Dingle but across Europe and back in the United States.

James Aubrey, aka the Smiling Cobra, had one of the most fearsome reputations in the American entertainment industry, and he enjoyed a lifestyle that was shocking even by Hollywood's standards of debauchery. A Princeton graduate from a wealthy family, he was not one who had to worry unduly about the consequences of making enemies. In fact, he regarded that as a virtue more than an occupational hazard. Aubrey had successfully turned around the fortunes of the CBS television network, largely by chopping quality content – *Playhouse 90* being the most notable casualty – and introducing laugh-a-second programming such as *The Beverly Hillbillies*. Aubrey's brief, as presented to him by Kerkorian, was to do something similar at MGM when he was appointed president in October 1969, and he set about the task with considerable relish. Aubrey immediately put a ceiling of $2 million on the production cost of all movies, and he decided to inspect the books of movies already in production, pledging to scrap commercially unsound projects. The consequences of this rapid review were drastic. Stanley Kubrick's *Napoleon* was iced permanently. *Man's Fate*, which David's great friend Fred Zinnemann had already put into pre-production, was scrapped, even though the sets had already been constructed at Pinewood Studios near London and the commencement date for filming was only a week away. Zinnemann, who had worked on *Man's Fate* even longer than the time Lean had devoted to *Ryan's Daughter*, phoned Roy Stevens, one of his staff on an earlier movie, *The Sundowners*.

'He was in a terrible state because MGM wouldn't pay for whatever it had cost to get to that situation – which was several million dollars – as he didn't have a production and distribution contract. He felt that if we hadn't been so far down the track with *Ryan's Daughter*, it would have happened to us as well. He was right, because Aubrey would have pulled the plug on anybody. God, he was a terrible man.'

Scrapping *Ryan's Daughter* so late in the day would have made no sense, but that didn't stop Aubrey trying to wield his influence over Lean and impose his ideas. Herb Solow, whose light touch couldn't have contrasted more sharply with Aubrey's management style, was dismayed when he reacquainted himself with Aubrey at a meeting of senior MGM executives at Chase Manhattan Bank in New York in October. Solow had worked with him at CBS and was shocked to discover that the Smiling Cobra was going to be his boss again. Aubrey's deeds were about to be fictionalised in Jacqueline Susann's steamy new novel, *The Love Machine* – 'make me mean, a real son of a bitch,' he had told her – but Solow already knew the legend. Men or women, it didn't matter to Aubrey. According to Solow,

> Jim had his own preferences in many different fields. He had a huge ego in knowing what was best, which would ultimately play against him. Jim felt he knew exactly what was needed in order for MGM to make some money or at least how the film should be, so he would stay here [in Los Angeles] late at night re-cutting everybody's films. To the point where a number of directors – Blake Edwards, Paul Mazursky and Robert Altman – protested to the Directors Guild that the president of MGM was re-cutting their films.
>
> He would call me at three o'clock in the morning when I was in a hotel in London and say, 'I'm here re-cutting Bob Altman's film.' You couldn't argue with him because he had a vicious temper. He could be very nice one moment and then turn on you like a viper. Business people saw him as a challenge, but creative people shuddered at the prospect of meeting him. I've been in rooms with him where an agent has come in to pitch an idea and said something that Jim didn't like. Jim would chop this guy down into little pieces.

Solow had briefed him on *Ryan's Daughter*, but Aubrey decided to see for himself what the hell Lean was up to in Dingle. Having cancelled *Man's Fate* and ignored Zinnemann's angry demands for a face-to-face explanation, a meeting was arranged with Lean at the Great Southern Hotel in Killarney. Not just a meeting; Aubrey wanted to view rough cuts from the film, even though it wasn't anywhere near ready yet. This was not necessarily a bad omen. On *Doctor Zhivago*, Bob O'Brien at MGM had thought the rushes so good that he had urged Lean to pull out all the stops to get the completed film ready for the Oscar season. However, now the vibe was different and David's antennae were tuned in to danger. Lean's agent, Phil Kellogg from the William Morris Agency, was instructed to fly over from Los Angeles and be in attendance.

Aubrey's people weren't happy with that, but Lean told them 'no agent, no meeting'. Aubrey's own entourage spoke plenty about the man. Douglas Netter was a hard-headed distribution man and shared Aubrey's taste not just for slashing movies but for living hard. A meeting with Lean was not going to cramp their style. 'Jim and I arranged to meet in London,' Solow recalls. 'They used to go out and carouse. The first stop was the Playboy Club in Mayfair. They were partying late at night and The Dorchester got so annoyed at what was going on that they threw them out, luggage and all, on the street. I stayed in my room.'

The group then flew to Shannon Airport and took a helicopter, which landed on the back lawn of the Great Southern. Joining them at that point was another young MGM executive, Mike Curb, a musician by trade, whom Aubrey employed to write songs that he tagged onto the start or end of films where he felt something was lacking. *Zabriskie Point* (1970), Antonioni's arty film made at a cost of $7 million, was a case in point. It didn't deliver what Aubrey was looking for, so he commissioned Curb and Roy Orbison to write a song that provided a more upbeat ending. Aubrey decided *Ryan's Daughter* needed a song, too, and he also started telling Lean how to cut his film.

In Lean, however, Aubrey had met his match. David was the only director at MGM with a written guarantee in his contract of having final cut on his movies, and it was clear that while he would humour Aubrey, he wasn't going to do much more than listen. Other MGM executives took their frustrations out on Roy Stevens when they visited the set. 'They cleaned me out over the film falling behind schedule and being well over budget,' says Stevens.

> I told them to go and talk to David, because if the weather and the seagulls aren't right, he doesn't shoot. They could bawl me out and fire me, but it wasn't going to make any difference.
>
> I told David on the radio that they were coming so he was waiting for them and he said, 'Cut, everybody go to tea.' And he sat in a chair and they sat around him, so fawning that it almost made me sick to listen to them. Finally, one of them said, 'David, shouldn't you be getting on?' David told them he would answer all the questions they wanted to ask since they had come such a long way. They left the next morning, but they came with the idea of getting the big stick out and seeing the film wrapped in a couple of weeks.

Still, Lean finally knew he had to do something, even if it meant moving to a different hemisphere. To finish off the sun-kissed beach scenes, Cape Town it was, over the Christmas period and afterwards, right in the middle of the South African summer. To capture the storm, it was decided that while the main unit would go to South Africa, another would stay in Ireland over the winter and decamp to the most storm-hit location in the country. This was a ninety-minute drive away in Co. Clare, at a stretch of coastline called the Bridges of Ross, which the film company had renamed The Slabs. For insurance and cost reasons, the stars would not have to make this trip, with doubles being used as necessary.

With those two issues parked, it was time to deal with the central fork in this trident of tribulation: the love-making scene in the woods. Bolt was particularly keen on this working well, as he knew how nervous Lean could be when it came to shooting a sex scene. From his base at Fermoyle House, Bolt wrote a letter to David on 20 September 1969 entitled 'STORM AND WOOD SEQUENCES'. The tone was constructive, but there was also a real sense of urgency and concern:

Dear David,
My last brief on the Storm Sequence was to split it between the beach and the slabs, excluding Robert and Sarah from the slabs where the genuine storm stuff was to be shot. We've not yet had time to discuss the rewrite which I gave to you then. Roy [Stevens] now tells me that you and he both think it may prove a great convenience if not a downright

necessity to rewrite again in such a way that Johnny [Mills] and Leo [McKern] can be shot exclusively from off the sea. That is, that the deeds of Ryan and Michael can be faked, with hosepipes, wind-machines and tanks, so that you need only take extras and less expensive actors with you when you go to shoot the actual storm. I'm sure that with a bit of ingenuity this can be managed, but obviously it will not be so good and it will take a bit of thinking out too. Please let me have a definite decision on this and also an opportunity to discuss it with you at leisure.

I have been with Stephen [Grimes, production designer] to see the rushes of Sarah and Chris in the woods, the woods themselves and the tower where they are to meet. I am not so pleased with the woodland rushes as everyone else seems to be. They are beautiful certainly but, perhaps because they are artificially lit, they are beautiful in a distinctly theatrical manner and look to my eye more like an unusually good Stratford production of *Midsummer Night's Dream* than the rest of our film, where the quality of light is so natural, the sense of wind and cloud and weather so true as to be almost palpable. Moreover, though I am not a naturalist, the woods in those rushes have a distinctly autumnal feel to them, something dark and opulent and damp, rich and fruity rather than lyrical and budding. And we are in the last week of September now.

The decision is for you to take, but I think there is a problem. I see four possibilities:

(a) To stick to the script as it is and the locations already chosen, relying on a sufficiency of good weather between now and late October when the woods will certainly be failing.

(b) To come back here next Spring.

(c) To take Chris and Sarah and a small unit forthwith to other woods in Italy or even New Zealand.

(d) To unlock ourselves entirely from the woodland locale and rewrite the lovemaking in a locale where we shall be less dependent on the vagaries of the weather.

Bolt favoured option 'd', with the lovemaking taking place in an abandoned old tower, where the couple meet before riding into the forest. This was a dilapidated place, but one overrun with nature in all its glory, which would still tell us, as Bolt put it, 'that their lovemaking is simple, natural and passionate like the lovemaking of Adam and Eve, without dark overtones and undertones'.

Eddie Fowlie had also put his thinking cap on, but rather than write a long, hand-wringing letter, he busied himself in his customary manner. Fowlie wasn't concerned that he had rubbed virtually everybody up the wrong way; as long as he still had David's ear, that was all that mattered. 'He was so far up David's arse that all you could see were his boots,' according to Trevor Coop.

Eddie was probably the best prop man that I ever worked with. He was also an expensive prop man because the props would always be there. If we moved, the props would still be there, because he would have a second set of props. He had worked with David so often that he could second guess him and David thought he was the best thing since sliced bread. He really was the biggest actor – Eddie Fowlie – he used to enjoy getting people in trouble and goading them. Although he was the best prop man I ever worked with, he was also quite a nasty piece of work.

Lean encouraged Fowlie's behaviour to some extent, and was happy for his prop man and others to be at each other's throats. Lean did, after all, as Nicolas Roeg pointed out, run 'a very political set which meant lots of rivalries and jealousies'. Eventually, the *Ryan's Daughter* production designer Stephen Grimes had had enough. 'If the property master is running the show for David Lean, you're kind of lost,' said Grimes's assistant Josie McAvin.

Normally a property master would be close enough to the director, but he wouldn't be calling any shots. When it came to locations, Eddie and Stephen would both go out, separately, and they would hand their photographs to David Lean. David would go along with Eddie as far as possible and then he would say 'that's the one' and that would be Stephen's choice, but you don't need all that pressure because you had got enough on your plate. Eddie was the property master. It was nothing to do with him, but we had that right through the film.

Grimes was also a bit of a ladies' man, and there was a suspicion in the art department that Fowlie had been in

David's ear with a little story that was completely untrue. The row over Jocelyn Rickards hadn't helped either, as Grimes felt that he had been misrepresented in his role as an intermediary. In late autumn, Rickards was eventually granted her wish to leave the film – her work was more or less done – and Grimes left around the same time. 'Steve never actually told me why he was going,' said his second-in-command, Roy Walker. 'He just said that he was going to have to go. He said, "I can't live any more this way." He knew that wherever he went after that, Eddie was going to torpedo it, which I had seen before from Eddie. He could bury you with David in a flash, if that is what he wanted.'

Others were more sanguine about the Lean-Fowlie dynamic. 'He was assistant director, art director, locations manager. Call him what you like,' said Michael Stevenson, an assistant director on more than 100 films. 'He was David Lean's right-hand man. Greatest prop man I ever worked with.'

Discovering South Africa was a notable coup for Eddie, but his champagne moment on *Ryan's Daughter* was close at hand. In October, David made one last desperate attempt to finish shooting the lovemaking scene in the forest, but the weather was more disobedient than ever, and rather than a carpet of bluebells, the woodland floor was a sea of mud. Bolt's four options had to be seriously looked at, but Fowlie had come up with a fifth one: a studio. 'Studio' had become a dirty word for Lean since he had started making his epics. Breaking away from what he considered the drawing-room stuffiness of post-war British cinema, he had left the country and vowed never to return to shooting in a studio. MGM had hoped David would avail of the studio they had built in Galway for *Alfred The Great* (1969) a year earlier, but that had been dismissed out of hand by Fowlie, who called it a 'white elephant', and Lean was in agreement. Now, Eddie was about to prove himself David's white knight once again.

Driving David back from location via a back road after another frustrating day trying to shoot the woodland footage, Fowlie stopped his Rolls-Royce outside an old dance hall in a hamlet called Murreigh, about eight miles west of Dingle. What Lean didn't know was that the hall had been rented out and turned into another of Eddie's props. When Fowlie pulled back the heavy curtain hanging behind the door, Lean got an almighty surprise. In front of him was a veritable jungle, more like something out of *Bridge on the River Kwai* than *Ryan's Daughter.*

The prop man had covered the dance floor with soil and laid a layer of thick underfelt. He had then sown a variety of seeds – grass, watercress, mustard. With heavy-duty lighting added in – Fowlie had borrowed a few Brutes off Freddie Young – the hall was hot and humid, so the foliage was growing even more luxuriantly than in Mitchum's greenhouse. That was only the start of it. Fowlie had his team dig up plants and small trees, which he had kept in cold storage before transplanting them into the dance hall, which was now effectively a massive greenhouse. The scene called for fluttering butterflies, always problematic, especially indoors, but not for Eddie, who added a couple of small birds just for good measure. Covering the roof and sides was a cyclorama depicting blue skies. It was late October, but Fowlie had produced one of the few hot summer days on the Dingle Peninsula. 'David was amazed,' Fowlie says. 'In fact, Havelock-Allan gave me a nice cheque for that, because I had saved them a lot of money. We were able to shoot the scene in nice, pleasant circumstances which was better in any case.'

Problem solved, or so Lean and Fowlie thought. What they could hardly have expected, after all that they had been through, was the caprice of one of the actors.

'David used to say, "As far as I'm concerned, actors are just a prop. All they have to do is what I fucking tell them",' said Fowlie. Christopher Jones was about to challenge that assertion in a manner that David hadn't come across before. Confronted by the sight of the dance hall, the actor decided he didn't like the look of it. And neither did he like Sarah, for that matter, nor anything else to do with Lean. After months taking abuse from the director, he was about to exact a touch of revenge, just as Mitchum had done by peeing in the sand, baring his backside to onlookers and insulting the producer, all while the cameras were rolling.

Lean and Bolt were expecting some difficulties when it came to Jones and this particular cinematic climax, but not on the level that transpired. Bolt was also expecting opposition from Lean as to what he had in mind now that the butterflies were in place and there was about to be union between Rosy and her British officer, after their initial clinch in the pub. Bolt wrote again to Lean on 28 October 1969, from his base at Fermoyle House:

> I've been thinking about the butterfly scene. It's not primarily a love scene; the butterfly incident is its core. Hold on to everything – could they play it naked? The opening and closing shots would not then be a mere repeat of the first lovemaking. And their both concentrating on the butterfly, forgetful

for a moment of their nakedness, would show how far their affair has advanced and would give a terrific poignancy to the situation and what follows. We see Rosy in the first lovemaking, shy and inexpert in the opening stages and then, as you say, 'swimming in her own water'. Here we would see what Randolph has done for her. It may be too much, but it may be very good. What do you think?

I haven't mentioned the idea to Sarah who might take off and hit the roof, but then again she might not. If she's feeling pretty and liked I think that secretly she doesn't really mind being photographed au naturelle. Whether she'd relish it with Christopher is another matter. And whether he would hate it or like it is unguessable. Anyway, the real question is whether or not it is right for the film. I have a feeling that if it were done just exactly right, it might be marvellous. Done any other way of course it would simply take the audience's attention from the intended content of the scene. But if for a moment we had Rosy and Randolph sitting side by side and apart, hostile almost, naked in a wood, I think it would be eloquent and moving.

Love, Robert

PS: The image of Randolph stalking that butterfly, naked, is somehow much less of a cliché than his doing it in uniform. Then his going and sitting, angry, at a distance from her (by his folded uniform, boots and cap), waiting to reclaim him for the Army is very poignant. And finally her throwing herself in his arms at the end of the scene would be marvellously erotic.

PPS: If he just unconsciously rested one hand on his uniform for the line: 'Why should you think I was going to kill it?' with his brows knitted and his face dark with resentment, the gesture and the excess of his reaction together would give us the answer to his question. But oh boy – how do you get Chris to focus on the butterfly with such intensity that Rosy mistakes it for a killing impulse?

It wasn't just Chris's acting they were worried about. Nudity had never featured in any of Lean's previous seventeen movies. Nor in *Ryan's Daughter* up to that point. Rosy losing her virginity to her husband on the night of her wedding had been filmed – in another converted shed, as it happened – and Lean was nervous enough at that, even though both Mitchum and Miles were wearing long nightclothes and were covered by heavy bedding. Lean's instinct when it came to both violence and sex on screen was to have them implied rather than shown explicitly. Now, Lean was prepared to bow to Bolt's wishes regarding matters of the flesh, but he was anxious and somewhat nervous about losing this celluloid form of virginity.

What he hadn't reckoned on was Jones refusing to play the scene. Some felt the problem might have started with Sarah, who felt her performance was being dragged down by Jones and took exception to the fact that he had alienated himself from the rest of the group. The nurse, Noreen Curran, had even been sent over the Conor Pass to give Miles an injection on the instructions of a Harley Street specialist who used to come to Dingle regularly and issue instructions. Sarah ate like a bird, existing on Complan energy drinks, cigarettes and the occasional injection to fight off anaemia. In an interview in the *Sunday Express* on 19 October 1969, she said she had lost a stone and a half, was getting lines on her face and was 'beginning to feel quite old'. She loved slagging off the Women's Liberation Movement which was spreading from the United States to Europe and, in the same interview, returned to one of her familiar themes concerning the differences between the sexes: 'I've always been aware that girls are not very interesting. A young girl is a young girl. She's either pretty or she's not. Girls are boring unless you're a man and you want to make love to them. It's only when they get older that they get more interesting.' What changes had marriage brought? Miles was asked. 'I'm quieter and less rude. I used to be much too outspoken, I'm afraid.'

At the time David Lean said he found Sarah 'divinely dizzy', but he was flagging as well. 'I used to inject Mr Lean every fortnight with energy boosters,' said Nurse Curran. 'And Sarah then would have to get her love potion to help the scenes with Christopher Jones, who she couldn't tolerate. She never liked being in the same area as him at all. I was never quite sure what we were giving her. I would have thought it was some sort of hormonal thing to excite her and get her going. It could have been a placebo. We don't know.'

On Sunday, 2 November, however, Sarah was ready to go. It was rare for the company to work on the Sabbath, but David had finally decided it was time to get a move on. He first wanted to rehearse the love scene in his caravan outside the dance hall, where he was joined by Sarah and Chris. Sarah knelt on the floor of the caravan where the rehearsal was to take place, but Chris remained seated, staring out the window. David instructed him to join Sarah on the floor so they could choreograph the love scene, but Chris ignored him. Sarah tried to coax him off the settee with loving words – 'embracing his fears', as she called it. Miles and Lean performed a curious good cop, bad cop act. Lean's cajoling turned into threats concerning breach of contract and lawsuits, but to no avail. Poor David shook with anger and frustration, twitching madly as he sucked on the cigarette held between his thumb and index finger. He changed tack again, reminding Chris that there was a whole crew outside waiting to work and a beautiful girl on the floor of his caravan who was feeling very unwanted now. Finally, Chris spoke. 'I don't work on a Sunday.'

David could have swallowed his cigarette holder, but instead he dismissed the company, telling them to return the next morning, when they would get down to it. Over dinner, David spilled out his frustrations to Havelock-Allan. 'He was enraged with the boy for having taken the role and being so unprofessional and being so absolutely stupid about what to David and everybody else seemed perfectly simple,' said Havelock-Allan. 'To fake the beginnings of a screw in the open air ought not to be difficult, but to the boy it was a nightmare.'

A part of Jones was enjoying it, however. After months of being sworn at by Lean and having his manhood questioned by others, Jones was exacting a form of revenge. When they reassembled the next day, it was the same story, Chris refusing to do the rehearsal with Sarah, everybody else hanging around waiting for the action to start.

They were making all kinds of threats to me. I wasn't hearing it. I didn't hear anything, you know?

David said to me, 'Christopher, you go back to your caravan and you stay there. You come to work every morning, you put on your costume and you sit in your caravan till you're ready to come out.' So we sat in the caravan all day long. We did that for about a week. And he kept coming to the caravan and saying, 'Are you ready, Chris?' and I said, 'No.' I flatly refused. I don't know why I was refusing, I just did and I'm not saying I was right.

There were more dire warnings. Eddie Fowlie had been buzzing about, on hand to ice Sarah's nipples when they wilted as Jones refused to engage on the floor of David's caravan. He pointedly warned the director in front of Miles and Jones that the butterflies and the dragonflies in the hall were dying, as was the vegetation; unusually for Eddie, he didn't have any replacements. Jones was implacable. Everyone kept waiting. One or two bawdy electricians tried to keep Sarah's spirits up, telling her that if they were in Christopher's shoes, there would be no such problems. Sarah loved the banter, but Jones was oblivious to it all. 'I just felt that if I did it over and over again [in rehearsals] that she would get used to it and she wouldn't have any reaction to it. So I decided that I wasn't going to do it until I did it on the take, but I wasn't going to tell them that.'

Jones was also racking up overage, like he did on his previous film. It was a dangerous game to play, because Miles, Lean and one or two others hatched a rather desperate and dangerous plan, which involved spiking Jones's drinks, even down to the milk going in his breakfast cereal. While his fears of assassination for walking around in a British army uniform hinted at delusions of grandeur, it is the case that a number of different people were conspiring to do Jones no good. Various parties have said that the actor was being highly medicated without his knowledge. According to the accounts of Sarah Miles and Olivia Hussey, this was done in a secret manner, which probably explains why in the end the dosage went horribly wrong. The driver of the Jones entourage, Walter Sheehy, says that one of the managers, Stuart Cohen, confessed to putting a sedative in his breakfast cereal every morning, but that probably would not have been connected with the dance hall stand-off. Hussey reckons Jones was drugged to stop him mentally unravelling. 'Watching his deterioration, witnessing each morning his panic as the waves of paranoia washed over him, broke my heart, making it impossible to even consider leaving him,' Hussey later recalled in her autobiography, *The Girl on the Balcony.* 'To slow the tide of his unravelling, the production – cynically in my view – decided to medicate him. It fell to me to see that he took his meds – that's what certain members of the production (who shall remain nameless) called them. I assumed they must have been Valium or some such thing. Not knowing what to do I would crush and blend the things into his morning cereal.'

The illicit drugging appeared to have been going on for weeks, and and was known by a handful of people, except for poor Chris, although the actor had his suspicions. 'He got it into his head, correctly, that he felt too good, that he must be being poisoned,' Hussey wrote. 'It was a nightmare. Rushing over, a wild snarl on his face, he would throw the bowl of oatmeal at me and scream, "I want you to eat this. I want you to eat this". Then he'd laugh ghoulishly and storm off.' Hussey felt for Sarah, who she said was having a 'horrid time' working with her 'glassy-eyed and silent' boyfriend. Chris sat staring off at nothing, or would throw a tantrum, as when he accused a crew member of stealing from him and stomped away.

Hussey pined for Rome and a return to Italy, but she says a sense of duty kept her in Dingle, believing, as a naïve 18-year-old, that Jones wouldn't be able to cope without her. Her boyfriend had been panicking and suffering waves of paranoia, but with the meds things settled down and Chris was calmer, less prone to mood swings.

Christopher had a number of people gunning for him now that he had refused to do the love scene with Sarah. One of the locals assisting with the catering on the set, Seamus O'Ciobhain, says that Lean gave him a spiked cup of black coffee to give to Jones in his caravan, with the connivance of Cohen, though he was unsure what exactly they were giving him. Of course, Sarah couldn't just wait patiently in her own caravan. Miles says she discussed the possibility of an aphrodisiac with Mitchum, who was waiting impatiently in a nightdress and make-up to play one of his final scenes.

'What the fuck's his problem?' she remembers Mitchum asking.

'He doesn't want to touch me.'

'Bullshit. He just wants you to bugger him, that's all.'

Sarah found this a bit crude, but she had been wondering openly why Jones spent so little time with Olivia Hussey. She said it took a stretch of the imagination to imagine Jones getting up to 'hanky-panky' with his managers, but when she shared her doubts with Mitchum, she received a 'withering look'.

At one point it looked like they were queuing up to take credit for wrecking Jones's head. Incredibly, Miles herself also admitted that she had drugged Jones, in cahoots with the director himself. 'David was well "in" with the local chemist [Vera O'Keeffe's husband] and got him to provide a white powder which would "help matters considerably",' Miles wrote. Just as Hussey had done, Miles says she then added the powder to the milk Jones used for his breakfast cereal.

It amused the film crew that while it was illegal to sell a packet of condoms in Ireland, strong sedatives were available over the counter, quite legally, and the chemist was doing nothing wrong.

'They had to keep him quiet,' says Vera O'Keeffe, the local chemist.

So what did they give him?

'I can't tell you.'

'Why not? Do you not remember?'

'I can't tell you. They gave him a potion anyway. I'd say she [Miles] was afraid of him [Jones].'

Sarah's mother, Clarice, on a trip over from England, also intervened, and managed to act as an intermediary, reporting back from Jones's caravan (which was out of bounds to virtually everybody else) that Christopher was unhappy about Lean bullying him.

Jones finally emerged from his caravan after a week to take his place in the dance hall, even though Miles said he looked unsteady on his feet and his pupils were dilated. Miles reckoned he was completely out of it as they removed each other's clothes, but Lean was so grateful just to get the scene underway that he wasn't his usual scathing self and tried to nurse Jones along.

Sarah pretended that it was Laurence Olivier as Heathcliff that she was making love to as she breathed heavily and panted. It felt like Jones was asleep on top of her, and she couldn't move. Lean came over and whispered in her ear, 'I know we're [shooting] on his back, but it looks dead'. Miles then moved her hand down his back and put her finger up his bum. 'He liked that alright. He went from a dead fish to a live fish wiggling about on a hook. Oh, the unsavoury things that actors have to do. Furthermore, I had to look into camera and make as if it was the most sensational, earth-shattering orgasm of my whole life.'

The following day, Sarah noted, when they were shooting on Christopher rather than her, he was a Don Juan. 'He got really keen,' Miles wrote, 'couldn't get enough of me. So we shot his close-ups again,' wrote Miles. 'Too late for my performance, the butterflies, dragonfly, bluebells – and my Oscar!'

There was a major feeling of relief all around when it was finally over. As Bolt feared, they had to forget about the butterflies and just get it in the can.

Whatever it was that was put in Jones's cereal was as far as the chemistry went. Chris says the notion that Miles had inserted a digit in his backside as she claimed was 'bullshit', but he had been violated in one way at least. 'Everything seemed pretty weird that day and I thought, "Man, I feel fucking awful. What the fuck is happening to me? Am I having a nervous breakdown or what? Is it all getting to me?"'

Jones didn't know which part of Miles's account he should be more enraged by. 'Sarah is out of her mind. For her to come out and say that they drugged me, she must be nuts. For her to admit it. I would like to know more about it, I really would.'

Probably what offended Jones more than anything was the suggestion that he was a homosexual and that he might be carrying on with his gay managers – a smear, he suggests, borne out of the fact that she was a woman scorned.

> It's total bullshit. I don't know what the fuck she's talking about. Probably because I didn't react to someone like her. But if you have somebody like Olivia Hussey that you're going with … at the time Olivia was exceptionally beautiful and still is, right? I just didn't have any eyes for Sarah. Plus she was married. And plus I wasn't reacting to her. I don't know what she was reacting to. Maybe it was because my managers were gay, but it had nothing to do with me. They lived their lives and I lived mine.

Passionate lovers on the screen, off it the relationship degenerated into name-calling. As for Sarah's musings about whether Jones had been making out with his managers, Altobelli replied, 'We never crossed the Mason-Dixon line. He doesn't have that side to him.'

Ensconced back at the Skellig, Jones used the door of his hotel bedroom for knife-throwing practice. His friends on the set, Roy Walker and David Tringham, learned to be careful around him.

'Dingle got to him. He went stir crazy, the whole thing with the film and the way it was run,' Tringham commented, but the main problem lay elsewhere, in the assistant director's view.

> I always thought *Ryan's Daughter* was semi-autobiographical. Mitchum was Robert [Bolt]. Sarah was Sarah. He [Bolt] had this problem with

Sarah. He's not charming, he's not good looking, he doesn't have a personality. He's got this woman who's not even at all sexually attractive, has no charisma, no presence and no personality. She used to walk around the set so desperate that she'd goose people, to try to be provocative. She didn't turn anybody on. And she didn't provoke anybody. And that was her problem. Chris Jones, she didn't turn him on sexually. Initially, they did her close-ups but she said that Jones didn't turn her on. Later, when they went to do Chris, he got his own back and said she didn't turn him on. That was in the barn, on that awful set. Those cobwebs. How pathetic.

It didn't work out between Olivia and Chris either. They wanted to get married, there and then in Ireland – at one point seeking out late at night a priest or a judge who might perform the ceremony – but Dingle wasn't Las Vegas, nor were the managers keen on the idea. They played for time and persuaded Jones to wait, which greatly displeased Hussey, and there were arguments. Their driver, Walter Sheehy, remembers Olivia's engagement ring – purchased at John Ross Jewellers in Tralee – going out the window of the Ford Zephyr as they drove along the road near Inch Strand, with no effort made to retrieve it. Mitchum and Dino Martin – one to her face and the other calling long-distance from Los Angeles – also advised Olivia to cut her ties with Jones. In this case, Hussey reckoned that Mitchum's motives were entirely chivalrous, while Martin clearly wanted her for himself.

Was it any wonder that Jones's head was wrecked, even without the car crash and the Mickey Finn that various members of the production team had concocted? The Jones entourage started to fragment, with Hussey heading over to Los Angeles. In the back seat of the Zephyr, Chris swung a punch at Cohen, whom he had grown to dislike intensely.

'Have you ever spent a year in Ireland, just coming from Rome?' Jones asked. 'Boy!' He was just desperate to get out of there.

# 14. Black and white

Slowly, ever so slowly, Lean ticked the boxes on the to-do list. But there remained the job of saying goodbye to Mitchum. David had a going-away present for Robert, to be delivered by Eddie Fowlie. There are no prizes for guessing which side Eddie had taken in Mitchum's battle of wills and wits with Lean. Eddie described Mitchum as a 'behind-the-scenes troublemaker from start to finish'. Lean was determined to have the last laugh as they filmed the scene outside the schoolhouse in which the mob turns up to lynch Rosy, believing she has betrayed the freedom-fighters to her British lover, and the cuckolded husband gallantly comes to her aid. Lean told Fowlie he would be playing the part of the villager who floors Mitchum with a punch to the gut in the melee. It was a suitable piece of casting notwithstanding the animosity between the two men, because Fowlie had one of those wild gypsy faces that David was so anxious to get in the film.

It was a good wind-up by David. Mitchum, however, could see trouble coming, not just with Fowlie but with the hired group of Irish extras, who had no proper training in how to pull their punches, and would have enjoyed bragging in the pub afterwards about leaving one on Mitchum. 'Believe it or not, I don't like getting hit,' Mitchum growled.

Fowlie delivered the punch all right, but Mitchum was already falling by the time it arrived, and the contact was minimal. When he picked himself back up, it was time to leave Dingle, for good.

Mitchum had been there for eleven months, the longest time he had ever spent on location on a movie by some distance. Dorothy came over to help him pack and settle up his bills in the shops and pubs around the town. A strange airline ticket left around the house in the name of a woman she didn't recognise was claimed by Harold, who was promptly informed by Dorothy that he would have to pay for it. It was not a time for recriminations. The assistant director Michael Stevenson adored and admired Mitchum and Lean, probably in equal measure.

'Did you say goodbye to Bob?' Roy Stevens asked Stevenson up on the village set on the mountain on the day Mitchum was returning to America.

'No, he doesn't like goodbyes,' Stevenson replied. Then he thought a moment. 'Roy, I should go.'

Michael drove back to Milltown House, where Dorothy greeted him warmly at the door and invited him in.

'Bob's in the shower. Will you have a drink?'

Stevenson waited in the lounge where he had spent so many evenings, delivering messages from David and talking with Mitchum. It was a long and hot shower, with steam coming out of the bathroom and across the living room. After about half an hour Stevenson said, 'Dorothy, as much as I want to see Bob, I have to get back.'

Dorothy shouted into the bathroom: 'Bob, honey, Michael wants to say goodbye to you. He has to go back on the set.'

There was a pause and Stevenson heard Mitchum say, 'Tell Michael I really can't make it.'

'So I said my goodbyes to Dorothy and left. Then Bob wrote me a lovely letter, seven pages on lined yellow American paper: "Some people can't say goodbye. I hate goodbyes. Ryan's Daughter was so long and then it was gone."'

Mitchum left Dingle, but he also left a going-away present around the back of the house for somebody to pick up – anybody, in fact, who wanted it. The Gardaí came calling to the production office, enquiring about the whereabouts of Mr Mitchum. They spoke to Roy Stevens, who told them the actor had left the country, probably for good.

'You know what he's been growing, don't you?'

'No,' Stevens replied.

Anyway, I was more or less cautioned and taken back to the house. And he'd built a greenhouse longer than this room [twenty feet], a complete greenhouse, and it was stacked with marijuana plants. The chief of police said to me, 'There's more pot here than we've ever seen.' And I had to wait there while they burnt it all. The clouds of smoke. You'd get high on it. It was funny, really. You always knew that Robert was going to get you in the shit somewhere. I phoned him up in America and said, 'You bastard. I got into trouble over that.' He laughed, but he was a very genuine man.

David Lean needed to get away from Dingle and the wild west of Ireland more than Mitchum, an unfortunate fact of life recognised more by his nearest and dearest around him than by the director himself. Even though South Africa had been pencilled in, Lean desperately wanted to finish his film where he had intended, in Ireland, if he could. Some last attempts were made to film the important missing sequences, such as the one involving Howard and Mills in the currach that had ended in near disaster in rough seas at Coumeenoole, so many months back that people could hardly remember it. An alternative, quieter bay was found, but it hadn't worked to David's satisfaction, because the weather conditions were far too dull.

Lean was also hoping that he could get some storm footage before any possible move to South Africa, which would have avoided the unit having to split in two, one going all the way south to Cape Town in search of sun and the other staying in Ireland to shoot a storm. Having wrapped the bluebell wood scene, mercifully, there were the usual forecasts of November storms.

Lean returned with the unit to the storm location in Co. Clare in hope rather than expectation. It was a treacherous business, even in normal weather conditions, as the wind and rain blew in. The huge Brute lamps stood up to the task, though they grew red hot once they were covered to prevent the rain getting in, short-circuiting them. But how do you stop the rain and hail driving at the lens and obscuring the action? They came up with a Clear Screen, a revolving piece of glass driven by a motor that acted like a windscreen wiper in a car, albeit invisibly. Lean said he came up with the idea having seen the Clear Screen in operation on a warship in the first movie he directed, *In Which We Serve*. 'Absolute rubbish, absolute lies,' said Freddie Young of that claim. 'Nothing to do with David Lean.' Young said he had come up with the idea, along with a camera mechanic.

Young's touchiness reflected strains in his relationship with Lean, as the cameraman felt that he hadn't got the credit he deserved for the famous scene in *Lawrence* when Omar Sharif is introduced to the world emerging from a mirage on a camel. 'They were bitter enemies but had huge respect for one another,' said Trevor Coop. 'It was a relationship I've never come across before in forty years in the business.'

Young was 67 years old, and there were concerns that both he and Lean weren't up to the rigours of shooting the storm scene. David really struggled when it came to dealing with the wintry conditions, even if he said that it was his Rolls-Royce he was more worried about than his own well-being after a day filming in the rain. A Rolls-Royce had twelve coats of paint, as he liked to point out when he talked about the hidden work that went into movie-making. Lean himself wasn't quite so indestructible.

I always drive myself to and from work; it's an enormous relief to be on my own and driving a car. I love driving a car, and as I put my hands onto the steering wheel, I felt a rush of water going down the sleeves. You drive for an hour, absolutely soaked and cold. Sheets of water are coming up in front of you. It's got darker, but you can see these great sheets of water. It's waves bursting onto the cliff road and you go through this absolute torrent of sea water. You have to pull up and you think, 'God, what's all that salt going to do underneath me there?' But great fun, you know. Terrific.

While David put up a brave face, there was a touch of Lean as Lear about it all. At one point in November, the director had a turn, and the doctor had to be called when they reached the Old Ground Hotel, in Ennis, Co. Clare, where his party were staying on one field trip to the storm site.

'He was getting very tired,' says the art director, Roy Walker.

> The weather was bashing him for a start. The problems he was having with his cast. Trevor falling off his horse. John Mills getting hit on the head by the currach. Sarah doing what she had to do. Robert Mitchum getting popped in the eye. And then there was Chris. He was the grand finale really. David was a pretty tough old bird and he could stand a lot, but he did keel over. He was exhausted. Whether it was the heat coming in from the cold, he actually collapsed.

Sandy was there for that incident when a local doctor was called. 'What happened was that David had a very bad back at one point while we were there in Ennis. And it was coming up to winter and they were running out of light and running out of time.'

It was time to get David out of Ireland and to organise a second unit to finish the storm sequence. 'It was just a ridiculous thing to take David to Ireland. He has to be somewhere sunny,' said Roy Stevens. 'He's like a flower. He can't operate when it's cloudy or wet or whatever. Which is totally true of the storm sequence. He kept saying, "I can't handle it, I can't handle it."'

The unit were given the week off leading up to Christmas, but on December 26 – St Stephen's Day as it is known in Ireland – a pared-down crew, led by David, flew out to Cape Town via Johannesburg in a chartered plane. On board was the old currach that had knocked Mills on the head on Coumeenoole beach, some live Atlantic lobsters, the costumes, the dummy explosives, and one or two loose cannons. Of the principal actors, only Sarah, Trevor, John Mills and Chris were required to travel to South Africa, but there had to be an infantry when it came to the crew, so the party consisted of fifty people in total.

What a transformation! The sun shone brightly out of a clear blue South African summer sky. Trevor Howard, who had just experienced what he called a 'year of misery' in Dingle, puffed on his pipe and declared it a crying shame that they hadn't made *Ryan's Daughter* in its entirety in South Africa. Howard was in his element, with a Test match coming up between South Africa and Australia in Cape Town and the prospect of a few days touring Kruger National Park. David too started blossoming again, becoming more like the Lean his Dedicated Maniacs had once worshipped.

'He was so depressed in Dingle,' says David Tringham. 'In Cape Town, David became a different person. He actually played cricket – bowling – on the beach. You could never imagine him doing that.'

What made David happier than taking any wicket was being able to shoot some footage. 'We're only here for fifteen minutes, of screen time,' Lean told bemused locals, who found it difficult to grasp what was going on. 'That is about six scenes in all. Just one single, sunny day in Ireland. That's what we've come for, all fifty of us. I know it looks mad to fly them all the way here. But four days of sitting around waiting for sun in Ireland, that alone pays for the air fares of this operation. It's as expensive as that.'

*The Sunday Times* of South Africa described David after a few days under the southern hemisphere sun as 'mahogany-tanned and healthy'. He was also at his diplomatic best: 'This country has everything in its favour – lots of willing extras – and everybody has been so helpful, it has made things easy for us. It has been absolutely terrific. The weather, the sun, everything. And the light is just right.'

White rocks around the Cape Town beaches were painted black to match the Kerry exteriors. Fowlie solved another problem which arose when a big tide covered an ancient shipwreck in sand on Kommetjie Beach. Lean wanted to feature the old wreck in the movie. Fowlie got back in the helicopter and instructed the pilot to hover over the shipwreck. 'We all laughed and thought, "what an idiot", but we were the idiots,' said the sound recordist Mickey Hickey. 'The helicopter actually blew all the sand away.' Otherwise, those who came along to gawk at the filming quickly got bored when Lean took three hours for a brief shot of Sarah walking along the beach, but this was rapid-fire filming in comparison to what had gone on before. There was only one location on the call sheet, instead of five. Actors wore sunhats and nose guards to stay pale and anybody who didn't take proper precautions suffered. Rudi Altobelli, who insisted on sunbathing surrounded by tin foil to work on his tan, ended up back in the hotel for days with sunstroke, with Mario Puzo's *The Godfather* to keep him company, a newly published book he had to smuggle into the country after hearing it was banned by the censors.

There were labour problems, from within, probably borne out of frustrations festering since Dingle. 'We had to be on location by the seafront at 4.30 a.m. and Lean arrives at 1 p.m.,' the gaffer, Bernie Prentice says.

> So that's when the electricians, the cameramen, the whole lot of us got together. I went up to Lean and said, 'At 2 p.m. we're finishing.' And he said, 'I can't be dictated to like this.' So at 1.30 p.m. he gets out of his tent, walks along the beach and says, 'Lay the track here.' And at 2 p.m. the camera boys said, 'We're going back to the hotel now.' He didn't like that. When the film finished, I got back to Lee Electric and instead of saying, 'All right? How's it going?', it was like, 'We were going to sack you. You pulled your labour off the job.'

David wasn't too put out. He knew the sun wasn't going to go hiding for weeks behind mist, cloud and drizzle. Around the corner from one of the Cape Town beaches there was a seal and cormorant colony that he was keen to observe from a small boat. He told David Tringham: 'Get rid of the mob, they just want to go to the bar. Just you, me and Freddie [Young].'

It was really only Bolt who found himself getting caught up in the growing controversy over the apartheid system and how best to challenge it. Bolt had been in Cape Town before, during the Second World War, when he was training for the Royal Air Force. He had a great time back then, with no fighting going on in that part of the globe. In 1943, Cape Town had a vibrant artistic community, made up largely of refugees from war-ravaged Europe. A communist at the time, Bolt even went as far as to say that his trip to South Africa made him understand that 'life could be pleasurable without doing harm to anybody', and his Marxist views about right and wrong started to be eroded.

Now, three decades on, so much had changed. Apartheid was introduced in 1948 and South Africa left the Commonwealth in 1960 after a vote in favour of the country becoming a republic. Growing opposition to its racist system around the world meant the country was banned from participating in international cultural or sporting events. Bolt's world of letters was divided over apartheid. He was one of a group of playwrights – which also included the likes of Samuel Beckett, John Mortimer and Harold Pinter – who refused to allow their work to be performed to segregated audiences.

Bolt was challenged by the South African novelist and war hero Laurens van der Post. Exiled in London after the election of the racist National Party, van der Post believed that performing *A Man for All Seasons* in South Africa could be a force for good. Bolt countered that 'the play's central character, Sir Thomas More, were he alive in South Africa today, would be in prison … the most effective way a playwright can declare his disapproval of racial segregation is to refuse to have his play performed for segregated audiences'.

Now, with *Ryan's Daughter* decamping to Cape Town, Bolt faced charges of being a sell-out. The character of Shaughnessy he had created in *Ryan's Daughter* was coming alive before Bolt's eyes in a way he had never imagined when he created the impotent but benign Irish schoolteacher. Though he insisted Mr Shaughnessy was a 'composite' of a number of teachers he had known, now he seemed more autobiographical than ever. Bolt, after all, had been a schoolteacher himself, and then went on to write about heroic characters such as Sir Thomas, a Catholic martyr from the Tudor times. Shaughnessy taught his pupils about Byron and Beethoven, but as he had warned his smitten former pupil Rosy when she had designs on him at the start of *Ryan's Daughter*, 'I'm not one of those fellas myself'.

Bolt was a man of strong convictions, and was also more courageous than most. However, he regarded himself as something of a coward, and his association with Lean had undoubtedly compromised him. As the theatre actor Frith Banbury told Bolt's biographer, Adrian Turner: 'I thought he was going to be a really important dramatist, but he preferred Sam Spiegel's yacht.'

Bolt's bar had been set high, by himself and others, who thought he might just be that man for all seasons. As a member of the Campaign for Nuclear Disarmament, Bolt had been sent to Drake Hall open prison in Staffordshire in September 1961 over incitement to commit a breach of the peace. He was given a month-long sentence but was told that he could be released at any time if he promised to behave himself in the eyes of the law. At the time, Bolt was supposed to be rewriting the script of *Lawrence of Arabia* for Spiegel and Lean, but he wasn't allowed to work in prison. Spiegel had issued him with all sorts of threats – he would never work again, hundreds of people working on *Lawrence* would lose their jobs, etc. – over his refusal to be bound to keep the peace. After a fortnight of this, Bolt relented and signed away his principles. He was driven away from Drake Hall in Spiegel's Rolls-Royce to a celebration dinner at the Berkeley Hotel. It was, said Bolt, 'the most shameful moment of my life', but no doubt he wolfed down his food as usual that evening, and he went on to complete an excellent script.

From a filmmaking point of view, Bolt didn't have to return to South Africa, but he wanted to be with Sarah. While Lean got the red-carpet treatment, the reception committee for Bolt wasn't entirely friendly. More a Lobster Thermidor socialist than a card-carrying Red, because of his trade union links the authorities in South Africa still regarded him as a communist, and every time he left his hotel he was tailed by plain-clothes detectives wearing coats and hats, as though they were from the comic books, rather than dressed for the height of the South African summer. 'Good morning,' Bolt would greet them jauntily, 'do you want my itinerary for the day?'

The heat, though, was enough to prevent Bolt from sneaking away to meet fellow writers, of any ethnicity, but he got criticism from both sides nonetheless. Athol Fugard, a well-known playwright and anti-apartheid figure in Cape Town, took Bolt to task in a local newspaper: '[He] doesn't allow his plays to be performed here, but writes a film that is not only free to be shown here to segregated audiences, but is made on the unhallowed soil of the country, with his wife in a leading role and himself in attendance.' As Fugard pointed out, Bolt's films earned him considerably more money than his plays, and he argued that the cultural boycott's main purpose was to satisfy the playwright's sense of righteousness.

Bolt quickly returned to Surrey, where he received a letter from a Cape Town journalist, to which he replied as follows:

You ask why I 'allowed' *Ryan's Daughter* to be shot in South Africa. The answer is quite simple: the choice of location does not rest with the writer. The film is set in Ireland and it was only our extreme ill luck in the matter of weather which forced the producer and director to find a few days of sea and sunshine elsewhere. Had the decision been mine, I should have tried to find somewhere other than South Africa. You are quite right in supposing that the financial sacrifice involved in disallowing stage presentations is slight. No moral kudos accrues from it, and indeed one is seeking moral kudos at very little cost. Many respected people, such as Laurens van der Post, take the view that more would be achieved by allowing stage presentations in South Africa than by the embargo. However, the South African citizens, both Black and White who are actively opposed to apartheid, are overwhelmingly in favour of the embargo.

My visit to South Africa did not change my views fundamentally but it heightened my sense of the poignancy of the situation there. The choice before a liberal-minded South African seems to be either to toe the line and go along with Government policy quite passively or else to invite trouble and even ruin and imprisonment. I do not blame anybody for making the less heroic choice. If I were myself a South African, not being made of heroic stuff yet unable to stomach the continuous injustice which subsumes South African society, I suppose that I would take the decision to exile myself from my homeland.

With the exception of Bolt, the South African government had done their best to make the film-makers welcome, and hold them up as an example of how the country was well disposed towards movie-making. Johnny Mills was very much in the nothing-to-see-here camp when it came to any controversy, and a special screening of his latest film, *Run Wild, Run Free* (1969), organised at the Pinewood Cinema in Cape Town, could hardly have been less portentous. However, his wife, Mary Hayley Bell, was her own woman, and didn't give a damn who she offended. 'She was like an older version of Sarah,' said Trevor Coop. 'Barking.'

At a drinks reception after the screening of the Mills film, she was reported in an Afrikaans newspaper as saying: 'I hear policemen here first sleep with non-white women and then arrest them.' This was in relation to the South African Immorality Act, which prohibited sex between whites and non-whites.

On reading the report, the police called to Mills's hotel, where Mary was arrested, brought to the local police station and interviewed at length by security police. The lengthy interrogation took its toll, and if Hayley Bell was barking, it was clear that she had been brought to heel. 'I was horrified to receive a translation of a statement reported to be made by me,' said her new statement. 'I categorically refute having made any direct statement to any member of the Press. It is quite apparent that some innocuous comments which were hearsay have been misinterpreted. I would like to emphasise that not only have I found this a very warm, friendly and delightful city, but I have also made many friends.'

Johnny was relieved, but his wife's work wasn't done yet.

'The first week or two we had nothing but white journalists presenting themselves,' says the director of publicity, Bayley Silleck.

Mary said to me, 'Why don't you get some of the African and Coloured journalists?' I actually met a couple of Coloured or mixed-race photographers in Cape Town and I thought they were great guys. I walked a couple of them down to the set, right on the beach, where we were filming the scene with the currach. All of a sudden this Land Rover came roaring up and this guy jumps out – a South African cop – and pulls a gun on me. He says, 'Where the hell are you going with these *kaffirs*?' and waved his pistol at them and told them to go. I got into trouble with David Lean over that. Doug Twiddy, the production manager, told myself and Mary in no uncertain terms that we weren't to do that again and we were there at the sufferance of the South African government. David wanted to keep a low profile. He didn't want to have any political trouble when he was there. He just wanted to get his movie done. That was his strength, in a sense, in that he never looked up from his work. He was so intent on making a great film that anybody who got in his way got into trouble.

According to Noreen Curran, some filming was done on one of the blacks-only beaches. Trespassing again, Eddie Fowlie described his own experience: 'I went on one beach and a blackman threw me off. He said, "You can't come on this beach, it's a blackman's beach". So it worked both ways. It was a lovely beach. It would have done us very well. They were very angry.' Most of the crew regarded it as segregation rather than discrimination, and were more worried that women weren't allowed into some of the bars they drank in. The fact that David would have faced arrest had he tried to check into his Cape Town hotel with his Indian wife Leila rather than with Sandy wasn't something that was going to stop the film being completed in South Africa.

In fact, with Mitchum back in California, the director was the star attraction in a town where international celebrities were as much of an oddity as they had been in Dingle, and he stayed away from the liberal press who might have challenged him with the same sort of dilemmas that Bolt was addressing. Unlike some members of his crew, however, Lean didn't block his eyes and ears completely to what was going on. While Bayley Silleck was chastised for challenging the status quo, Lean turned on the charm when it came to dealing with the guests Bayley had invited down onto the beach set.

The *Ryan's Daughter* people had decided to tap into the talent pool available at the University of Cape Town, a whites-only institution except for a couple of mixed-race young artists categorised by the authorities as 'Cape Coloureds', who had managed to get themselves enrolled. Amongst them was Gavin Jantjes, who was studying graphic design, as his parents wouldn't allow him to do fine art. Jantjes sidestepped the cops, but the beach was a dangerous place for another reason: the 19-year-old black man was allergic to direct sunlight. Sarah at one point placed Rosy's bonnet on his head while he chatted to her husband, after which Gavin had taken shelter under a giant beach umbrella. He happened to be sitting in David's chair when the director returned from shooting lower down on the beach. 'You're sitting in my chair,' Lean told him, before asking, 'What are you doing here?'

Whatever young Gavin said, Lean was disarmed, and invited him for lunch. Jantjes, a born networker whose attitude was to ignore apartheid as much as possible, then invited Lean to view his portfolio of artwork, and an arrangement was made to liaise on Sunday morning at David's hotel, the Grand, a majestic colonial structure on Strand Street.

'I walked straight through the front door, which was already very unusual because black people didn't walk through the front door. I walked up to the desk and said, "I'm here to speak to David Lean", and the receptionist looked at me. She probably had an instruction that nobody speaks to David Lean. She looked at me and went to the telephone and just then David walked out of the breakfast room and said, "Hi Gavin, I am just going to pick Sandy up."'

David suggested that they call a cab. Jantjes explained that it would be impossible for them to travel together in a hired vehicle. 'David just said, "Oh shit", went back and told the lady behind reception to call his driver. And along comes this stretch limo with a chauffeur. We drove into District Six where my parents lived.'

District Six, situated in a prime location in the heart of Cape Town, had recently been designated a whites-only area, but was populated by a wide variety of ethnic groupings and rich white folks from abroad were regarded as something of a novelty.

Gavin's mother, Freda, was on the veranda when she saw Lean's black limo approaching, being trailed by a load of

The discovery of sand in Rosy's riding hat is the moment her husband realises she is having an affair. Here Lean shows Mitchum how he wants it done and then gets behind the camera in this intimate scene at the schoolhouse.

On the village set, Lean relaxes with John Mills, wearing a duffle coat over his costume. Mills was one of the few actors Lean confided in.

All smiles as visiting MGM president Louis 'Bo' Polk tries out the Ford Model T, with producer Anthony Havelock-Allan, but problems were brewing.

In May 1969 An Taoiseach Jack Lynch and his wife, Betty, visited the set and chatted with Havelock-Allan, Mitchum and Miles outside the actors' caravans.

Robert Mitchum left a memento for his friend Bayley Silleck. 'I seethe,' he wrote, as Lean detained him on what he called 'Devil's Island'.

Lean directs local musicians for a rendition of 'The Gentle Maiden' at the wedding party for Rosy Ryan and her schoolteacher husband.

Main Street, Dingle, 1969: the production company took over all the local office space, not to mention Ashe's Pub, a favoured watering hole.

Lean and Miles figuring out an early scene on the beach, while the crew behind them wonder if they are on the right track.

First official day of shooting, 24 February 1969. Actor Barry Foster steers horse and cart behind the crew and all their equipment.

Wrapped in waterproofs, David Lean directs the storm scene, with Clearscreen wipers used to keep rain off the camera lens. The storm scene was hugely difficult for actor Leo McKern (*below*) as he battled with the Atlantic.

The filmmakers used a stretch of coastline in Co. Clare called The Bridges of Ross for much of the storm scene, where extras braved some treacherous conditions.

Apartheid South Africa, January 1970: local student Gavin Jantjes ignored local cops and braved his sun allergy, with the help of Sarah Miles's hat, to talk to Robert Bolt on a Cape Town beach.

David Lean pushed a reconnaissance trip down Inch Strand a step too far and the incoming Atlantic tide claimed the company Land Rover.

local kids, and got a shock when her son emerged from it and brought the Leans into the house. David spent most of his time there in Freda's kitchen, talking to her about her life, with Sandy doing the art appreciation in the front room. 'Every now and then she would drag David out from kitchen and say, "Shall we buy this one or this one?" They bought about six or seven pieces of work. As they were leaving Lean said, "Gavin, you should come work in the movies." I said I didn't want to work in movies. I wanted to be an artist.'

Jantjes brought a couple of his friends down to the set, one of them an 18-year-old student called Linnemore Nefdt, who was also classified as a Cape Coloured. She was frowned upon by the black staff working as waiters and waitresses in the tented catering facilities on the beach when she went to lunch with Bayley Silleck. 'I could have been seen as some kind of easy woman. Like a prostitute. Maybe not even that bad. People do know that white men are really charmed by the exotic person of colour and especially of my kind of colour – light-skinned – and that was very much the case.' While Jantjes grew in confidence as Lean purchased his art, Linnemore made the simple observation that: 'It might sound silly, but just realising that a beach in South Africa could look like a beach in Ireland showed the interconnectedness of the world ...'

Bolt would have appreciated the sentiment, but he had concerns about his wife mixing too freely. Before he had left South Africa and returned to Surrey, Bolt had asked his young friend Barry Jackson – an actor and martial arts expert who played the part of the British army corporal in the film – to look after Sarah. The writer was concerned that his wife had the potential to stir things up in South Africa in a way that could land her in all sorts of situations. Jackson was happy to help out Bolt, whom, along with most people on the unit, he regarded with enormous fondness. The writer had helped Jackson secure the part of his life in the first place – in *Ryan's Daughter* he had a touching monologue about the futility of the First World War – and the young actor was one of those who made use of all the spare time he had in Dingle. From an equity minimum wage of £17 a week playing at the Royal Court in London, he went to a minimum of £150 a week on *Ryan's Daughter* when he was waiting, and £300 a week when he was actually called.

Jackson bought a house near Dingle – he could have bought four or five with the money he was on – and did it up himself, putting in a septic tank, reflooring, making his own furniture, all the things resourceful actors with carpentry skills do while on David Lean downtime. And there was more. Jackson learned to speak Irish and appeared at the 1969 Rose of Tralee festival on the main stage, giving a demonstration of the Japanese martial art of aikido, in which he held a black belt. Playing the part of Major Doryan's sidekick in Lean's film, he had wet-nursed Chris through some of their scenes together. Now he was making sure that Sarah didn't end up in too much trouble as she ventured into District Six and hung out with bohemian types who aroused the suspicion of the security forces, such as Ben Dekker, a giant of a man who lived on the beach.

In so much as Miles thought about politics, her husband reckoned she was decidedly right-wing, but she abhorred what she witnessed in South Africa, particularly after she was also questioned for holding the hand of a black photographer – either Gavin Jantjes or George Hallett – who was helping her across a sand dune. Lean had to intervene again, which he didn't appreciate.

For all Lean was enjoying South Africa, he was at the end of his tether with Sarah, and wanted to see the back of her. After eight weeks, that moment was close at hand, but the actress had her party trick to perform one last time, at a farewell reception thrown by the mayor of Cape Town for the cast and crew. Sick of the whole thing, the art director Roy Walker and production manager Doug Twiddy decided to give the reception a miss, tie up a few loose ends at the hotel and then have a quiet drink together. 'Then the phone rings. "David insists you come." So we thought we better go along. Sarah sees Doug and I coming through the door. She makes a beeline towards us and as she comes she says, "Darling, how nice of you to come" and she grabs me.'

David had seen what was happening in front of their strait-laced hosts and put Walker on his shit-list. 'His face was like thunder. He blamed me for it – "your behaviour yesterday" – but I just put my arms out to her and she grabbed me. David never forgave me for that, I think.'

Shooting in South Africa had gone on for two months rather than the intended one. It was the end of the line for another Dedicated Maniac.

'I didn't go back to Ireland,' says Walker. 'I actually fired myself. There was Eddie to throw the parasols off the cliff, because that is all they had left to shoot. He had thirty parasols made in Japan or some bloody place. I didn't fall out with David as such, but I wasn't much enamoured with him at the end. To me, he had lost the magic that he had, and he was really getting old and grumpy.'

At least, though, he had what he was looking for: the currach scene featuring Michael, the priest and a lot of shots of the idiot copying Major Randolph as he limps across the beach, as well as Rosy being counselled on the beach by Fr Collins. Unlike the West of Ireland, South Africa didn't get a credit in the film. Instead, there was a lot of false rumour, the principal one being that Lean had gone to shoot the storm scene there. The truth was an entirely different story.

# 15. The storm waiters

The storm scene was hugely important to *Ryan's Daughter*, for it was the only real action in a film slated to run three-and-a-half hours. Lean had the ability to put up images on the screen that audiences had never seen before – the desert landscapes in *Lawrence* being the most powerful example of many – and now he wanted to capture the celluloid storm to end all storms. As Fr Collins comments when he watches the storm clouds gather: 'You'd think they were announcing the coming of Christ.' What he had to come to terms with after failing to master the elements on *Ryan's Daughter* was that he was not going to be able to capture it all himself, and would have to bring in a second unit.

Lean had done some second-unit work himself, standing in for George Stevens on *The Greatest Story Ever Told* (1965) when the American director fell ill. Selflessly, he asked not to be credited, out of respect for Stevens. Lean had observed how another friend of his, the director William Wyler, had his thunder stolen in another MGM film, *Ben Hur* (1959), as the famous chariot race was the work of the second unit headed by Andrew Marton. 'That will never happen to me,' Lean vowed. Lean would never barge in on the work of others, and he protected his own territory jealously as well. He despised second-unit directors to the point where he dumped all their work on *Lawrence*, after Sam Spiegel had brought them in to try to get that movie finished somewhere close to on schedule. If there was going to be a second unit on *Ryan's Daughter*, David was going to control the process.

Roy Stevens took the liberty of sounding out his old boss, Fred Zinnemann, about directing the storm scene – the Austrian director did, after all, have time on his hands, with MGM having scrapped *Man's Fate* – and Lean hit the roof when he heard about it. 'Get on the phone!' he shouted at Stevens. 'Get on the phone! Tell him there's been a mistake.'

'So who is going to direct the second unit?' Stevens eventually asked after Zinnemann had been stood down. The words were hardly out of his lips when he knew he shouldn't have asked, as Lean duly handed him the poisoned chalice.

Stevens protested, saying he was already overworked as associate producer, but was then promised that he could have David's 'eyes', the name Lean gave to his cameraman, Ernie Day. This was quite an offer. David relied on Ernie to capture the image he had in his mind but wouldn't see until the film was developed, and he could view the rushes. On one of the rare lighter moments on the *Ryan's Daughter* set, Lean played a little game with Ernie, zooming in on an image, then changing the focus and passing the camera to Ernie, who always managed to adjust the camera to achieve precisely the same composition. The cameraman was vital, and it was unusual of David to give up his 'eyes'.

It was no surprise, then, when the offer to Stevens was pretty swiftly withdrawn. During the Christmas break, Stevens took a call from Havelock-Allan. 'He said that

David couldn't work without his "eyes" and they were fixing me up with another cameraman. I was trapped.'

Stevens knew better than anybody what he was letting himself in for. Ever since the series of near disasters at the death trap that was Coumeenoole Cove, the storm scene had been put on the long finger, despite Stevens's best efforts. 'I couldn't get David interested in going to look at locations. He'd say, "Oh I can't, I've got to have a rest." Nobody wanted to take responsibility for the storm, because they thought it was going to be a complete cock-up. Even Eddie Fowlie, who used to look at all the locations for David, wouldn't touch it. He didn't want to get a bollicking.'

The location had to be stormy but safe, or at least as safe as it could be. The spectacular Cliffs of Moher drew the production team into Co. Clare, and would feature in the film, from a distance, but the sheer drop meant that filming actors there was out of the question. The area around the Bridges of Ross had been used by Lean the previous winter for some of the storm work, and that is where the second unit returned to now, in earnest. The Slabs were on a slight elevation and enormous waves could break in front of the actors and extras without them being submerged in a deluge. Getting camera equipment in to allow filming to take place in rough conditions was more of a problem. Again, the construction manager Peter Dukelow was called on to build a road across a field to the site, and plugs were drilled into the rocks to secure camera and lighting positions.

At last, the Dublin contingent of Hard Lads could earn their money, if they were up to it after idling about for so long. At the beginning of shooting, Lean had filmed the Hard Lads approaching Tom Ryan's pub as the storm brews, looking mean, taut and ready for serious action. Then *Ryan's Daughter* hit the doldrums, and it wasn't until nine months later that Lean got around to picking up that sequence, where he did the reverse shot of Ryan opening the back door to his pub and the men entering the premises, hard no more. One of the first men through the door in his dripping oilskins was the Dublin actor Emmet Bergin, playing the part of the rebel Sean.

'Emmet had at this stage put on three stone, and had a face like a balloon,' says Tóibín. 'Only somebody who was really watching would have noticed, but as somebody who had been there on both occasions, I just pissed myself laughing.'

The Kirrary pub and the real thing run by Tom Long were luxuries compared to what the Hard Men now faced into. With the main unit having left for Africa and the sun, the Hard Men headed north to Co. Clare. On hand were two units of the local fire brigade, sucking water out of a local stream when it was required to drench the players. Much of the time was taken up simulating storm conditions by using tip tanks that could pour hundreds of gallons of water onto the actors when it was required.

The second unit also managed to get some of the real thing. In eight weeks' shooting in Clare with McKern, Tóibín and the rest, there were five stormy days, and Stevens himself was hurt on one of them and taken to hospital with concussion. The crew carried on without him, with a top cameraman, Denys Coop, drafted in for the difficult scenes.

Technicians and actors returned with graphic stories of freak, monster waves, one of which – according to the stuntman Bronco McLoughlin – had darkened the skies. In stormy conditions it was said that every thirteenth wave was going to be a particularly big one, and the unit had a production assistant looking out from a raised area who sounded a klaxon so that the players knew when to withdraw. A camera hut and its valuable contents, which were chained down with drills driven into the rocks, were claimed by a wave that was so big that everyone was shaken, and Stevens ordered that shooting finish for the day.

That was the exception. The rule was a lot more waiting around. In the search for amusement, the second unit staged its own little show when the sun came out instead. 'I would get phone calls from David: "How are you getting on?" We're not doing anything. The sun is out and it's as calm as a mill pond.' Stevens sent over to Lean some Polaroids of the crew sunbathing on the rocks, wearing nothing but shades and shorts.

Leo McKern, whose character Ryan has to prove his bravery and nationalistic zeal by retrieving rebel arms from the seething ocean in the storm to disguise his role as a British informer, was the only one of the marquee names required for this part of the shoot. And so he had to remain on in Ireland for a second winter along with his stunt double, Bill Fisher. 'What I asked him to do wasn't half as bad as what we did with the double when the water hit him and we had to pull him out of the water,' says Stevens. 'We got him halfway down there into the water and I'd have somebody on top of the rock saying, "There's a big wave coming now." And you would hear it coming like a train, this great sound. The water would come right over. Also we had a tipper of water that would come down on him. He was quite safe where he was, unless there was some huge rogue wave.'

Mostly, it was the waiting that was killing McKern. He wasn't of the 'You crack the whip, I'll make the trip' school of acting to which Mitchum professed to belong.

McKern's daily routine was similar to Mitchum's. Unlike Mitchum, however, he tended to go in on himself, and had dealt with periodic bouts of depression all his life. In Dingle, McKern would sit at home waiting for the phone to ring and, increasingly as the months went on, sought the company of a bottle when it didn't. McKern had asked an experienced sailor to navigate his boat over from Southampton, and he had driven over to Dingle with his family in the Volkswagen camper. 'He deliberately rented a place where he could see his boat moored,' says his daughter, Abigail.

> He thought it would be nine months in Ireland with his family and he could sail his boat when he was not needed on the set. So he would sit at the window looking out at his boat, desperate to go sailing, and he felt very trapped, and that's when he got depressed. He suffered from depression throughout his life, and he was drinking as well. My mother doesn't drink, and she was worried about him, so that is when it went quite sour. Mostly my father would only drink red wine only after a show in the evening, but on *Ryan's Daughter* he was drinking vodka first thing in the morning, and that is when it got frightening.

McKern had lost respect for Lean, and his mental health started deteriorating further when his family returned to England and the second unit moved up to the Bridges of

Ross. 'To be told to prepare for a scene the next morning and have it postponed not once but twenty times is rather like preparing for a stage entrance, summoning up the blood and stiffening the sinews, as it were, only to find the curtain continually refusing to rise,' McKern wrote in his autobiography, *Just Resting*.

A reasonable comparison is that of a runner on the blocks; one false start is bearable, two maddening, but three impossible to contend with if the best performance is expected.

Towards the end of my time in Ireland I was beginning to feel like the head of a Pavlovian dog; the bell kept ringing, I kept salivating, but the food never appeared. Every morning we left Ennis from the hotel at about six o'clock for a forty-odd-mile drive to the location, the windswept barren rocks of Kilkee, and sat in Calor-heated caravans waiting for the bad weather and a few 'pick-up' shots. There wasn't many of us and our time was spent in endless and unsatisfying games of Scrabble or (for those who could) reading. The dull, cold, rocky foreshore held nothing but an affinity with the endless grey sky and an occasional disinherited seagull.

Niall Tóibín was also at the end of his tether. When not gainfully employed at the storm site, the Hard Lads were settling in for another winter of watching the world go by from the comfort of their bar stools – this time the Royal Marine Hotel in the small town of Kilkee – but Tóibín needed to be elsewhere. His one-man performance of Brendan

Behan's *Borstal Boy* was due to transfer to New York, and as far as Tóibín was concerned, with Broadway beckoning, Hollywood could find its next new star somewhere else. 'The Broadway date looked more and more like being firmed up, and *Ryan's Daughter* looked more like pissing around until Tibb's Eve,' Tóibín observed.

He instructed his agent, Tommy O'Connor, to secure his release date from *Ryan's Daughter*, but none was forthcoming. Tóibín complained, but the production company could keep him there as long as it liked once they gave seven days' notice of intention to extend the contract, a condition that applied to all the Irish actors. Had he broken the contract, he could be prevented from working on his beloved *Borstal Boy*. Very politely, Roy Stevens explained to Tóibín that there were still a number of scenes for which he was required. Grumbling over his Guinness, Tóibín became paranoid and figured the production company's insistence on dumping barrels of money into his lap was part of a British plot to deprive America of seeing him perform on Broadway.

It was the Royal Mail in England that came to his rescue. The letters of intent to extend the employment of the actors, posted out by the production manager Doug Twiddy, got stuck in a London letterbox on a Bank Holiday and, having failed to give seven days' notice to his agent, Tóibín was free to go.

'Ok, how much does he want?' the production company asked, realising they were now over the barrel.

He just wants out, they were informed.

Surely, he wasn't looking for billing?

No, just out.

Finally, they accepted that a year of overindulgence had taken its toll on Tóibín, and a swift rearranging of the schedule meant the actor could be wrapped before the week was out and he was free to go. What's more, they were terribly nice about it – far too nice, in Tóibín's suspicious mind. 'I don't trust these fuckers,' he thought to himself. So he took a detour of more than 100 miles (via Cork) to get on the road to Dublin, or, as he put it, the Golden Road to Samarkand.

His suspicions were well founded. Flying out from Dublin to New York a few days later, the plane stopped over in Shannon Airport, near where Stevens and Co. were camped to film the storm scene. The passengers disembarked, and who should be there to meet him in the duty-free section but the Hard Lads, who had discarded their oilskins, taken a break from filming to make their final farewells and somehow blagged their way into what was supposed to be the restricted area of the airport.

The production company, the Hard Lads told him, had contacted the Gardaí hours after he had left and sent a car out to try to intercept him, as there was one shot they had overlooked. The drink was flowing in the duty-free section, but the news was sobering to Tóibín, and he was happy to retire back onto the aircraft, where he felt safer.

The Hard Lads decided they liked the ambience of the duty free, and as there was no sign of a storm outside they made themselves comfortable, drinking at the bar. The singing started, and when they were asked to quieten it, they told security to 'fuck off'. Eventually they were thrown out, and would have been arrested were it not for the fact that they were connected to the film.

The Hard Lads would love to have packed Leo McKern off in fine style as well, but one minute he was there and the next he wasn't. His blow-out, described later in *Just Resting*, was more spectacular than Tóibín's – another self-sacking as he walked off the job.

Unable to put my mind to any constructive activity and poised in vain for the second assistant to rush into the caravan and call 'ready?' I couldn't take any more; in the middle of some footling game or other I said, 'I'm going home.' And I did. I knew, as well as anyone, that the pick-up shots could be perfectly well done by Billy [his stand-in]; had there been vital stuff to do, I couldn't have left, however frustrated and depressed. By evening I was at the ferry in my Volkswagen caravan, and home the next night, after eleven months.

I was not conscienceless, but not a word was said by the company. Enough was enough and I believe there was tactful recognition of the fact; but one aspect seemed to surprise various people. I was being paid daily what a skilled professional in some other pursuit would receive in a week, and some found it incomprehensible that I would voluntarily forego this sort of payment for doing nothing but play Scrabble, but I think I have explained why. As Orson Welles once said, 'No money is worth it.'

Stevens's view was equally bleak: 'The whole thing was murder,' he remarked, and the storm shooting in Co. Clare had nearly finished him off. They called it a wrap and went their separate ways. Stevens had a date with Lean back at base, a prospect he didn't relish.

# 16. Rid of the mob

David and Sandy had taken a week's holiday on the way back from South Africa, staying at the Mount Kenya Safari Club. David dipped into a copy of *Out of Africa*, which Barbara Cole had recommended to him a few years earlier as a book he might like to adapt into a film. The storyline, which involved capturing the animals and vast scenery of Africa, interested him much more than the devastating impact of syphilis on a woman's health, which Karen Blixen's novel also explored. Perhaps after he made *Gandhi*, David thought.

When he returned to Kerry in March 1970, it wasn't to the Skellig Hotel but to the more comfortable Great Southern in Killarney, where he had taken over a wing and one of the floors of the hotel. His construction team had already moved in, and one of the rooms was converted into an editing suite by the time Lean arrived. Since it was the off season, David was able to persuade the hotel to turn one of the restaurants into a theatre, and engineers were brought in to soundproof it. Another room was devoted to storage of the film.

While not as opulent as some of the hotels where this homeless man laid his hat, Lean was charmed by the hospitality and fascinated by its history. His was not the first British takeover of the hotel. The Crown's forces had requisitioned it during the 1920 War of Independence, and surrounded it with barbed wire and sandbags to protect themselves against the type of characters who featured in Lean's movie. There had been shootings, too, on the steps of the hotel during the Civil War, which followed after the British left, and the basement of the hotel had been turned into a prison.

When that all ended, the hotel got an upgrade. One of Lean's heroes, Charlie Chaplin, was a regular guest when he holidayed in Kerry, and likewise Grace Kelly and Jackie Kennedy, who came with her children to stay in the hotel for some peace and quiet after the assassination of her husband in Dallas a few years earlier.

The Great Southern was a curious choice when it came to editing a big-budget Hollywood movie. Lean had edited *Doctor Zhivago* at MGM Studios in Culver City, California, where Robert O'Brien had put aside space on the lot and reserved a suite for him at the Bel-Air Hotel, though David worked virtually round clock on the editing in order to get the film ready for that year's Oscars. Ominously, perhaps, MGM wasn't asking Lean to rush through the editing of *Ryan's Daughter*, and Lean wanted to stay away from the studio executives now that the MGM regime and culture had changed so dramatically.

David had another important reason why he didn't want to return to the US. This time, he was going to edit his picture at his own pace, so there would be no need for the vitamin injections he was given during the editing of *Zhivago*, and again when he was filming around Dingle. His attorney, Lee Steiner, had also advised him that the Inland Revenue Service was on to him, which was another disincentive for going back to the US. The advice was contained in a letter written by Havelock-Allan to Lean on 25 November 1968, which stated that Lean was vulnerable to claims for tax in the United States if he completed his films there, and in Switzerland if he chose it as a place of residence. Havelock-Allan went on to warn that eventually one country or another would try to make tax claims against Lean.

The Irish Taoiseach (prime minister) Jack Lynch, who had visited the *Ryan's Daughter* set and was shown around by Havelock-Allan, was naturally well disposed towards what was happening on the Dingle Peninsula. David had thought he might be offended by the sight of the Union Jack flying at the army barracks, a notion Lynch found laughable when he spotted it and was told they hadn't been able to take it down in time. Lynch had informed Havelock-Allan that he and his Finance Minister, Charles Haughey, were introducing tax breaks for film-makers in Ireland, and had been speaking to the director John Huston, who was living in a castle in Galway at the time and was involved in promoting Ireland's film industry.

Lean could work at his own pace in Killarney, not having to worry about the Irish taxman moving on him. What he was more anxious about was the quality of the storm footage his associate producer had managed to shoot in Clare, and he waited impatiently for Stevens so that he could view it.

Stevens drove to the Great Southern with the rolls of film in the boot of his car. Combined with what David had shot while he had been in Ireland, he thought it would be enough, but it wasn't his opinion that mattered.

Lean met him at the hotel alongside the film's editor, Norman Savage. They had a pleasant lunch together, and then David said to Roy: 'Come on, let's see what you got.'

Stevens again was on the defensive:

'No, David, I'm not going in there because you'll be saying, "Why didn't you put the camera two inches to the left or up two inches or down two inches?"' I went off to the bar and had a drink. After about half an hour Norman Savage came out grinning from ear to ear and said, 'Oh boy, are you in the shit. Are you in for a bollicking.'

We went to his little cutting room by the theatre. David sat there solemnly and said, 'I don't know how you fucking did it. I wish I'd done it. Now fuck off, I never want to see you again.' He meant it, too. He didn't talk to me for the rest of the picture. If he had to give me any instructions or whatever, he would send the message through Doug Twiddy and I would send one back through Doug. It was like having his wife screwed or something. It was his film, his baby, and there was something in it that he hadn't done and he had to put it in.

On David's side, there was a suspicion that Stevens was starting to get ideas about himself and was claiming more credit than he was due. Eddie Fowlie wasn't very impressed by Stevens's bearing during the film. 'Roy got himself an enormous desk in that office down on the Holyground and some huge cigars. That wasn't his scene up till now, but all of a sudden he's Sam Spiegel.'

Even Sandy got involved in defending David's behaviour towards Stevens, a year spent on location with Lean having taught her plenty about how the director operated. 'What David had done was write out in detail, shot by shot, exactly what had to be done,' Sandy told Lean's biographer, Kevin Brownlow.

Medium-close shot or medium shot, a bucket, a hand reaching down to pick a grenade out of the water, foaming water in the lower half of it. Absolute detail, because he wasn't going to let anyone do that kind of stuff. So he gave Roy a very, very precise list of shots that he had to get. Having said that, what Roy got was wonderful, the footage was extraordinary.

There was about seven hours of rushes which eventually was cut down into a ten-minute sequence, maybe. So yes, Roy did a wonderful job of shooting it, but he was in no sense responsible for the sequence. You can argue it either way, depending on whose side you're on. But I remember being dazzled by the stuff, because a lot of it looked very dangerous. The waves coming over the heads of those folks, it was terrific.

David was very touchy about that. There was often a case for second-unit directors claiming that they shot the film. It happened on *Zhivago* with a young man called Roy Rossotti, who actually went around afterwards claiming he shot the whole of the train sequence, having done two or three background shots. David was very cross with Roy [Stevens] afterwards because he thought that Roy was trying to pinch the credit. He did this thing which he always does, which was just to freeze him out.

Stevens might have dismissed himself at that point, as others had done, but he hung around, swallowed his pride and worked to the production manager, Doug Twiddy. Also lurking about, dangerously under-occupied, was Eddie Fowlie, who had parked up in his mobile home close by the Great Southern, ready to spring into action should his master come to the steps of the hotel. When David wanted to rough it a bit, he went to Eddie's trailer and got treated to bangers and mash. And, after sneaking around for so long, Eddie finally introduced Kathleen to polite society, and was happy that not just David but also Sandy warmed to his delightful teenage girlfriend when they went out to dinner.

It was time, however, for *Ryan's Daughter* to be entrusted to a new set of hands, the editing team led by Norman Savage. New in the sense that they were starting to get down to doing some work in earnest, even though they had been there already for the best part of a year. There were three members of the cutting room and a projectionist on location for the entire shoot, and they didn't cut a frame of film until the very end. They were there to support the unit, to screen rushes, make notes – to prepare, but not to edit. Most films are edited as they are shot, so that by the end of the shooting period the director is shown a first cut – warts and all – and from that point director and editor complete the film together.

Even though he didn't credit himself for his writing and editing roles, David needed to be involved in every part of the process. He was probably at his most comfortable in the editing room, where he didn't have to work much with actors and had the film in his fingers, an object he loved touching more than anything else.

Savage's assistant editor was a 25-year-old Londoner named Tony Lawson, who was starting out in the industry, unaware that he was living a part of movie history.

It was a huge crew and there was no expense spared in anything really. Nobody would put up with that nowadays. When I think, for instance, they gave us wet weather clothing for free and so we got Wellington boots, rain macs, etc. That's ridiculous. Why would an editing crew want Wellington boots and a waterproof mac? From that sort of scale of things, it was extraordinary. Moving an entire unit lock, stock and barrel, as large as it was, into a small town was very unusual.

About as busy as the Hard Lads but without an all-consuming drink habit, Lawson soaked in all that was going on around him instead. He lived for the duration of the film in the nearby village of Annascaul, close to Inch Strand, with his wife Christine and their two young children. Lawson's images from that extraordinary year were as graphic as any seen in the film itself, and David would have loved to capture them. 'I'll never forget going for a walk in Annascaul one Sunday morning with my wife and children and suddenly realising that everybody else was walking in the other direction, to church. The whole village.'

Lawson had seen it all – Mitchum ladling out the spiked beef chili at John Mills's party that had everybody off their faces, Sarah's outrageous behaviour, Chris acting like a lunatic – but he wasn't much interested in the tittle-tattle; it was the business of filmmaking that fascinated him. On a brief return to London, he'd got a sense of the hostility towards *Ryan's Daughter* from other directors when his contemporary, Alan Parker, a protégé of Fred Zinnemann, had buttonholed him and complained vociferously about how David Lean was taking almost the entire MGM budget for one film, and there was nothing left to go around. Lawson thought Parker should be addressing his complaints to MGM or to David, as he was only an assistant editor. 'I was so shocked and embarrassed that I didn't say anything,' Lawson recalled.

Lean himself, Lawson noticed during filming, was irascible and 'like a schoolmaster'. Lawson's immediate boss, Norman Savage, had told him there was a dress code – smart casual – and, specifically, no jeans. David didn't want his staff looking like slobs as they lolled around Kerry, and Savage was old-school like that as well. 'David was very much of his generation. Very correct. He wouldn't stand for what he would consider rudeness or off-handedness or any social behaviour that was out of kilter.'

One incident stood out for Lawson when they finally moved to the Great Southern and were editing the film.

It was the weekend, so we weren't working. We had been in the bar for some time. It was jovial, but we were all fine. My assistant, Peter Holt, was going to buy a round of drinks, and as he stood up, he knocked the glass table and it collapsed. Just at that moment David was walking into the bar, and in his eyes he saw a drunken lout falling about. He was very, very stiff and reserved towards Peter for several days after that.

Other than that, David started to unwind a little. He was no longer in a rush, and so the pace was unusually relaxed. He would bring down his short-wave radio from his suite, and the team would take a break from their work to listen to the cricket or live reporting of NASA's moon landings. David should do a space movie, Lawson thought. The grandeur. The schoolmaster in Lean meant that he liked to pass on the knowledge he had learned from five decades in the movie industry, and Lawson took it all in. There was the story about editing *Doctor Zhivago* in California, when David had spotted a fireman at one of the doors watching the film, which was strictly against all the rules. Instead of getting upset, David asked the roughneck what he thought of the film.

'He told us the story in a way to suggest that he liked to hear other people's comments, which actually is completely untrue,' Lawson said. 'He didn't, particularly if they were critical. He would listen to Norman or me and then tell me why I was wrong, essentially. If my assistant had said something, he would have kicked him out or told him to shut up. He was less receptive than a lot of people at the time to not even criticism, but suggestion.'

One of David's trickiest remaining problems was what to do about Christopher Jones's poor attempt at an English accent, which made the character of Major Randolph sound more like Gary Cooper than a member of the British officer class. Lean thought about getting Jones back from Los Angeles to re-voice some of the lines in the sound studio they had set up in the hotel, but Chris was having none of it, having given up on not only Europe, but the whole movie industry as well. He had returned to LA and moved into the gate lodge at 10050 Cielo Drive, where – surprise, surprise – he became more than a little freaked out. Olivia Hussey was living in the main house, where Sharon and four others had been murdered, but she wanted nothing to do with Chris as she snuggled up to Dino Martin. Belatedly, Jones had decided to become a hippy, and was seen walking around the street in his bare feet.

'David Lean had tried to turn me into a British officer, which was the epitome of "trained",' Jones told the Hollywood super-groupie turned bestselling author Pamela Des Barres.

> So I went in the opposite direction. I had to go to the totally opposite extreme, reverting to Tarzan, become totally primitive, otherwise I'd have been like the guy I played in the movie. If you have ever been under David Lean's iron fist for a year … he drove me crazy, man, trying to turn me into aristocracy. He shell-shocked me for that part. A call came through from David Lean, or somebody. They wanted me to fly back over and loop. So I said, 'Fuck that.' That's how all that bullshit started.

Using another actor to dub someone's voice was deeply frowned upon, and broke rules laid down by the actors' union, Equity, but it did happen in the movie industry. Under strict secrecy, the English actor Julian Holloway – who didn't have to stretch to reproduce the plummy tones

David required – was flown over to Ireland, and it was his voice that was used in the main when Randolph spoke. David had finally freed himself from his casting nightmare.

There were other bits and pieces to tie up. Shooting on *Ryan's Daughter* officially ran 135 days over schedule and $3,549,833 over budget, at a cost of $13,015,877. Much of that overspend was taken up in overtime for the actors. Mills, having signed for $200,000, was paid $387,500, huge money for the English actor, with the exchange rate at $2.40 to the pound. Howard's basic of $250,000 (plus a $1,000-a-week living allowance) had swollen to $443,000 by the end. Jones, who had done all the heavy lifting when it came to slowing things up, received more than double the salary for twenty-nine weeks in his contract, from $200,000 to $444,791. Mitchum's basic for twenty-six weeks of $750,000 had risen to $875,000, plus he had negotiated a tiny percentage of the net profits. The biggest multiple was achieved by the leader of the Hard Men, Barry Foster, employed on an original contract of fourteen weeks at a projected cost of £4,800, who was eventually stood down after fifty-one weeks having been paid £30,325. Sarah fumed that she was paid only a flat rate of $125,000 (plus a $600-a-week living allowance) for what she thought would be three months' work, while her colleagues all around her coined it on overtime.

Shooting of *Ryan's Daughter* was officially completed on 18 March 1970, but in reality it continued for months after that, for most of the time that the editing was going on at the Great Southern, in fact. Granted it was with a skeleton crew, by David's standards, but nonetheless some important shots were still not in the can, one being the opening of the film, which couldn't be faked in South Africa or in a studio. Trevor Coop, for one, had come back from South Africa and was reunited with his fiancée, Doreen McCann, who had been working in the production office and had then gone to Co. Clare with the second unit to shoot the storm. The couple were married in early May 1970, and then came back to work on *Ryan's Daughter* two months after the film was officially completed. 'Filming could have gone on for another ten years as far as I was concerned,' Coop observed. 'I was young, earning lots of money, working on the biggest movie of the last twenty years. Life couldn't get any better.'

As it was, he was required for a further twelve to fourteen weeks to shoot the opening sequence. This shows Rosy's umbrella being blown off a cliff and landing in the sea next to where Michael and Fr Collins were fishing in their currach. As they were just specks in the distance, stand-ins were used for Johnny and Trevor. Eddie came into his own to make sure that the umbrella, instead of flipping and landing on its head in the water, would drop elegantly to the sea like a parachute, just so.

David was never satisfied. He would see things such as clouds scudding over the mountains at great speed, and would suddenly stop what they were supposed to be doing and film this natural phenomenon instead. Then he would go back to the Great Southern and slip this piece of film in just before one of the beach scenes. One time, Lean spotted a certain reflection in a pool of water on a mountaintop and despatched Coop and others to film it. The image never reappeared despite the film crew – a third unit, if you like – waiting there several days while David edited away back in Killarney.

The film people were at each other's throats by the end, but there was no end of goodwill towards the locals. As a gesture of appreciation, Havelock-Allan offered to make good the work on the fifty buildings that composed the village of Kirrary and leave it as a permanent fixture, to be used by local people as they wished. That was a very generous offer, for the alternative – pulling down the structures and leaving the windswept mountain as they had found it – was the cheaper option. It became quite a talking point, whether to keep the village or not, as its potential as a tourist attraction was obvious. However, the locals feared disputes over who owned the village, and thought it would become a white elephant. They were also afraid of hippies moving in and squatting the place. Thanks, but no thanks, came the reply to Havelock-Allan.

A normal set could be dismantled using ladders and a few spanners. In the case of Kirrary, bulldozers and men with jackhammers moved in and flattened the village, a demolition job carried out by some of those who had built it in the first place. The set was struck. The rubble was carried away. The mountain was returned to nature and the sheep. Only the solid-stone schoolhouse at the bottom of the mountain was left, sitting incongruously in the middle of a field looking out on the Blaskets. The people of Dingle could sleep easy, secure in the knowledge that no hippy gang was going to come off the mountain and butcher them as they lay asleep in their beds.

# 17. Body in the bathroom

Back in the States, Mitchum had been recuperating post-filming at his ranch at Atascadero, 200 miles north of Los Angeles, where he kept his stable of Quarter Horses. MGM had been in contact, asking him to go on a promotional tour of *Ryan's Daughter* in the lead-up to its launch. He agreed, having been prodded by his two sons, both aspiring actors, who felt that their father must finally be in line for an Oscar, having worked with Lean on such a big project. Mitchum decided to play the game, albeit still on his own terms. He had picked up on the fact that David and Eddie Fowlie were still adding bits and pieces to the movie back in Dingle. 'They are probably still up there now,' Mitchum told reporters, 'chasing some parasol down a beach, waiting for the wind to blow right and an old crew man to pull the strings correctly. David going, "Oh bugger".'

With the exception of Chris, walking on the wild side in LA, and McKern, who had fled as far as Australia and said that he was giving up the business, it was all hands on deck when it came to generating as much publicity as possible. Sarah was confined to base, as she was on stage in the West End, but she did some interviews, reluctantly. 'I guess I hate the press because they have always treated me like a whore,' she told Rex Reed of the *Los Angeles Times*, who wrote that she spoke to him 'chewing away nervously on her bottom lip like a Velázquez child facing the Inquisition'.

The publicity drive was organised out of New York by MGM's resident longhair in the marketing department, Mike Kaplan, who had successfully strategised the rescue of Kubrick's *2001: A Space Odyssey* (1968) after it had been savaged, by Pauline Kael of the *New Yorker* magazine in particular. Kaplan realised that there was a problem with *Ryan's Daughter* from the marketing point of view. It wasn't based on a great figure, as with *Lawrence of Arabia*, or a great book, as with *Doctor Zhivago*. The media blitz he and his team dreamed up, after a brainstorming session with his staff at the Warwick Hotel on 54th Street, was a multilayered approach designed to make people believe that this was a great piece of filmmaking, even if they hadn't seen the movie. As a result, senior crew members were roped in for publicity work as well. Freddie Young addressed students in Toronto, but not before first lighting the stage on which the event took place. Even Eddie Fowlie went on a US tour of film colleges, while Jocelyn Rickards reluctantly headed to the States as well to do media work. She had to be talked around by Nat Weiss, the American director of publicity for MGM, who told her over lunch at the Connaught Hotel in London that 'the success of *Ryan's Daughter* is vital to the whole movie industry in this country'.

Rickards crossed paths with Mitchum in New York, where Bob was staying at the Plaza on Fifth Avenue, in a suite where the previous occupant had been the comedian Jerry Lewis. While Mitchum and his secretary, Reva Frederick, were unpacking, Rickards lay on the sofa with a tumbler of Jack Daniels and stared at the ceiling. Her artist's eye spotted something out of place, fifteen pieces of chewed gum stuck to the baroque plasterwork above her head. The hotel manager was called, and Mitchum remarked, 'If you hadn't noticed them, they'd have said that I'd slung them up at their precious ceiling during a drunken spree.'

Mitchum was watching Rickards's back as well. He was aghast that she was heading to New Orleans the following day without a minder there to meet her, so the actor put in a few calls to make the necessary arrangements for one of his people down there to pick her up and look after her. Mitchum himself was accompanied by Bayley Silleck, who had developed a good rapport with the actor, and they ended up doing two different publicity trips coast to coast over the course of four weeks.

> I was supposedly the only one who could handle Mitchum; everybody else was afraid of him. He was a very scary interview in a way for a publicist because you never knew what he was going to say. He would mimic David Lean holding his cigarette holder between thumb and forefinger, 'Well now, yes, yes.' I once got rather annoyed with Mitch, in Detroit or Cleveland. 'Goddammit Robert, you're here to publicise a movie, not make fun of people.' But it was difficult to be angry with him for too long. His whole stock-in-trade was being insouciant and cynical.

At Columbia University, Mitchum was showing off, producing a block of hashish for a student to take and pass on before he started talking about the movie. The picture he painted of Lean was not a particularly helpful one when it came to trying to counter the impression that Lean had been careless with the studio's money. 'He comes to work in the morning, he begins a scene with – I think – really no pre-conceptions, or at least no established or announced concept,' he told the compère, *Life* magazine film critic Richard Schickel, who countered that Lean's films looked so carefully composed. 'But, you see,' Mitchum replied, 'first he shoots the picture. Then he takes a look at it. Then he shoots it again. And then he looks at that. And then he finally shoots it. So, it's a bit expensive.'

Dressed in a dark suit and dark glasses, Mitchum looked every inch a movie star, and he warmed to his theme as the audience listened agog.

> David found it very difficult working with me because I would be over joshing with the grips, with the electricians and he'd say, 'Action'. And I'd go in, without explaining, and do it in one take, which would just, I'm sure, infuriate him. He'd be almost tearful and say [plummy imitation], 'Bob! That was spot on! I can't tell you how beautiful that was – simply marvellous.' I would say, 'You don't think it was too Jewish?' And he'd say [Lean imitation], 'What's he on-n-n about?' It would drive him just crazy. I kept putting him on.

With Mitchum and his tongue on the loose and dining out on his dealings with Lean, the producers had little hope of keeping a lid on what had been going on in Dingle. 'I've made it a practice of never looking at rushes of my films,' he told Bob Lardine of the *New York Sunday News*.

> In fact, I haven't seen half the movies I've made. But in *Ryan's Daughter*, the director insisted that I examine some footage. I agreed just to keep him quiet. The first thing that comes on the screen was Leo McKern completely gassed in a pub. Then the scene shifted to a shot of Trevor Howard staggering up the beach, absolutely stoned [drunk]. And then Lean cut to a shot of me on the beach – wiped out. All I could say was, 'The camera never lies.'

In Detroit, Bayley insisted they get out of the hotel, despite Mitchum's reluctance, as he wanted to see some real life, and he had been told of this great steak house they had to try.

> These two big truck drivers came over and they insisted he autograph pictures for their girlfriends. He brushed them off: 'Look, I'm eating. I'll do it later.' They came back again, he brushed them off again, they came back a third time and this time one grabbed him on one side and one got him by the other and one smacked him on the head. The table went over, a chair went up in the air and Bob got a few swings in. The waiters came rushing over, the cops were called. Afterwards, Mitchum was brushing himself off and he looked at me and said, 'I fucking told you so. We're not going out from now on.'

David was also due over. He had grown to love the United States. Whereas in Britain the establishment tended to be either sniffy or condescending towards movie-makers, in the US they were lauded. Lean's films were loved and received with rapture, the director himself was fêted in Hollywood, strangers on the street stopped him and congratulated him on his work and all doors were open when it came to what could be achieved, with the money there on the table. How could someone wholly obsessed with making movies not fall in love with the place? Columbia Pictures had announced before shooting *Lawrence of Arabia* that it was 'the first motion picture to go before the cameras without a budget'. Robert O'Brien at MGM had promised much the same, and both giant studios pretty much delivered. While James Aubrey had wanted to get his fangs into *Ryan's Daughter*, he was stymied by Lean's bulletproof contract, and even his attempts to tag a 1960s song on at the end were dismissed by Lean – 'It Was a Good Time' by The Mike Curb Congregation was only released after the film.

After attempting to at least hurry Lean along, MGM in the end made a virtue of his pyramid-building ways, as it announced the unveiling of *Ryan's Daughter* on 15 October 1970, while David was still working on the film, supervising the sound mixing in London and working on the musical score with the composer Maurice Jarre. 'David Lean is among the world's most honoured and successful film-makers and *Ryan's Daughter* is the best film he has made to date,' said an MGM release, which at least tied David to an opening date. 'The Nov 9 premiere will culminate three years of intense work.' An accompanying retrospective of Lean's films was to be shown at the Museum of Modern Art (MOMA), including a full-length version of *Oliver Twist* (1948), which had previously been censored in the US because of charges of anti-Semitism in Lean and Alec Guinness's portrayal of Fagin.

Everything was in place for David's triumphant arrival in New York, but rather than eager filmgoers queuing around the corner, that was where disaster and humiliation lay.

For a start, the retrospective at MOMA inevitably led to comparison between the intimate and epic sides of Lean's filmmaking. The acid critic John Simon had taken an aggressive stance at a question-and-answer session beforehand, which featured Lean and Bolt at the top table, with Mike Kaplan acting as the moderator, Willard Van Dyke, the director of the museum's film department, having cried off with a bad case of stage fright. From the floor, Simon had started attacking the film and Sarah Miles in particular, remarking at what a bad actress she was and how terrible she looked. Kaplan reminded the critic that Sarah's husband was on the stage, and when the critic insisted on further personal attacks, Kaplan had him slung out. 'I was amazed at myself for having the audacity, the smarts to tell him to go fuck himself,' Kaplan later remarked.

Further inklings of trouble could be detected when a few titters were heard at the press viewing during that love scene in the woods with Chris and Sarah. So lifeless and sedated had Chris's performance been when it came to the love-making scene that David had kept cutting away, literally, to the birds and bees that Eddie Fowlie had placed in the dance-hall set. White dandelion petals, carefully cultivated by Eddie, were blown onto a stream to symbolise the moment of climax, and buds started sprouting. The symbolism had been intended all along, but David had rather overdone it in the editing stage, repeatedly cutting from the couple's lovemaking to other images of nature in all its fertility. Pens were dipped in poison, and the reviews were cutting. 'There isn't a joke in all the three hours (three and a half hours including intermission), except maybe the idea that an Irish girl needs a half-dead English man to arouse her,' Pauline Kael wrote in the *New Yorker*.

'Lean has opted for bombast rather than character development,' wrote Mark Goodman in *Time*, 'scope instead of dramatic tension.'

'The [Irish] coast has most of the best lines. The original love story which Robert Bolt has set in these desolate seascapes seems both too frail and too banal to sustain the crushing weight of 3 hours and 18 minutes of Super Panavision.' – Charles Champlin, *Los Angeles Times*.

'The film hovers above the category of Dr Johnson's Bridge, the one that was worth seeing but not worth going to see.' – John J. O'Connor, *The Wall Street Journal*.

'Most fatuous of the current big films … but I could believe even in this dime fiction more than in Robert Mitchum as a shy, sensitive, somewhat repressed, Beethoven-loving Irish schoolmaster … Lean is an altogether stranger case: a man afflicted with gigantism, who wants to make bigger and bigger movies even though his small and medium-sized ones are often very good.' – John Simon, *The New Leader*.

Kael's review in the *New Yorker* was the most savage of all: 'The only reasons for setting the film in 1916 were to legitimize the fact that every idea is shop-worn and to build sets … *Ryan's Daughter* is gush made respectable by millions of dollars tastefully wasted, an awe-inspiring and tedious lump of soggy romanticism … The emptiness of *Ryan's Daughter* shows in every frame and yet the publicity machine has turned it into an artistic event and the American public is a sucker for the corrupt tastefulness of well-bred English epics.'

There was more epic venom from Kael spread over two pages of the *New Yorker*, 21 November edition, and it was surprising that Lean accepted an invitation to spend an evening with Kael and her fellow members of the National Society of Film Critics (NSFC) the following month. It was meant to be an informal exchange of ideas, but it turned out to be an inquisition that shook David to the core, and he later blamed it for his subsequent lengthy exile from the movie industry.

The NSFC was founded in the 1960s as a counterweight to the more conservative New York Film Critics Circle. Literary New York had discovered that film was an 'art' and the critics were lionised and became, as one of them put it, 'demi-celebrities'. The organisation published an annual anthology, met six or seven times a year to discuss the film scene and issued declarations on film censorship and other issues, such as studios re-cutting films. They also invited directors to what were supposed to be informal, off-the-record dialogues and exchanges of ideas.

The venue was the Algonquin Hotel in Times Square, where the dining room was closed to the public on Sunday evenings and turned over to the critics, free of charge, in return for a bit of publicity. Members of the circle, such as Kael and the *Village Voice* critic Andrew Sarris, were more likely to feud with each other than any visiting director, but they seemed to find one voice with the arrival of Lean.

David had come in straight from a transatlantic flight, feeling jet-lagged but looking forward to a convivial dinner with his hosts. Sandy accompanied him, along with the MGM head of publicity, Natt Weiss, and his wife. Ominously, there was nobody from the Critics Society at the hotel to meet them, so David's party waited in the lobby. 'All of a sudden, almost together, this gang appeared, it was almost like a funeral procession of these creatures. They were such a strange assemblage of people,' Sandy told Kevin Brownlow. 'In they came, they opened up this private dining room, turned on the lights, went in and sat down at this huge *Citizen Kane* table and interrogated David for the next two hours, while we sat outside toying with cashew nuts and waiting, wondering what on earth was going on.'

'I remember Pauline Kael meeting me at the door,' Lean said, 'and she sat me at the head of the table. I remember the way she crossed her legs and you can practically see right up them. She's a peculiarly sexy woman, ugly, but very sexy and it sort of spreads around her. She's got an aura of sex around her.'

In the circumstances it was a pretty extraordinary observation, but Lean had withdrawn into himself, and the recidivist side of his nature emerged. 'They just took me to bits,' said Lean, who was particularly upset by the demeanour of Richard Schickel, the *Life* film critic whose work David greatly respected. Lean said that Schickel opened the meeting by asking: "How could the man who made *Brief Encounter* come up with a piece of shit like *Ryan's Daughter*?"

'It cut me to the heart,' David said. 'And that was Richard Schickel.'

The battering continued. Pauline Kael was particularly vociferous, and David could hardly believe it when she asked, 'Are you trying to tell us that Robert Mitchum is a lousy lay?'

Even though Kael was in full flow, she still sensed that the meeting was getting out of hand, and she tried a new approach. 'About halfway through the meeting,' says Sandy,

> Pauline Kael burst out, on her own and said, 'Let's get some dames in here, we've got to break up the tension.' And she grabbed me by the hand. She didn't know who I was, and she grabbed Nat Weiss's wife's hand as well and said, 'Come on in and join us.' She wouldn't go back in either. So Pauline Kael went back and then there was just nothing till David came out and then the whole lot of them came out and filed off. It was the most extraordinary piece of rudeness just on that level, to invite him at eight o'clock in the evening and sit him down for this interrogation.

David couldn't remember ever being spoken to with such hostility. Normally he was the one who tore strips off others, and he couldn't deal with being on the receiving end. 'The meeting was one of the most horrible experiences I have ever had. It was very *Citizen Kane*, this huge dining room. They had a big table in the middle. The light was not strong enough to illuminate the whole room, so it was very sinister and very heavy,' David said, regretting the fact that he didn't cut out early and go for dinner with Sandy. 'I was a fool to stay there. I remember saying to Pauline Kael at the end, "You won't be content until you've reduced me to making a film in black and white on 16mm." And she said, "We'll allow you colour."'

The recriminations continued for years. Richard Schickel, who chaired the meeting, was prepared to shoulder some of the blame, but pointed the finger also at Kael and at Lean himself in a lengthy letter to Kevin Brownlow, Lean's biographer. This also cast an interesting light on the duality of Lean's career, and how he was frowned upon by highbrows.

> At that time the standard American critical line on Lean was that his small films (*Brief Encounter*, *Hobson's Choice*, the Dickens adaptations) were superior to his spectacles. I didn't hold with that view. I liked them all. And indeed, my review in *Life*, which accompanied a big color picture act, was credited with turning the tide on *Dr Zhivago* after it had been savaged critically a few years before.
>
> Indeed, a year or so after that film opened, the president of MGM, Robert O'Brien, sought me out at a party to impart that information and to thank me almost embarrassingly for the notice. Still, I didn't like *Ryan's Daughter* any more than anyone else did.
>
> In welcoming Lean to our gloomy revels I tried to prepare him for the hostility that I felt was sure to come. In introducing him, I listed his past triumphs, paid tribute to his distinguished career and added that although I knew there were 'mixed' feelings about his latest work I was sure – although of course I wasn't – that all assembled would bear in mind the distinguished filmography that lay behind it. There followed a period of polite sparring – questions about his 'intent', some neutral enquiries about casting and staging etc.

Then, however, Pauline Kael launched a brutal critique in the form of a question. This was always her public style. She was sort of the Camille Paglia of film criticism, especially when she was in public, showing off. I myself had once or twice been victimized by her at panel discussions.

This opened the floodgates. And, I must say, it was an angry torrent. Other than Kael, I can't recall who Lean's most savage assailants were, but there were several. I was not among them. But that doesn't mean I covered myself in glory. I pretty much lost control of the meeting, caught between a director I revered and colleagues for whom I had more respect then than I do now. Lean did not counterattack; instead he went into his shell. I seem to recall plaintive bleats from him, to the effect that he was unprepared for a dialogue of this intensity – and for the lack of respect being shown him. This was a legitimate complaint and I tried once or twice to intervene and divert the discussion to calmer areas. But to no avail. Lean, of course, grew less and less responsive. At some point he said, 'I don't understand all this; why are you doing this to me?' Or words to that effect.

It was in this context that the words he has since made demi-famous escaped my lips. It is given in Stephen Silverman's book [*David Lean*] as 'How could the man who made *Brief Encounter* come up with a piece of shit like *Ryan's Daughter*?' He has me 'greeting' Lean with this remark, which is not true. What I was doing was all-too-bluntly summarizing the subtext of the questions that were being put forward, answering his question about their all-too-apparent animus. I think the way I put it was this: 'What they are trying to say, Mr Lean, is that they don't understand how someone who made *Brief Encounter* could make a piece of bullshit like *Ryan's Daughter*.' There is, I hold, a substantial difference between a 'greeting' and a summary offered up well along in a difficult discussion when tempers had grown short. There is also a nuanced difference between 'shit' and 'bullshit' in American colloquial usage.

In other words, mine was a perfectly accurate summary of the meeting's tenor. But of course it was not felicitously or kindly put and I regret that. On the other hand, I confess to a certain amount of impatience with Lean at that point – his evasions and his silences. I was an impatient younger man – 37 at the time – and in those days a believer in the value of free, open exchange of opinion, the more outrageous the better.

Around the same time, on 9 December 1970, *Ryan's Daughter* had its British premiere at the Empire Cinema in Leicester Square, where the giant screen was able to do justice to the 70mm print. However, the projector failed in the Empire halfway through, and everyone tramped home without seeing the end. Reading the reviews in the newspapers, they may not have been inclined to return. The critical reaction in Britain was only mildly warmer than in the US. 'SIX MILLION POUND BORE' screamed the headline in *The Sun*, while Alexander Walker in the *Evening Standard*, armed with intimate knowledge of much that had gone on in Dingle, wrote cuttingly that 'instead of looking like the money it took to make, the film feels like the time it took to shoot'.

The Academy of Motion Pictures in Hollywood also wasn't terribly impressed, as Lean – who had either won or been nominated for his previous four films – wasn't shortlisted in the Best Director category, nor was *Ryan's Daughter* for Best Picture.

Bolt wasn't nominated either, but Sarah was, for Best Actress, and John Mills was also nominated for Best Supporting Actor. Miles set off for Los Angeles without her husband, who stayed in Surrey working on his next screenplay, in spite of Sarah's protestations that she didn't want to go to the ceremony without being on her man's arm. Bolt's decision to stay in England turned out to be a life-changing one, for otherwise, Sarah says, she wouldn't have allowed David Whiting come into her life.

Whiting was the young, handsome, dapper west coast show business correspondent for *Time*, as well as being a conman and fantasist. An open book such as Sarah was easy prey.

Sarah was staying with her English assistant in Bungalow 14 at the Beverly Hills Hotel, where she received Whiting, expecting just another run-of-the-mill media interview. It was 14 April 1971, a day before the Oscars ceremony, and a boil had erupted on her face. Whiting spotted his opening. He rushed off and returned with creams and pills he said would make the boil disappear. He also expressed his huge admiration both for Sarah and for *Ryan's Daughter*, and said he had convinced his editors to put her on the front cover. The medicine did the trick, and Miles was suitably impressed, but she didn't think that much more of it. She was, after all, about to see the Mitchums at their home nearby in Bel Air. After a pleasant evening, Dorothy applied her red lippy and drove her guest back to her hotel bungalow. According to Sarah, Dorothy kissed her on the cheek before telling her with a gentle smile, 'Robert will never leave me.'

Miles went to the Oscars in the Mary Queen of Scots outfit she had worn on stage during *Vivat! Vivat Regina!* The regal look didn't quite come off as she was dropped off several hundred metres from the venue, the Dorothy Chandler Pavilion, because of heavy traffic on North Grand Avenue, and was hot and sweaty when she arrived. She also caused something of a stir when collecting Freddie Young's Best Cinematography Oscar for *Ryan's Daughter* when she refused to read the corny cue cards, which included the line 'my husband keeps his two Oscars in the toilet'. Hollywood reacted coldly when she said she had forgotten her spectacles. Miles, having lost out in the Best Actress category to *Women in Love* (1969) star Glenda Jackson, felt a little vulnerable when she flew to New York the following day for more promotional work and booked into the Sherry-Netherland on Fifth Avenue.

Somehow, she didn't spot trouble when she discovered that David Whiting had booked into the neighbouring room. Armoured with his cover story, Whiting trailed Sarah around New York, reassuring Miles about her acting skills and convincing her that there was more he could do to boost her career besides getting her on the front cover of *Time*. Sarah says she rang the magazine to check out Whiting's credentials and was given a glowing reference. When they were back in her suite, Sarah's assistant having returned to Los Angeles, Whiting produced some pot and suggested they have a smoke together. When Sarah agreed, he guided her into the hotel wardrobe, saying it would result in a better high from inhaling in an enclosed space. They smoked several joints and then had sex in the wardrobe.

The following day Sarah was full of remorse. She knew all about her reputation as a scarlet woman and the stories that had been flying around Dingle about her liaison with Mitchum. It had been open season for the gossip-mongers.

'Did you enjoy making *Ryan's Daughter*?' Mitchum was asked by the chat show host Dick Cavett around that time, in front of an audience of millions.

The audience laughed and Mitchum raised an eyebrow.

'Very much,' Mitchum replied, also grinning.

'Let me put it another way,' continued Cavett, still leering. 'Was the film a pleasant experience for you?'

'Yes.'

'We have a clip from the movie.'

'I think you better get it on as quickly as possible.'

Miles dealt with the rumours, but her protestations as reported in the *Los Angeles Times* of November 15 1970 had a curious ring to some of those who had worked on the film and knew how frequently she had been in and out of Milltown House. 'When they aren't dumping on our work, they're printing lies about our private lives. I read in one paper that I was having an affair with Bob Mitchum while we were making *Ryan's Daughter*! My husband was there the whole time and I hardly ever saw Mitchum off the set.'

Much later she said she was drawn to his 'sheer animal magnetism' but had remained faithful to Bolt, up to that point. 'Mitchum and I were soul-mates,' Miles told Bolt's

292

biographer, Adrian Turner. 'We were very close, but we weren't doing it. People always assume you're doing it and we both knew what everybody was thinking and I find that a bit tacky. But I knew the truth and Robert [Bolt] knew the truth.'

Now she resolved to tell her husband about Whiting and the wardrobe. She was returning to England the day after the liaison in the wardrobe, and when Whiting told her that he would have to come too, she put her foot down and replied that she didn't want to see him again, regardless of any cover story. They parted at John F. Kennedy Airport. Sarah was delayed at Heathrow waiting for her bags. Pulling up to her house in Surrey in her MGM limousine, she saw Bolt waiting, with a tall, young man beside him who looked very much to the manor born. Whiting.

After leaving Sarah at the airport, Whiting, the son of a Pan Am pilot who made full use of his flying privileges, had hopped on a flight and arrived at the Bolt family home near Heathrow airport before her. Bolt was at home and his usual hospitable self, accepting at face value Whiting's spiel about the cover story and the need to intrude in their lives for a further month or so. A spare bedroom was hastily prepared for their unexpected guest. Bolt himself was 'bowled over' by Whiting, and Sarah decided not to mention the wardrobe. Instead, there was an attempt to convey a sense of normality. Bolt and Miles did an interview that appeared in the *Daily Mirror* on 14 May as part of the newspaper's Candid Couples series, which was headlined 'A Marriage For All Seasons' and written by the highly respected feature writer Donald Zec. 'A marriage which, Mrs Bolt gaily admits, took place despite the dark warning to her husband by her friends: "Don't marry Sarah Miles. She'll devour you, chew you up, and spit you out for breakfast".' Zec wrote that the word 'trust' was used a lot, and quoted Miles saying, 'he knows I am never going to have an affair with the carpenter', a clear reference to how Bolt was cuckolded in his first marriage.

Still hovering in the background was Whiting. His role was evolving, and Bolt had him working on publicity for his next film, *Lady Caroline Lamb* – the story of the nineteenth-century politician's wife who has a disastrous infatuation for the poet Lord Byron – which again had Sarah in the title role. Bolt not only had written the screenplay but was directing for the first time, and it was during this that everything started to unravel.

Miles says that Whiting had sneaked into her bedroom and stolen explicit love letters written to her by Laurence Olivier during their secret seven-year affair, which ended when she met Bolt. To complicate matters further, Olivier was starring in *Lady Caroline Lamb* alongside Miles and, according to Sarah, had told her to do anything to get the letters back when she had told him what was happening. This included hopping back into the wardrobe with Whiting, who Sarah says was blackmailing her by threatening to publish the letters unless she slept with him again. Bolt heard about the rumours, and decided not to do anything. Whiting was an increasingly manic and controlling figure on the set.

It was difficult to know who would crack first: Bolt, Sarah or Whiting. As Sarah told the *Evening Standard*: 'Caroline Lamb is the nearest to me of all the ladies I have played. She is very highly strung, not quite mad or neurotic, but could go either way.'

Sarah could hardly believe it when her normally placid husband lost his temper and beat up Whiting at the house in Surrey and threw him out. When remorse set in, Whiting went to live at Sarah's London house in Chelsea, with the couple's permission, and there he took an overdose of pills. The Bolts started treating him with kid gloves, as two people who Sarah had previously taken under her wing – Johnny Windeatt and Thelma Andrews – had already committed suicide in her London house, on separate occasions. Olivier had told her that people tended to 'vampire her light'. Sarah now knew that another disturbed individual had been drawn towards her.

'There was nothing erotic about him,' she wrote in her autobiography, *Serves Me Right*. 'He smelt of disinfectant, potions, strange chemical creams. He turned me into a numb, fear-ridden alien. That's what terrified Robert, the fact that I was teetering on the edge.'

Whiting was a speed freak who derived his extraordinary energy through taking amphetamines, which might also have contributed to his deranged behaviour. However, his sudden death and the discovery of his body in Miles's bathroom was a different matter altogether.

Acting now as Miles's agent, Whiting had secured Miles a part in a western with Burt Reynolds called *The Man Who Loved Cat Dancing* (1973), and he formed part of her entourage that went to Arizona for the filming in February 1973. At the motel where the crew were staying, Sarah was mixing in her inimitable style with some wranglers who were also working on the movie. Whiting complained, but Sarah was determined to enjoy herself and not listen to her adviser/agent-turned-jealous lover any longer. Whiting again went into manic mode back at the motel late at night, this time physically attacking her with punches and kicks. She fled and found refuge in Reynolds's bedroom.

She says that when she returned to her room in the morning, she found Whiting dead in her en-suite bathroom. There was a star-shaped wound on the back of his head and pills scattered on the floor. The press weren't slow to link Sarah to the killing, and fingers were also pointed at Reynolds. Both actors made statements to the police, but they were still ordered to attend the inquest despite the best efforts of MGM's lawyers to keep them out of the courtroom. Reynolds's testimony to the inquest was interrupted by Whiting's mother shouting 'murderer'. Sarah gave evidence, in tears, lashing out at MGM and Reynolds for trying to stop her doing so. A verdict of suicide caused by overdose of drugs was eventually returned.

A heap of questions, particularly about the star-shaped wound on the back of Whiting's head and blood found on the bed sheets in his own room, remained unanswered. The cops believed that Whiting had been involved in a fight with Reynolds, spurred on by a jealous belief the actor was having an affair with Sarah. The finger of suspicion was also pointed at the actress. Yes, she had shoved Lean down a small flight of stairs at the Skellig, but this was on an entirely different level. She reckons being branded as a 'murderess', as she described it, badly damaged her career.

The upward trajectory of Reynolds's career wasn't affected, but Sarah quickly found that she had been unofficially blacklisted in Hollywood. Back in England, she and Bolt became tabloid newspaper fodder. Bolt wrote an article in the *Daily Mail* about the continued intrusive scrutiny into their lives.

There have been some pretty evil innuendoes in the press, hints even of homicide ... Why is speculation in the press nearly always ugly? I blame you, the reader. The gentlemen (and ladies) of the press write as you want them to write. Tragedies big and little pile up on their desks, reduced to words: they are probably unaware of the distress their words are causing. They say they write as you want them to write. I wish I could think they were wrong.

Below another interview with Bolt published a few days earlier (5 March 1973), the *Daily Mail* republished Whiting's piece on Sarah, which had finally appeared in *British Cosmopolitan*. The *Mail* headline read: 'My Wicked Wonderful Friend: By the Man Who Died for Sarah'.

While her affair with Whiting stayed out of the public eye, her marriage to Bolt couldn't stand the strain. The couple separated late in 1973 and were divorced in 1975.

Sarah moved to Malibu, where she was regularly visited in her apartment by Mitchum. It was during her California sojourn, Miles insists, that the mutual attraction turned into an affair. Sarah also bumped into, of all people, Christopher Jones from time to time. *Ryan's Daughter* was supposed to make them both stars; instead it brought notoriety. Jones's fall from grace was so dramatic that many people thought he had actually died shortly after making *Ryan's Daughter*. When Miles met him, she said he was dishevelled and had run away with the keys to her Volkswagen Beetle and she had only got the car back when she complained to Stuart Cohen.

Eventually, Jones found peace and was living quietly in the San Fernando Valley of south California, painting and raising a family. He offered Sarah an explanation for his strange behaviour on the film: that he was due to elope with Sharon Tate before she was murdered. Miles remembers him asking, 'It is true that Polanski can't return to these shores, isn't it? If he can, I'm a dead man.' Jones laughed when I mentioned that to him. 'I might have been just goofing on her head.'

Bolt could have done with another Lean project to sink his teeth into, particularly since he was such a spendthrift in his own right. David, however, was going through a post-*Ryan's Daughter* crisis of his own. He had suffered bad reviews before, particularly for *Doctor Zhivago*, but the cinema-going public had flocked to his rescue, and Lean had emerged triumphant in the end. This time, word of mouth hadn't helped David's cause. Cinema owners complained that customers were leaving early, and that the movie was too long, allowing for only two performances a day. MGM sent him a list of suggested cuts. About twenty minutes was removed, much of it concerning the rebel gunrunning subplot. It was another kick in the teeth for the Hard Lads and brought to mind what the critic Adrian Turner had said about *Doctor Zhivago*: 'Robert wanted to make a film about humanity in the grip of the Russian Revolution, while David wanted to make a film about fucking.' Still, Lean cut *Ryan's Daughter* back with a heavy heart. 'By that time the navel cord was severed,' Havelock-Allan said. Middlebrow man was a chastened figure.

'With the highbrows I'm highly suspect,' Lean said.

I'm too popular and the critics really act like a pack of wolves. In some curious way, word gets around. I don't know how it happens, but [it's like] 'it's time we got hold of this chap and clobbered him'. They certainly did it with me in a big way. After *Ryan's Daughter* I thought, 'what the hell am I doing making films?' I was in a miserable state. I didn't like going out to a restaurant because I thought that I'd be sort of pointed at as the chap who did that disastrous, terrible, horrible film. I felt very ashamed.

Quick to withdraw into his own shell, David didn't do himself any favours.

I used to go to a well-known tailor in Los Angeles, and the owner always came up and greeted me. Some time after the film came out, I walked into the shop and suddenly saw a face looking at me from between the suits at the other end of the corridor. It dived straight through the suits and into a door and never came out again. I suppose one has to have a certain amount of sympathy because if you have just read the most horrendous review – 'this is a real turkey, take it away' – there is not much to say, is there? Except a sort of funeral-parlour approach. I thought, 'What the hell am I doing if my work is as bad as this?' I didn't want to do another film. I thought, 'I'll do something else.' I went travelling around the world and I didn't make another film for fourteen years. I thought, 'What's the point?'

# 18. God save our Lean

It was not as though David walked away from filmmaking; it was more a case of the filmmaking world walking away from him. He had been flirting with the Gandhi project for more than a decade, with Alec Guinness having agreed to play the title role. Lean had put the project to one side to make *Lawrence of Arabia*, and he had returned to it only intermittently since. Bolt was also on board to write the screenplay, but similarly had been easily drawn away from it, particularly when, at one point, David had suggested they both go to India to work together on the project. While making *Ryan's Daughter*, David had spoken of the Gandhi project as though it were a done deal, and told his favourites to prepare themselves for the rigours of India. However, when he attempted to get the film up and running, he ran into a series of delays and lost heart again, handing over the project to Richard Attenborough.

David took a step back, reacquainting himself with his brother Edward, the brainy one in the family who was director of external broadcasting at the BBC and lived in Camden, North London. The man who had suitcases of clothes stashed in some of the best hotels in the world also bought a house in Rome, just off the Appia Antica, which Sandy busied herself on.

'We did, actually, have a wonderful time,' Sandy told Brownlow.

We had the house in Italy that for a while we certainly enjoyed. We did a lot of travelling. He was always looking for something to make, make no mistake. It was just that he couldn't find anything. Certainly he was devastated by the critics, but I think if he had found the subject he would have been after it like a terrier after a rat. It was paralysing. This happens with so many directors, their very success paralyses them and he's always got to top the one before. It was some record he was trailing, some trail of tin cans, as he would have said, *Kwai* and *Lawrence* and *Zhivago*.

*Ryan's Daughter* was the first time the critics really got their heels into him. No, that's not true. You see I am following the party line there. He got some terrible reviews on *Zhivago*. He got some frightful reviews on *Lawrence*, but they were both huge popular successes so that was okay. *Ryan's Daughter* was neither, so I suppose the critics really had the last word.

It wasn't that *Ryan's Daughter* was a total flop at the box office. It was, in fact, the seventh-highest grossing film of 1970 in North America, bringing in more than $30 million. Lean was also consoled by the fact that the film ran for a year at the Empire Theatre in Leicester Square. However, cheques were clearly slow coming through, and Bolt for one was getting anxious, as he had bills to pay.

Bolt had been working on his script for *Gandhi*, but clearly still had *Ryan's Daughter* on his mind when he wrote to Lean in Rome on 23 April 1973, referencing a letter from his solicitor, Laurence Harbottle.

> He, Harbottle, says that Phil Kellogg says that MGM say that *Ryan's Daughter* is still short of her break-even figure, so don't yet put in [accountants] Solomon and Finger. Well of course MGM say it's short of break-even. Columbia say *Lawrence* is short too. That's why you put in Solomon and Finger isn't it? It'll be short of break-even on MGM's books if it plays round the clock in every cinema in both hemispheres, because Aubrey and Netter are as selfish as the rest of us and so clumsier that they are quite apparently criminal. So put in the bloodhounds now, I say. They've certainly hidden away the missing eight million and it may be possible to disinter four or five of them. That bloody film goes on and on everywhere. It's been to Staines [West London] six times. Love to you both, Robert.

Havelock-Allan expressed similar sentiments when asked whether the film made money, replying:

> I suspect that it has, but there's nothing you can do about it because once a film has failed on its initial release, every possibility for cooking the books, every possibility for inventing – indeed it happened in the very first accounting at the end of the year – unless you want a lawsuit you will never know if it made

money or not. I think Metro did alright with it. In fact, I am sure they did. I think it grossed in America $21 million or something like that, and the rest of the world. I am sure they made money. I don't know if they actually made a profit with the percentage for the distribution and the percentage they charge, but the very first accounts they sent us at the end of a year when we thought that the film wasn't doing too badly, they had $5 million down for publicity and exploitation. And it was made at a time when Metro was on the point of going bankrupt. We had not paid publicity at all, no paid television, nothing.

David was trying to look forward rather than back. A trip to Los Angeles to collect an award from the Directors Guild of America was followed by a working holiday in Tahiti, where David had long wanted to make a movie, having seen another Robert Flaherty movie/documentary called *White Shadows in the South Seas* (1928). David was reinvigorated by the trip, and then found a subject when Eddie Fowlie gave him a copy of the 1972 book *Captain Bligh & Mr Christian*, an account by Richard Hough of the infamous mutiny aboard the *Bounty* that was sympathetic towards Bligh. At a stroke, David decided to sell up in Rome and move to Bora Bora, a picturesque island next to Tahiti. The house in Rome had been burgled while David and Sandy were sleeping upstairs. David's two Oscars were stolen and alcohol was consumed – all sufficiently upsetting for David to pack up, and he was also frightened away by the kidnapping of the teenager John Paul Getty III in the Italian capital. Once again, he was an air-conditioned gypsy.

David started to assemble a team in Bora Bora. First, Eddie Fowlie and young Kathleen, who was about to embark on the adventure of her life, having been whisked away from Dingle by Eddie. Normally, Fowlie came back from a film with a few props he fancied for himself, such as the gleaming brass-plated door from *Nicholas and Alexandra* (1971), which he had decided would be a showpiece for the front of a hotel he was building back down on the Mediterranean in Carboneras. Returning instead with a pretty Irish teenager who was about to be made his wife had caused a few problems with Conchita's brothers in Madrid, but he had got that sorted out. Nonetheless, he was thrilled to get the call to go to Tahiti, particularly as the new project was partly of his own making. With Kathleen and Sandy getting along so well, he felt that not only was he David's Dedicated Maniac in chief, but the four of them were 'family'.

David also looked on Robert Bolt as a younger brother – he reminded him of his intellectual sibling Edward – though Robert wasn't a maniac, and didn't see it this way. Nonetheless, Bolt, having read the Bligh book and seen the dollar signs, was also keen to come on board as the scriptwriter. He agreed to relocate to Bora Bora, as did John Box, Lean's trusted production designer. Warner Bros agreed to make the picture for $17 million, but it was obvious that costs would quickly escalate, as David was demanding that they build a full-scale *Bounty* from scratch rather than refit an existing boat. There were other problems, and then came the deal-breaker: Lean and Bolt wanted to make two films out of the book rather than just the one Warner was expecting, at double the agreed cost. John Calley, the president of Warner, was a huge Lean fan, and longed to produce one of his movies, but he was now getting cold feet, and David found his reputation coming back to haunt him.

'Building the *Bounty* was emblematic of the kind of extravagance which David had got a name for,' Calley told Lean's biographer, Kevin Brownlow. 'If I'd gotten a call from Phil Kellogg [Lean's agent] saying, "David's got his next project. He and Bolt are working on a really extraordinary two-part action adventure about the mutiny on the Bounty, the whole thing is going to cost 37 million", I think we might have said yes, but it was the slide that got to me.'

Warner pulled out, and then the producer Dino De Laurentiis agreed to take it on. De Laurentiis put his own man on the production, Bernie Williams, who explained to David that the age of the big movie was over, and that Paramount had spent just $6 million making *Saturday Night Fever* (1977), which would gross more than $100 million. He may as well have been talking to the coral reef found in such abundance in Bora Bora. Arguments over budgets continued interminably, and John Box left the project, telling people in LA as he made his way back to England that David had become grandiose, and was behaving like a megalomaniac. Bolt might have gone as well, as he had tired of David's 'royal command', but he still needed to stay away from the Inland Revenue.

Then disaster struck. Bolt was miserable in Tahiti and was having health problems that required travelling to Los Angeles, where he had a triple heart bypass and then suffered a severe stroke at St John's Hospital in Santa Monica. David came to visit and bumped into Sarah.

'Don't you feel a little bit responsible?' Sarah asked him.

'No more than you must feel,' David replied. David paid Bolt's enormous medical expenses as a friend, not out of a sense of guilt.

It didn't require Bolt's stroke to kill off the *Bounty* project, but David had spent four years in Tahiti to no avail. He did eventually get another project off the drawing board and in the can when he adapted E. M. Forster's *A Passage to India* (1984). David was even more cantankerous fourteen years on from making his previous film. It didn't help his mood that, for the first time, he would have to forfeit his salary if he went over budget. Also, because of funding problems, he had to go to HBO as well as Columbia and EMI to get the finances he needed, and in the process was forced to compromise on how he shot the film, dispensing with 70mm and the widescreen format with which he was so in love, and shooting the picture instead in television ratio. In his pomp, David would have swatted away such a proposal as though it were a fly.

It was when *A Passage to India* was released that the controversy over *Ryan's Daughter* flared up again. The world premiere was held in Los Angeles on 13 December 1984, and David snubbed the New York opening the following night because of his continued bitterness over what had happened in the Algonquin Hotel all those years before. By then, Richard Schickel had become the film critic for *Time* magazine and, along with another Lean devotee, Jay Cocks, was campaigning for a David Lean cover story. This was the real deal, not a Whiting piece of fiction, even if the *Time* management took some convincing that Lean merited such an accolade. Schickel and Cocks were despatched to London, the former to watch and review the movie, the latter to interview the director. 'This was in no sense an act of atonement as I didn't know at the time that I had anything to atone for,' Schickel insisted. 'We meant this to be a tribute to a great figure on what we imagined might be his last film.'

Just before the screening, Schickel got a telephone call from the Warner Bros publicist informing him that Lean – or Sir David, as he had now become, having been knighted that year – had barred him from the screening, citing the ambush at the Algonquin. 'I was astonished and also placed in a highly embarrassing position,' Schickel said. 'After my campaign for this story – and after having spent the company's money on this venture – how could I explain what seemed about to happen?'

The film's producer, Richard Goodwin, intervened, and told Schickel to come along to the screening. 'I'll never forget Goodwin's comments: "Don't worry, after what we've been through on the picture, this is nothing".'

Schickel wrote the *Time* piece and Lean got his cover story, which he regarded as a great honour. 'My story, may I say, was a nightmare to write,' Schickel said, 'for knowing what I now knew, I found myself almost totally blocked when I sat down to write it. Now that it had been pointed out to me, I did feel compelled to atone for my youthful indiscretion. At the same time, I had to fulfil the usual journalistic obligations to judiciousness and objectivity.'

Schickel was invited to contribute to a David Lean special made by the flagship ITV arts programme *The South Bank Show*, but the interview wasn't used, and instead Lean would use any suitable platform to continue to blame his fallow years on the Algonquin incident, and Schickel in particular.

'The implication that I was largely responsible for a great director's 14-year absence from the movies is intolerable. And nonsensical,' Schickel wrote to Kevin Brownlow in 1993.

Are we really to believe that this vast silence grew out of a single inconsiderate remark? Or even out of one unpleasant hour in the Algonquin Hotel? No, the silence was his choice and it must have stemmed from something more than this incident, or, for that matter, the generally poor reception accorded this film.

Why, given all the honors and general acclaim he received for the body of his work, could Lean not himself contextualize *Ryan's Daughter*, treat it as an unaccountable failure amidst 16 beloved successes? Why this obsession with a single flop? Or maybe it was the very fact that it was his only large failure, that he had largely been spared the contempt that most people in films experience quite regularly, that made him so vulnerable.

For myself, I for years remembered the occasion simply as an extremely awkward social event, another bad evening in a lifetime's list of, shall we say, brief encounters that didn't work out as well as they might have. That it involved a director whose work I had praised and defended, and which meant – and means – a great deal to me as a critic and an ordinary moviegoer, made it perhaps a little more vivid than my other minor bad memories. But if I thought of it at all it was as one of several turning points in my relationships with my fellow critics. It was the first – though not the last – time I witnessed the misapplied passions and the dismaying self-importance of the breed. In later years I have tried very hard to maintain a certain civility – the sense that 'it's only a movie, Ingrid' – both in my reviewing and in my less formal public comments about pictures. In any event, it never occurred to me that Lean was recasting it as a turning point in his personal history and, thus, as a footnote in movie history as well.

When Schickel's protestations were put to David by Brownlow – namely that he was summing up the mood of the meeting rather than offering his own opinion with his 'bullshit' remark – the venerable director snapped back: 'This is not true and I don't want to take it up again, so please don't do it. Schickel did say that and I think they were pretty well all pissed. I would not mistake that. No good taking it up and I don't want to start it again.'

Lean seemed to think that Kael had chaired the meeting rather than Schickel, which was an important point in the context of what was said. Kael herself also says she chaired the meeting, but wasn't prepared to go into quite the same detail as Schickel when she replied to Lean's biographer in 1991, pointing out that the meeting was 'privileged ie not to be reported'.

Kael continued:

I consider myself bound by that agreement. Even if I weren't bound, I wouldn't trust myself to report what various people said at a talkative gathering 21 years ago. I always felt bad about the evening because everything that was said [about *Ryan's Daughter*] seemed to go wrong and Lean was so offended. He seemed determined to misunderstand the remarks made and to take even jocular comments and attempts to be soothing as affronts. With the years, this got worse and as chairwoman of the group at the time of his visit, I figured as a leading villain in his print and TV interviews. There's really nothing I can do about this. As you know, critics are always a handy target for moviemakers and, in this case, he somehow put the blame on us for his bum picture.

One of David's sharpest critics turned out to be the producer himself, with Havelock-Allan lining up alongside Kael in his criticism of the casting of Mitchum. 'David said, "They're telling me that I don't even understand my own business" and in a sense that was true, about that particular thing. It wasn't a good idea, but both Robert [Bolt] and Sarah were in favour of it,' Havelock-Allan said. 'You're playing him as a weak man, he's a strong man, he's a tough guy, he's a reactor and a violent one at that. And I don't believe in him in his nightdress looking out of the window and watching his wife go to meet a man half his size who he'd half kill in real life.'

Lean's preference for casting against type, as he put it, produced the equivalent of a derisive snort from Gregory Peck, who was desperate to play the part and be reunited with all his cousins in Dingle [of which he counted thirty-eight]. 'Lean did consider me for that role, and as I heard it, decided to cast "against type", whatever that means.'

Miles, too, in Havelock-Allan's opinion, couldn't really sustain such a big part. 'She's certainly a strange girl, very talented, but strange and unlucky for her that it doesn't fit into any sort of star quality thing. She has got what I would describe as piquant looks, it's not just straight uncomplicated looks, there is a feeling that there's something more complicated about her personality and if she was a comedienne it might work, but she is a serious actress. So she has never found the right niche for herself.'

Lastly, there was criticism for Jarre's bubble-and-squeak score.

> There is a wealth of marvellous Irish music and every Irishman in the world will have tears in his eyes if you hear echoes of Irish music in the background. David said that was going to be too difficult. The composer had done the music for *Lawrence of Arabia* and *Doctor Zhivago* and David said to him, 'You do what you like.' And there was not one note of Irish music in the background. The film would have been far better if there had been.

David had some of his own criticisms of what he did on *Ryan's Daughter*. They are contained in more than forty A4 pages of Lean talking about his film, which Lean's biographer, Kevin Brownlow, kindly made available to this author.

> I made a great mistake, one can do it very easily. The photography of *Ryan's Daughter* was dead straight as it were until the appearance of the Major, and she falls in love with him. Suddenly the whole world changes, everything centres around that man or that girl and you are swept off your feet. I decided

that when they fell in love, when particularly she, that we would change the photography and the sets into wildly romantic and so I went at it, full tilt. We had exotic lilies growing in the garden of the school house, that sort of thing and the music and the woods, the bluebells and everything photographed. I said to Freddie make it as lush as you can, think of the times you first fell in love, that first wonderful week and we did that, and the critics all laughed at it. It's my fault. They wouldn't have laughed if, as it were, Father Collins had said to Rosy, 'Rosy, you are seeing everything through rose-coloured glasses' and you had cut to something wildly romantic; in other words, if you told them what you were doing. If I'd told them what I was doing, what I was up to, it would have been alright.

David's other regrets about *Ryan's Daughter* revolved around the 'absolutely desperate' weather. 'Nobody at the time realised that we were doing *Madame Bovary* fairly thinly disguised, but we took the main things and put it in Ireland. We had a choice. We had the idea of either doing it in Ireland as we did or putting it in India and making the Charles character an English civil servant and the lover an Indian prince. I rather wish we'd done it in India come to think of it. Very glamorous.'

Robert Bolt's reservations were far more profound. Even at the end of his ten-month collaboration with Lean in Rome at the writing stage, he was unhappy with the final outcome. A letter written to David on 11 October 1968, but never sent, had expressed his dismay at the last quarter of the movie, and the final scene in particular, when it looks like Rosy and her schoolteacher husband might stay together after all. 'In short,' Bolt wrote, 'I feel this happy ending is terribly sad.' Bolt had wanted Randolph, Rosy and Charles to meet a 'disastrous end which I feel was really in store for all three if they really were what they pretended to be in the first three-quarters of the film.' This would have left the two men dead and Rosy tarred and feathered for her traitorous adultery.

> We have had this argument a dozen times, over several weeks, and as an argument it is played out and I have lost it. When you tell me that Rosy is not Joan of Arc, that Sarah is not Greta Garbo and I am not writing *Tristan and Iseult* I am not only silenced, I am undermined within; all my more ambitious ideas suddenly appear pretentious and tasteless. I feel I am about to make an ass of myself and Sarah and that I am asking you to risk your enormous reputation on some highly personal spree of my own.

They turned out to be prophetic words, but Bolt spun the party line for years about *Ryan's Daughter*, perhaps out of loyalty to Lean. If only David had stuck with the original script, Bolt wondered years later. 'He dragged it down. *Madam Bovary* would have been a superb film,' said Bolt, when he was recovering from his stroke. 'He couldn't bear somebody to give him and say, "This is your screenplay".'

Bolt eventually remarried Miles when she returned to England from Los Angeles, and helped him recover from his stroke. Sandy tired of David's difficult ways and went

off with John Calley, the Warner executive, who didn't get a
Lean movie but took his wife instead. David then met and
married his sixth wife, Sandra Cooke. Eddie, who made no
bones about disliking Sandra, wanted David to leave his wife
to come and live with himself and Kathleen in Carboneras,
so that they could all be family again, but David refused.

'He was a lonely man,' said Bolt. 'Very. I don't know
anybody who came near him, with the possible exception of
myself. He stopped short – about that short [Bolt places his
thumb and forefinger an inch apart] – of being a great film-
maker. Really great. Like *Citizen Kane*.'

Lean and Mitchum met again, years later, not quite by
chance, shortly before David died. David was having lunch
with Sandra at the Colombe d'Or Hotel in Saint-Paul-de-
Vence, near the house they had bought in Provence. Also
at the director's table was Serge Silberman, the producer
for Lean's last project, the filming of Joseph Conrad's
*Nostromo*, along with some other backers. David and his
party were dining on the terrace of the hotel, enjoying the
balmy weather. Sandra saw Robert Mitchum entering the
restaurant with a group of friends. David was sitting with
his back to the entrance and Sandra said nothing, knowing
this was a delicate situation. Mitchum didn't seem to notice
David either.

'All went well until Bob, fuelled by good wine and
encouraged by his friends, started telling tales from the
movie. I shuddered, hoping that the conversation would be
drowned by the laughter from our own table,' Sandra wrote
in *David Lean: An Intimate Portrait*. 'He was telling them
all sorts of stories about how I told David this and he told
David that and you know what he's like and this and that.'

David's splendid elephantine ears had also picked up the drift, but he said nothing. The gaiety at the Mitchum table grew. Sandra heard

> wafts of 'And we waited and waited for David to find the perfect shot, the perfect cloud formation and the perfect light.' His guests were highly amused and the laughter at Mitchum's stories about this ridiculous director resounded over the terrace. I watched David and he seemed unaware that this was going on. My illusion was shattered as Robert's party got ready to leave. David crunched his chair against the stone, made a sudden turn and said, 'Hello Bob. Made any good movies lately?' It was perfect timing as usual on David's part and the look of embarrassment on Bob's face, now even redder than it was from the wine, made the finale perfect. Mitchum, lost for words, gave a slight gesture of a wave and took his leave.

Mitchum was due to meet Lean the next day to discuss playing a role in *Nostromo*, which David was due to film on a set in Nice and elsewhere. However, they still clearly rubbed each other up the wrong way.

'He's difficult, also a monkey you see in various ways,' said Lean, pointedly.

Asked whether Mitchum was an alcoholic, Lean replied:

'Yes, he was very fond of the bottle and poor old Mitchum he had a drug problem which was well known. He's sort of a hangover from what do you call those chaps, what do they call themselves? Tearaways. You know, Peter

O'Toole was a tearaway in his young days. Some grow out of it, some don't.'

Mitchum's attitude to Lean softened as the pain of his time in Dingle subsided, and he complimented the director on going to the trouble of getting the best out of him rather than take shortcuts. However, the misunderstandings and differences continued right to the end, even when the American Film Institute asked the actor to present Lean with their Lifetime Achievement Award in March 1990.

'They came and asked me to make the presentation,' Mitchum remarked the following year. 'And I said, "You had better check with David and ask him if I'm acceptable or not." Instead, they told David that I had refused. And he cried.' Johnny Mills flew over and delivered the tribute instead.

Mitchum's reflections were made eight weeks after David had died of throat cancer, at the age of 83, on 16 April 1991. 'I suppose that I would have had the script for *Nostromo* and I suppose I would be over in France working on that now, but the bum died on me.'

In Dingle, they weren't quite so flippant. It was, after all, the town where the cry 'God Save Our Lean' often went out. When news of David's death reached Dingle, the Irish flag over the Phoenix Cinema was lowered to half mast.

# Acknowledgements

I am indebted particularly to David Lean's biographer, Kevin Brownlow, for all his help on a number of fronts. Robert Bolt's biographer, Adrian Turner, was also a strong arm to lean on, as was the *Financial Times* film critic Nigel Andrews. I would also like to thank Tony Reeves of the David Lean Foundation for all his help, and Ben Bolt likewise. Bayley Silleck in New York was a huge help, and kindly handed over his personal collection of fine photographs. Thanks also to Gavin Jantjes and George Hallett.

A big thank you to the following:

Amy Rowan, a fine manuscript reader as well as casting director. John 'Taoiseach' Murray for a strong guiding hand, and Kathleen Rowan for all the support. Fergus Rowan (RIP) and Paud Mahoney at Met Éireann for Kerry weather reports. Ray Wells, Eileen Martin, Jason O'Neill and Dermot Kavanagh for some sage picture advice. Noreen Curran, Kevin Devane, Kate Ashe and everybody in Dingle who made visiting and staying there such a joy. Peggy, Joe and all the Keelaghans for all their help and support in Los Angeles … 'turn right at the giant doughnut' … and making my time there so memorable. Anna Rowan for helping me to get there. Alan English for his enthusiasm. Tina Dillane, Olive Moriarty and Tommy O'Rourke at Kerry Library. Ray

317

'Mock-Up' Molony; David Sweeney, for covering the Washington angle and Lee Server. Rory Godson, who I didn't thank properly before. To my editors Rachel Pierce and Aoife K. Walsh and all the staff at New Island Books. Also many thanks to Ivan Mulcahy for pointing me in the right direction, and Emily Hourican for same. My dear friend Fintan Keyes also helped me greatly.

Finally, a big thanks to all those interviewees who gave generously of their time and asked for nothing in return.

# Credits

**Quotes:**

Jocelyn Rickards's description of Sandy Lean on page 16 is quoted from Rickards' autobiography, *The Painted Banquet*.

Sir David Lean and Sir Anthony Havelock-Allan letters on pages 21, 22, 30-31, 51 and 113 are reproduced by kind permission of A.A. Reeves of David Lean Films Ltd.

Extracts from Kevin Brownlow's biography of David Lean, *David Lean: A Biography* on pages 27, 180, 236, 155, 156, 157, 285, 286, 298, 299, 309 and 315–316 are reproduced by kind permission of Kevin Brownlow.

Robert Mitchum's description of the hotel on pages 67 and 68, his stories about Christy Brown on pages 70 and 71 and his version of being asked to present David Lean with the American Film Institute's Lifetime Achievement Award on page 316 are quoted from Jerry Roberts's book, *Mitchum: In His Own Words*

Mitchum's account of days spent not shooting on pages 90–91 was recorded during an episode of 'The Michael Parkinson Show' in August 1972.

The story of the eavesdropping telephone operator on page 91 was recounted to me by Niall O'Brien.

The quote by Lean about his casting nightmare on page 110 was recorded during my interview with Roy Stevens.

The story of Christopher Jones's British accent on pages 115 and 116, losing cars to the Dingle tide on page 153 and Mitchum's story of the crane on pages 203 and 204 were recounted to me in an interview with Nigel Andrews.

Leo McKern's observations on pages 130, 259 and 262 are extracted from his autobiography, *Just Resting*, by kind permission of the McKern Estate.

The mention of Edna O'Brien's night-long affair with Robert Mitchum on page 171 is fully recounted in her autobiography, *Country Girl*.

Mitchum's take on his miserable existence in Dingle on page 173 is quoted from George Eells's book, *Robert Mitchum: A Biography*.

Sydney Bolt's opinion of the relationship between Robert Bolt and Sarah Miles on pages 104 and 105 is quoted from Adrian Turner's book, *Robert Bolt: Scenes from Two Lives*, by kind permission of the Adrian Turner.

David Tringham's poem on page 196 is reproduced by kind permission of David Tringham.

Robert Bolt's letters on pages 213–215, 219–221, 224, 302 and 313 are reproduced by kind permission of Ben Bolt.

Richard Schickel's recollections of Robert Mitchum on page 279 are extracted from an interview with Schickel in *Sound on Film* in April 1971. His letters to Kevin Brownlow on pages 308 and 309 are reproduced by kind permission of the Richard Schickel Estate.

Pauline Kael's letter to Brownlow on pages 309 and 310 is reproduced by kind permission of Kael's daughter, Gina James.

**Photographs:**

All photographs are by Ken Bray and reproduced courtesy of Bayley Silleck except for:

Plate Section 1: page 2 (bottom): photographer unknown, courtesy of Noreen Curran; page 5 (bottom): photographer unknown, from collection of Olivia Hussey; page 8 (top and bottom): photo by Ken Bray, courtesy of Noreen Curran.

Plate Section 2: page 1 (top): photo by Ken Bray, courtesy of Noreen Curran; page 2 (bottom): photo by Ken Bray, licensed from The Kennelly Archive; page 3: photo by and courtesy of Bayley Silleck; page 4 (bottom): photo by and courtesy of Bayley Silleck; page 8 (top): photo by George Hallett, courtesy of Gavin Jantjes; page 8 (bottom): photo by Ken Bray, courtesy of Noreen Curran.

# Notes on Sources

INTERVIEWS

Rudi Altobelli
Ken Bray
Trevor Coop
Tom Fitzgerald
Bernie Goggin
John Irwin
Christopher Jones
Stevie Kelleher
Frank Kelly
Fred Lane
David Lean
Josie McAvin
Sarah Miles
Robert Mitchum
Joanna Ney
Bernie Prentice
Gladys Sheehan
Bayley Silleck
Roy Stevens
John Trehy
Roy Walker
Freddie Young

Kate Ashe
Bob Bremner
Con Cremins
Eddie Fowlie
A. Havelock-Allan
Barry Jackson
Pauline Kael
Timmy Kelleher
Sean Kerry
Christine Lawson
Sandy Lean
Bronco McLoughlin
John Mills
Sean Moran
Vera O'Keeffe
Richard Schickel
Margaret Sheehy
Bernard Smith
Michael Stevenson
David Tringham
Maureen Whitty

Robert Bolt
Denis Butler
Noreen Curran
Kathleen Fowlie
Michael Hickey
Gavin Jantjes
Mike Kaplan
Des Keogh
Douglas Kirkland
Tony Lawson
Liam Long
Peter Miller
Tommy Mitchell
Linnemore Nefdt
Terry Pierce
Jack Redshaw
Walter Sheehy
Herbert Solow
Niall Tóibín
Pedro Vidal
Bob Willoughby

All interviews conducted by author, except for interviews supplied by David Lean biographer, Kevin Brownlow, with David Lean, Sandy Lean, Freddie Young and Robert Bolt. Plus correspondence from Richard Schickel and Pauline Kael. Robert Mitchum interview courtesy of Nigel Andrews and Harlan Kennedy.

Most of my interviews were carried out between 1999 and 2004.

Thanks to the following libraries and their staff for their kind assistance: Margaret Herrick Library, Beverly Hills, California; National Library, Dublin; British Library, London; British Film Institute Library, London; Dingle Library, Co. Kerry; Tralee Library, Co. Kerry; Killorglin Library, Co. Kerry; Steve Baker and all the staff at News UK Library, London; Science Museum Media Dept, Bradford, West Yorks, UK.

## SELECTED BIBLIOGRAPHY

**Books**

Bart, Peter. *Fade Out: The Calamitous Final Days of MGM* (Anchor, 1990)

Bronfman, Edgar M. *Good Spirits: The Making of a Businessman* (GP Putnams, 1998)

Brownlow, Kevin. *David Lean: A Biography* (Richard Cohen, 1996)

Bugliosi, Vincent. *Helter Skelter* (WW Norton, 1974)

Eames, John Douglas. *The MGM Story* (Octopus, 1975)

Eells, George. *Robert Mitchum: A Biography* (Pavilion, 1998)

Falk, Quentin. *Anthony Hopkins: Too Good to Waste* (Virgin, 1989)

Flaubert, Gustave. *Madame Bovary* (Wordsworth Classics, 1994)

Fowlie, Eddie & Torne, Richard. *David Lean's Dedicated Maniac* (Austin & Macauley, 2010)

Hussey, Olivia. *The Girl on the Balcony* (Kensington, 2018)

Kellerman, Sally. *Read My Lips* (Weinstein Books, 2013)

Lean, Sandra & Chattington, Barry. *David Lean, An Intimate Portrait* (Andre Deutsch, 2001)

Love, Damien. *Robert Mitchum: Solid, Daddy, Crazy* (BT Batsford, 2002)

MacLaine, Shirley. *My Lucky Stars* (Bantam, 1995)

McKern, Leo. *Just Resting* (Methuen, 1983)

Miles, Sarah *A Right Royal Bastard* (Macmillan, 1993)

Miles, Sarah. *Serves Me Right* (Macmillan, 1994)

Miles, Sarah. *Bolt from the Blue* (Orion, 1996)

Mills, John. *Up In the Clouds, Gentlemen Please* (Weidenfield & Nicolson, 1980)

Mitchum, John. *Them Ornery Mitchum Boys: The Adventures of Robert & John Mitchum* (Creatures At Large Press, 1989)

O'Brien, Edna. *Country Girl* (Faber and Faber, 2012)

Pettigrew, Terence. *Trevor Howard* (Peter Owen, 2001)

Rickards, Jocelyn. *The Painted Banquet: My Life and Loves* (Weidenfield & Nicolson, 1987)

Roberts, Jerry. *Mitchum: In His Own Words* (Proscenium, 2000)

Roberts, Jerry. *Robert Mitchum: A Bio-Bibliography* (Greenwood, 1992)

Server, Lee. *Robert Mitchum: Baby, I Don't Care* (Faber & Faber, 2001)

Silverman, Stephen M. *David Lean* (Andre Deutsch, 1989)

Strasberg, Susan. *Marilyn and Me* (Warner Books, 1992)

Susann, Jacqueline. *The Love Machine* (Simon and Schuster, 1969)

Tóibín, Niall. *Smile and Be a Villain!* (Tower House, 1995)

Tomkies, Mike. *Robert Mitchum Story* (Harpercollins, 1974)

Turner, Adrian. *The Making of David Lean's Lawrence of Arabia* (Dragon's World, 1994)

Turner, Adrian. *Robert Bolt: Scenes from Two Lives* (Hutchinson, 1998)

Walker, Alexander. *It's Only a Movie, Ingrid* (Headline, 1988)

Willoughby, Bob. *The Star Makers: On Set with Hollywood's Greatest Directors* (Merrell, 2003)

## Newspapers, periodicals and documents

*Ireland*
*Clare Champion, Cork Examiner* (now *Irish Examiner*), *In Dublin, Irish Times, Irish Press, The Kerryman, Sunday Independent.*

*United States*
*American Cinematographer, Buffalo News* (NY), *Chicago Sun Times, Chicago Tribune, Citizen News* (Hollywood), *Daily Breeze* (Toronto), *Daily Post* (NY), *Esquire, Hollywood Reporter, Hollywood Studio Magazine, Life, Los Angeles Herald-Examiner, Los Angeles Times, The New Leader, New Yorker, Newsday, Penthouse, Port Chester Daily Item, Rolling Stone, St Louis Post Despatch, Time, TV Guide, TV Time, Variety, Village Voice, The Wall Street Journal, Washington Post.*

*Great Britain*
*Cosmopolitan, Daily Express, Daily Mail, Daily Mirror, Evening Standard, Fair Lady, Financial Times, The Guardian, International Herald Tribune, Independent on Sunday,*

*Manchester Guardian Weekly*, *News of the World*, *Observer*, *The People*, *Reveille*, *Saturday Review*, *The Sun*, *The Sunday Times*, *Time Out*, *The Times*, *TV Times*.

*South Africa*
*Cape Times*, *Newscheck*, *The Argus*, *Sunday Times* (Johannesburg).

*Others*
*Cairns Post* (Queensland), *Sunday Herald Sun* (Melbourne).

## Broadcasts

*A Bit of a Fillum: Ryan's Daughter in Dingle*, RTÉ, 25 December 2008.

BBC Film Night Specials: *We're the Last of the Travelling Circuses*, 1969.

Champlin on Film, Z Channel, 8 June 1988.

Dick Cavett Show, ABC, 29 April 1971.

Sound on Film Radio Programme 10, November 1970.

The David Frost Show, Syndicated, 1970.

The Michael Parkinson Show, BBC1, 19 August 1972.

*Sir David Lean – A Life in Film*. A South Bank Show Special (1985).

*Spré Rosy Ryan,* Adare Productions for TG4, 1997.

# Index